Supporting the Child and the Family in Paediatric Palliative Care

of related interest

Children Also Grieve
Talking about Death and Healing
Linda Goldman
ISBN 978 1 84310 808 5

Talking with Children and Young People about Death and Dying
2nd edition
Mary Turner
Illustrated by Bob Thomas
ISBN 978 1 84310 441 4

Grandad's Ashes
Walter Smith
ISBN 978 1 84310 517 6

Empowering Children through Art and Expression
Culturally Sensitive Ways of Healing Trauma and Grief
Bruce St Thomas and Paul Johnson
ISBN 978 1 84310 789 7

Palliative Care, Social Work and Service Users
Making Life Possible
Peter Beresford, Lesley Adshead and Suzy Croft
Foreword by Dorothy Rowe
ISBN 978 1 84310 465 0

Lost for Words
Loss and Bereavement Awareness Training
John Holland, Ruth Dance, Nic Macmanus and Carole Stitt
ISBN 978 1 84310 324 0

Music Therapy in Children's Hospices
Jessie's Fund in Action
Edited by Mercédès Pavlicevic
Foreword by Victoria Wood
ISBN 978 1 84310 254 0

Dying, Bereavement and the Healing Arts
Edited by Gillie Bolton
Foreword by Baroness Professor Ilora Finlay of Llandaff
ISBN 978 1 84310 516 9

Supporting the Child and the Family in Paediatric Palliative Care

Erica Brown with Brian Warr

Foreword by Dr Sheila Shribman

Jessica Kingsley Publishers
London and Philadelphia

First published in 2007
by Jessica Kingsley Publishers
116 Pentonville Road
London N1 9JB, UK
and
400 Market Street, Suite 400
Philadelphia, PA 19106, USA

www.jkp.com

Copyright © Erica Brown with Brian Warr 2007
Chapters 3 and 20 copyright © Ann Smallman 2007
Foreword copyright © Sheila Shribman 2007

Library of Congress Cataloging in Publication Data
A CIP catalog record for this book is available from the Library of Congress

British Library Cataloguing in Publication Data
A CIP catalogue record for this book is available from the British Library

ISBN 978 1 84310 181 9

Printed and bound in Great Britain by
MGP Books Group, Cornwall

The book is dedicated to John Overton, former Chief Executive of Acorns Children's Hospice, in recognition of his vision and commitment to life-limited children and their families.

Contents

Part 3   Meeting Individual Needs

Part 4   The Way Forward

Foreword

Children's palliative care is receiving increased attention and this book is very timely in contributing to the discussions on the future of this essential aspect of care for increasing numbers of our nation's children.

Putting the child and their family at the centre of all we do is a key value, central to a focus on the quality of life, as well as its length. A holistic team-based approach is essential. Working as part of a palliative care network, hospices have an important role to play, as do all children's services, whether tertiary, secondary, primary, acute or community.

Supporting the Child and the Family in Paediatric Palliative Care contains a wealth of useful information and reflects innovative research findings from Acorns Children's Hospices that raise key issues for future consideration.

Dr Sheila Shribman,
National Clinical Director for Children,
Young People and Maternity Services,
Department of Health,
May 2007

Introduction

Be careful, then, and be gentle about death. For it is hard to die, it is difficult to go through the door, even when it opens. (D.H. Lawrence)

Over the centuries poets, playwrights, novelists and authors have wrestled with bittersweet experiences of death and dying. Perhaps this is because grief incorporates a myriad of emotional, behavioural (affective) and cognitive manifestations, in both adults and children. Amongst the most traumatic events a family can experience is the death of one of its members. Children are not supposed to die, but they do. Their death is not only a loss, it is a turning point; the world will never be the same again.

Since 1984, the children's hospice movement has made an enormous contribution to the care of life-limited children and their families. There are now over 35 residential facilities in Great Britain and several more in the planning stages. There is little doubt that this expansion is in direct response to need. Through advancements in technology and medicine, many children with congenital abnormalities are surviving. Indeed, over 80 per cent of babies born with a birth-weight of less than one kilo will live. Some of these children have complex medical needs for which there is no reasonable hope of cure. Others may have conditions that cause progressive deterioration, rendering them dependent on their families and carers.

The ACT/RCPCH joint report (2003) suggested that in a district with 50,000 children, eight are likely to die as a result of a progressive condition for which palliative care is appropriate; between 60 and 85 are likely to have a life-limiting condition with some palliative care needs, for half of whom the needs will be substantial.

Since Acorns opened its first hospice at Selly Oak in Birmingham in 1988, we have cared for more than 1200 families. Acorns Walsall opened in 1999 and, most recently, Acorns Worcester has been providing care in a ten-bedded unit since 2005. The defined catchment area of Acorns covers the counties of Warwickshire, Worcestershire, Herefordshire, Gloucestershire and the West Midlands, as well as parts of Staffordshire and Shropshire. Caring for the child and supporting the family lies at the heart of the philosophy of Acorns. Hence the title of this book, *Supporting the Child and the Family in Paediatric Palliative Care*, was born.

The opening sentence of Tolstoy's novel *Anna Karenina* rings unquestionably true for many families with a life-limited child. He writes, 'All happy families are alike, but an unhappy family is unhappy after its own fashion.' In other words, families may have shared experience of events, but the consequences will be unique to each person within the family unit.

The book is first and foremost a book with practical ideas, supported by references from the literature and the findings of recent research projects at Acorns. In writing this book I have attempted to reflect on the role of the children's hospice in caring for life-limited children and their families. It has been necessary in many cases to make generalisations, but at the heart of the text are the children and families with whom we work.

The United Nations Convention of the Rights of the Child defines a child as someone under the age of 18. Throughout the book the words 'child' and 'young people' are used interchangeably. Rather than using combined personal pronouns such as s/he, his/her and him/her, which are not congruous with the way in which we speak, I sometimes use personal pronouns which relate to the female gender and sometimes those which relate to the male sex. I also recognise that many adults act in caring roles or are part of extended families. Therefore the term 'parents' does not refer exclusively to biological parents.

The right for families to have their views heard is of prime importance. This right extends to research, and it is my belief that studies do not accurately or adequately represent the reality of lived experiences unless accounts from service-users are taken into consideration. Therefore, throughout the book, I will share short case studies with you. The quotations used are exactly as the children and their families have told them to me, save for any names which have been changed to protect the anonymity of the people concerned.

Small-scale research findings on their own are unlikely to play a crucial role in policy-making or provision. However, as Parahoo (1997) advocates, the impact of the evidence may gradually enter into the thinking of policy-makers and practitioners. It is my dearest hope that others who support life-limited children and their families will draw on the findings from Acorns' experience as a catalyst for their own imaginative initiatives. Developing our own skills and capacities is good and it is impossible to provide guidelines which will fit every situation. As families live through grief, life goes on. Palliative care services have rich opportunities to support children and their families through living out their stated ethos in practice.

In the course of writing I have drawn on the ideas, memories, advice and support of a great many people who have helped me directly and indirectly. Some are colleagues, kind enough to share their knowledge with me; others are children and families who have been brave enough to trust me and to share their stories. I never cease to be amazed by the courage and openness of families which has been both challenging and humbling. As families live their lives in the shadow of death, life around them goes on. The hope that they hang on to is that their child's life counted for something. Their ability to survive in the face of adversity is an example to us all.

My two colleagues Brian Warr and Ann Smallman deserve special thanks. Both are at the forefront of the care we provide at Acorns. In spite of many challenges, they found time to write without compromising the standards of care for which they are responsible. Were it not for the support of all my colleagues at Acorns, the book would not have been completed. I am indebted to Sandy Walshe, a volunteer at our hospices, who has transcribed many hundreds of hours of interviews with families and she has done all the audio typing for the book. Anne Healer and Lynne Cohen have given generously of their time to proofread and have offered encouragement, friendship and support along the way. Brian Warr read and commented on the manuscript. Geraldine Mannion and Christine Randall have been trusted friends and 'props' when I was tempted to give up writing.

By far my greatest gratitude is to Alan, my husband, who has contributed over the years to putting back together the pieces of my own life more than he will ever know. Throughout the writing of this book he has constantly and unselfishly made sacrifices so that I have been able to pursue my professional quest. I thank him for his unconditional love.

The book is divided into four parts:

- Introduction to Paediatric Palliative Care
- Responding to Holistic Needs from Diagnosis through to Terminal Care and Bereavement Care
- Meeting Individual Needs
- The Way Forward.

Chapter 1 discusses 'The Historical Background of Paediatric Palliative Care'. References are made to the holistic nature of care and the challenges posed to service-providers striving to meet the increasing complexity of children's needs. The problem of a sustainable revenue stream to support children's hospice care is addressed.

Chapter 2, 'Working Collaboratively', challenges service-providers to find ways of working collaboratively in order to safeguard against fragmented provision. Reference is made to recent policy initiatives and the new proposal for National Mapping of life-limited children and children's palliative care services is discussed.

Chapter 3, 'Assessment of Needs and Models of Care', describes and debates the strengths and weaknesses of some traditional existing models.

Acorns' approach to matching care to a detailed assessment of individual need is described.

Most parents advocate that symptom control and ensuring their child's comfort is of paramount importance. **Chapter 4**, 'Managing Children's Pain', makes reference to some of the many origins and types of pain which children may experience during the trajectory of the illness. The particular challenges posed by receptive, expressive, articulatory and interactive problems encountered by many children is discussed. Particular attention is paid to meeting the needs of children with profound and complex learning disabilities, in addition to life-limiting illness.

Chapter 5, 'The End of Life Phase of Care', acknowledges the tremendous emotional, physical and spiritual anguish experienced by families during the terminal stage of their child's life. A plea is made for parents to be partners with professionals in managing their child's care for as long as they feel able to do so. The stress felt by professionals is also acknowledged.

Chapter 6, 'Administrative and Practical Requirements when a Child Dies', provides a summary of the legal, administrative practicalities after a child dies, whether this is at home, a hospice or in hospital.

Chapter 7, 'The Child's Funeral', emphasises the importance of enabling the family to care for their child's body, if they wish, up until the funeral. Some rituals and ceremonies are outlined as well as the processes involved in burial and cremation.

Chapter 8, 'Counselling Support', argues that support for family members is crucial to the care of the child. Individual differences in coping with grief are outlined together with reference to the intense anticipatory grief felt by many parents when their child is diagnosed. The importance of differentiating between professional counselling and counselling skills is discussed.

'The Financial Impact of Caring' is the focus of **Chapter 9**. The importance of enabling families to access financial support from voluntary organisations and benefit agencies is acknowledged as a vital component in how well families cope.

Chapter 10, 'Children's Developmental Understanding and Emotional Response to Death and Dying', discusses both life-limited and non-life-limited children's ideas about death and dying and how they are likely to respond to sad news. The text is supported by some examples of children's art work. Suggestions are given to adults endeavouring to answer children's questions about death.

At the heart of children's palliative care is support to the family. **Chapter 11**, 'The Impact of Life-limiting Illness on the Family', describes the interdependency of family members and the likely impact of a child's life-limiting illness on family members from the time of the diagnosis to the child's death.

Reference is made to the struggle that many parents encounter as their nurturing and protective roles are challenged by the fact that they are unable to stop their child dying.

Chapter 12, 'Continuing Bonds', explores how some parents may find solace in being helped to continue the bond they have with their child after the child's death. Professionals are urged to consider ways to help parents maintain links between the past and a continuing relationship with their child.

Chapters 13 and 14, 'Working with Siblings of Life-limited Children' and 'Grandparent Support', extend the idea of holistic care to include brothers and sisters and grandparents.

Until fairly recently it was considered that a family's own spiritual leader or a chaplain had sole responsibility for faith matters. **Chapter 15**, 'Religious, Cultural, Secular and Spiritual Aspects of Care', suggests that service-providers should recognise how cultures change in response to local, national and international situations and how the influence of religion on people's lives varies greatly. Research findings into the experiences and expectations of Asian mothers with a life-limited child at Acorns are described. Stereotypical views of ethnicity and culture are challenged.

At the time of writing, post mortem, organ donation and tissue retention have been topical subjects for discussion. The Human Tissue Act, which became law in September 2006, has highlighted the importance of providing parents with appropriate and accurate information if they agree to a post mortem or tissue or organ donation. **Chapter 16**, 'Post Mortem, Organ Donation and Tissue Retention', discusses the protocols of both a hospital and a Coroner's post mortem and provides information that professionals may find useful when working with families.

Chapter 17, 'The Education of the Life-limited Child', stresses that education is a statutory duty and a right for all children and young people. Maintaining educational continuity provides important ways of celebrating children's achievements, encouraging peer group relationships, minimising isolation and promoting equality of opportunity. A detailed framework is offered for the assessment of children's physical development, perceptual development, intellectual development and personal and social development. The resulting profile may have potential for informing the child's nursing care plan, physiotherapy assessment and meeting social needs.

Improvement in medical and nursing therapies means that children with life-limited conditions are surviving longer. **Chapter 18**, 'Transition from Paediatric Palliative Care to Adult Services', discusses transition as a philosophy as well as a process. Professionals are urged to involve young people in choices and decision-making at every level.

Working in palliative care settings can be extremely stressful on individuals and costly in human terms on the individual and to the employer in resource terms. **Chapter 19**, 'Acknowledging Staff Stress and Providing Support', discusses how the quality of care that families receive is dependent on the quality of care that staff receive.

The penultimate chapter of the book, **Chapter 20**, 'Maintaining the Quality of Care', focuses on the crucial role of audit in recording and evaluating progress within the quality agenda of an organisation.

Finally, **Chapter 21**, 'The Role of Research and Development in Children's Hospices', acknowledges that paediatric palliative care is at a critical stage in its evolution. Service-provision should always be based on the best possible evidence of what families need so that care truly matches the unique needs of individual family members.

A book is a platform for ideas and opinions. Inevitably my own views and life experience of loss is held between the cover. Because we are all different, the ways in which we cope in the face of adversity and the strategies which we adopt will be individual. There will be areas where your skills exceed my own. The implications for practice at the end of each chapter are intended as a springboard for your own creativity and innovation.

There is no single way to support life-limited children and their families. Yet there are avenues open to each one of us. Keep travelling alongside those who hurt and listen to the words they use, and be aware of the ways they choose to communicate. Pace yourself with the child and their family and be sensitive to people's own need to be a part of what is happening. Give your support at all times, but do not intrude. Care, but do not lose sight of the emotional price which you pay for your own commitment. Seek solace, guidance and comfort for yourself. But most importantly, be there, and trust the children and the families with whom you work to be your guides.

Erica Brown,
Acorns Children's Hospice

Part 1
Introduction to Paediatric Palliative Care

The Historical Background of Paediatric Palliative Care

Erica Brown

Palliative care has its origins as long ago as 460BC in Greek medicine prac-
tised by physicians such as Hippocrates. In the first half of the twentieth
century most adult deaths in the United Kingdom occurred at home. Care for
dying adults in hospices has become a well-recognised and valued area of
service-provision since the foundation of the modern hospice movement by
Cicily Saunders in the 1960s and the opening of St Christopher's Hospice in
1967. Children's hospice care is much newer and only began in the 1980s
with the opening of Helen House in 1982.

Paediatric palliative care embraces a philosophy that attends to the psychological, physical, spiritual and social needs of the child and their family.
Farrell (1996) describes this care as a concept where there is a shift of emphasis
from conventional care that focuses on quantity of life towards a commitment
to care which enhances quality of life. The Joint Report of the Association for
Children with Life-threatening or Terminal Conditions and their Families
(ACT) and the Royal College of Paediatrics and Child Health (RCPCH)
(2003) recommends that palliative care should be an integral part of clinical
practice, available to all child patients. Such a philosophy presents a major
challenge both clinically and culturally, demanding that all providers work
together to ensure seamless care that will meet the needs of medically vulnerable young people and their families.

The trajectory of childhood illness from diagnosis to the end of life phase
of care may be sudden, but often onsets gradually. Whatever the pattern, each
family's circumstances and experience are unique. Hynson (2006) describes
the changes that each child and family encounter as 'multiple', with some children experiencing the transition from 'person' to 'patient', 'home' to 'hospital'

and 'able' to 'disabled'. Often parents become experts in caring for their child, taking on clinical interventions and complex tasks.

Increasing numbers of very sick children are surviving as a result of advances in medicine and nursing (Olsen and Maslin-Prothero 2001). However, the ACT Joint Report (2003) suggested that in a population of 50,000 children, eight are likely to die in a year as a result of a progressive condition for which palliative care is appropriate; between 60 and 85 are likely to have a life-limiting condition with some palliative care needs, for half of whom the needs will be substantial. It should be recognised, however, that the prevalence of life-limiting illness in children is dependent on how life-limitation is defined. Generally it is estimated that 1.5/1000 children between birth and 19 years are likely to have an illness from which they will die prematurely. About half of children in need of palliative care have malignant diseases (Chadwick 1999). Neurodegenerative diseases, congenital disorders and chromosomal disorders account for more than 55 per cent of illnesses (ACT 2001). However, Horrocks, Somerset and Salisbury (2002) in their scrutiny of data relating to non-malignant diseases in childhood concluded that there was no reliable way to identify children with life-limiting illnesses at the time of diagnosis. Indeed, available data is based on incidence of death rather than diagnosis.

Life-limiting conditions have been described in four main groups (ACT/RCPCH 2003):

- those which are a threat to life because although curative treatment is available it may not be successful in every case, e.g. irreversible organ failure and cancer
- those for which treatment may lengthen life expectancy but for which no cure is known, e.g. muscular dystrophy and cystic fibrosis
- those conditions which are progressive and for which there are no curative options and treatment is palliative, e.g. mucopolysaccharidosis and Batten disease
- those conditions that involve severe neurological disabilities and deterioration may be rapid and unpredictable, e.g. cerebral palsy or brain damage.

The very special care needs of children with life-limiting illnesses has been recognised and acknowledged for over two decades. The move away from invasive medicine to holistic care for these children has challenged clinicians, and a range of models of care has emerged, including children's hospices (Chapman and Goodall 1980). At the time of writing, there are 39 fully operational children's hospices, four hospice at home services and one day care service. A further five units are currently in the building or planning stages (ACH 2006). Epidemiology within other European countries indicates similar statistics.

However, the contribution that children's hospices make in ensuring quality care for life-limited children and their families over many years is sometimes discounted by those who perceive the primary role of hospices as providing places where children go to die. Such a misapprehension is no doubt borne out of experience of adult in-hospice care which primarily focuses on the last days of a patient's life.

The first children's hospices were often opened as the result of individuals working tirelessly to raise sufficient funds to provide care. Early in the establishment of the children's hospice movement, paediatricians were sceptical about the hospice contribution to the care of life-limited children and their families. Indeed, their views were often perceived by the hospices to be misinformed and critical. Hain (2002) speaks of 'a division between the children's hospice movement and the rest of palliative care' that in some cases still exists today. However, the Joint Report between the Royal College of Paediatrics and Child Health and ACT (2003) has endorsed the distinct role of children's hospices in caring for children and young people with life-limiting disorders. It is hard to realise that less than two decades ago Carlisle (1988) wrote that it was thought that England and Wales would need no more than four children's hospices.

As children's hospices have increased in number, they have developed distinctive identities. In some cases the only common element has been the title 'children's hospice'. Fortunately, most have found common ground through membership of national bodies such as the Association of Children's Hospices (ACH) and ACT, and they have been able to pool knowledge and examples of good practice.

Children's hospices are usually relatively small units with 8–10 beds that offer a wide range of services including community support, respite care, end-of-life care, bereavement support, counselling and group work. Some children's hospices such as Helen House and Martin House grew out of a Christian tradition. Others have secular origins whilst welcoming families from the variety of cultures and faiths represented in their geographical area. For example at Acorns Selly Oak in South Birmingham, over 40 per cent of families using the hospice are members of South Asian communities.

Respite care was the primary focus for the foundation of Helen House, the first children's hospice which opened in 1982. Specialist respite services remain the predominant role of many children's hospices nearly a quarter of a century later, with the emphasis on creating an environment for holistic child-centred and family care.

The development of children's hospice services in Great Britain has often been perceived and described as a sequence of events. Such a view is unhelpful because it does not recognise that the voluntary sector has made a major contribution to paediatric palliative care, meeting the in-depth needs of individual family situations and plugging gaps in statutory provision. Thus Helen House Hospice was built primarily to provide respite care for families with a life-limited child, whilst the Acorns organisation has also embraced the philosophy of providing community support for families. More recently community projects such as the Diana Community Nursing Teams have taken forward a model of home-nursing support. Outreach nursing was first provided by Martin House and has become the blueprint of newer organisations such as CHASE Hospice Care for Children, in advance of the opening of their hospice buildings.

Individual hospices have concentrated on specific areas of care and have become centres of excellence in areas such as sibling support, fathers' support, mothers' support, grandparent support, bereavement support and counselling. Medical and nursing practice has been developed alongside other professional groups. Working relationships have not always been harmonious but, nevertheless, collaboration has been successful in providing a seamless service for children and their families. Recent healthcare initiatives have focused on the importance of patient and family involvement in the care that patients receive. In 2003, ACT recommended that development in paediatric palliative care should be a 'continuous process that is regularly reviewed' and the principles of Clinical Governance state that practice must be evidence-based (DoH 1998). Without research it is impossible to ascertain what merits the term 'best practice'. To this end some hospices are appointing staff with responsibility for research and development within their organisation.

As children's palliative care services have evolved, they have done so in response to local initiatives, the recognition of individual healthcare personnel for holistic family-centred care and through a desire to enhance the quality of experience for life-limited children. Hain (2002) notes that children's hospices are predicted by some as likely to develop into specialist units as adult hospices have done, providing the clinical base for paediatricians specialising in palliative care.

Children's hospices have not developed to a national or local plan, however. Rather they have sprung up where a local person or persons have had the finance, charisma or drive to make it happen. Carlisle (1988) wrote more than a decade and a half ago that 'there is a growing concern that the mushrooming of hospices is not appropriate to children and family needs. There are worries that they are not being planned, coordinated or strategically placed.' (p.20) Provision of paediatric palliative care is still extremely uneven in the

United Kingdom and this has been recognised by ACH and ACT, who have recently embarked on a mapping exercise.

The majority of staff recruited to children's hospices live locally. With no other children's hospice in the area, many will have little experience of hospice care. Staff who formerly worked in busy paediatric hospital departments will be experienced practitioners in that environment. The concept of empowering parents as partners in their child's care, undertaking complex medical tasks, may be a new and challenging philosophy. Hospice managers, who are usually very experienced and competent, will be faced with some staff that see the unit as an intensive care environment. Other staff may perceive the unit as a thera-peutic community with good quality nursing. Notwithstanding, most units have recruited, trained and developed a multi-disciplinary, multi-skilled pool of staff committed and enthused to take forward the philosophy of hospice care. Today, with more hospices and more posts, the children's hospice move-ment can offer professionals a career structure which attracts highly skilled staff.

New hospices are opened with staff who are vastly experienced in their own professions, for example nurse managers, nurses, doctors, counsellors, social workers and care assistants. However, as we have already seen, many of these people will have no past experience of hospice care. Placed in a new environment it is understandable that they fall back on their experience and qualifications. Nurses will be nurses; social workers will expect to provide psycho-social support. At the very time that it is vital for a staff group to work together and communicate with each other, they are likely to revert to type, speak in jargon and create tensions.

The idea that a children's hospice is not a building but a philosophy of care is widely argued. Few professionals engaged in paediatric palliative care would disagree with this viewpoint, but every hospice building still needs to be managed. Managers will have to combine the philosophy of care with organisational and logistic considerations. For example, when a hospice design is discussed architects advise: 'Calculate storage space carefully and then double it!' However, when the unit opens, either the head nurse bemoans the lack of storage space or families rattle around in large rooms!

All children's hospices have developed within the voluntary sector. Each will have had founder members driven by their own dreams and visions, com-mitted to the building and running of the service. The relationship between the founders/trustees and paid staff in a hospice is crucial to the wellbeing of the organisation. Indeed, the founders would not have succeeded had they not had the drive to complete the building and fund the staff group. In 1988, Huntly wrote about the potential difficulties which may occur when hospice founders hand over responsibility of a hospice to paid officers. In any group there will be a range of opinions. Tales abound about hospice managers being unable to change the décor or furnishings without the express permission of the founders! Later on, trustee fatigue may set in after initial capital costs for building are achieved.

Paediatric palliative care is costly. A ten-bed respite facility will cost in the region of £1 million a year to run, with additional resources needed for care in the community. On average children's hospices in England receive just over 5 per cent of their income from statutory sources, mostly from local Primary Care Trusts. Over one-third receive no form of statutory funding at all. The situation in across the United Kingdom is different. In Scotland, for example, in 2005 CHASE received 18.5 per cent of its income from statutory sources. In South Wales, Ty Hafen Children's Hospice received 13 per cent, but in North Wales, Hope House only receives 4 per cent from statutory sources. In Northern Ireland, Horizon House receives no government funding at all. Admittedly the Department of Health has little control over the demography of children's hospices, but this does not negate the need to support a neglected area of care.

In 1989 Virginia Bottomley, the then Health Minister, said, 'The Government's objective is to work towards a position in which the contribution from public funds available to voluntary hospices and similar organisations matches that of voluntary giving' (DoH 1989). The funding has not been forthcoming and it has become increasingly hard to explain to volunteer fundraisers why the Government are not prepared to fund the healthcare of life-limited children. At Acorns we have three times more volunteers than paid staff, contributing about £1 million a year to each hospice. Volunteers themselves probably contribute in excess of £1 million annually to each children's hospice, together with Community Fundraising and Grant Making Trusts which play an important part in helping match the provision of paediatric palliative care to demand.

Sheldon and Speck (2002) expressed concern that children's hospices were likely to face economic challenges as they became an established part of children's palliative care services, yet with minimal funding from statutory sources. Often children's hospices meet care costs for children with life-limiting illnesses which, under different circumstances, would be met by Health Services. For example, many children's hospices pay fees to local GP surgeries for doctors to visit regularly and for out-of-hours services. In a parliamentary debate on 1 May 2003, the Under Secretary of State for Health, David Lammy, said:

> We as a Government have long recognised that respite, short-break care is essential, as it allows the family time to rest and enables them to continue to care for their ill child, siblings and themselves. It also brings the opportunity for peer socialising of children and young people, who can be difficult to access elsewhere.

It is arguably far easier to obtain corporate support for the capital costs for building a hospice than it is for the running costs of any charity. Indeed, in recent times there has been a downturn in charity funding with money for children's hospices in very short supply. In order to secure the future financial stability of children's hospices, Primary Care Trusts (PCTs) need to recognise the needs of children with life-limiting illnesses in the communities they serve. In order to do this, they must develop open and honest relationships with the voluntary sector and work collaboratively with Strategic Health Authorities to secure funding. All those concerned need to think intelligently and compassionately about the individual needs faced by families with a life-limited child.

Children's hospices provide unrivalled flexible and responsive care, meeting the individual needs of the child and their family. It takes courage, determination and very hard work to provide a service worthy of being called excellent. Children's hospices might rightly be proud of their achievements to date, but never complacent. They must ensure that their desire to respond to need is supported by sustainable revenue, which will guarantee that vulnerable families receive the care and support they deserve.

At the end of October 2006, the Health Minister Ivan Lewis announced that 35 children's hospices in England would benefit from emergency funding of £27 million. He also confirmed that an independent review of England's children's palliative care services headed by Professor Sir Alan Craft (Professor of Child Health at Newcastle University) and Sue Killen (a Director General in the Civil Service) would be carried out. The findings of the review are expected in spring 2007.

Key points

- Children's hospice care is a relatively new service, beginning a quarter of a century ago in the UK, with the opening of Helen House. Provision of paediatric palliative care is still uneven in the UK.

- The distinct role of children's hospices in supporting life-limited children and their families has been recognised by the Royal College of Paediatrics and the Association for Children with Life-threatening or Terminal Conditions and their Families.

- Available data for children with life-limiting conditions is based on incidence of death, rather than diagnosis.

- Children's hospices provide a variety of support, including community care, respite care, end of life care, bereavement support, counselling and group work.

- Individual children's hospices have become centres of excellence in areas such as sibling support, parent support, cultural and religious care, grandparent support, bereavement support and counselling.

- Paediatric palliative care embraces a philosophy that attends to the psychological, physical, spiritual and social needs of the life-limited child and their family.

- Volunteers probably contribute in excess of £1 million annually to each hospice. Hospices also rely on community fundraising and Grant Making Trusts to enable them to provide a service, matched to demand.

- Children's hospices are likely to develop into specialist units, providing the clinical base for paediatricians specialising in paediatric palliative care.

Implications for practice

- The success of paediatric palliative care demands that all providers work together to provide seamless care matched to the needs of medically vulnerable young people and their families.

- Practitioners should recognise that parents often become experts in caring for their child, taking on clinical interventions and complex medical tasks.

- Managers need to combine the philosophy of paediatric palliative care with organisational skills and logistic factors.

- The relationship between the founders/trustees and paid staff in a hospice is crucial to the wellbeing of an organisation.

- If the financial security of children's hospices is to be achieved, PCTs need to develop open and honest relationships with the voluntary sector, and work collaboratively with Strategic Health Authorities to secure funding.

Working Collaboratively

Brian Warr

The care of children with life-limiting illnesses is holistic and multi-disciplinary requiring a range of services and skills (ACT/RCPCH 2003). In order to provide flexible comprehensive support to all members of a child's family, services must be coordinated so that the wide range of agencies across health, social and voluntary sectors are able to make a valid contribution. This requires effective networking, cooperation and commitment to collaborative partnerships in practice.

Models of care are different. Some children with life-limiting illnesses are cared for in the community, some in children's hospices and some in hospital. Wherever the care setting, the overall aim is to meet the needs of the child and their family and to maintain the equilibrium of life as far as possible (Callery and Smith 1991). Seamless care follows the child from one environment to another and recognises the skills and expertise of the multi-professional team. There will be occasions when families use palliative care and curative therapy owing to the trajectory of a child's life-limiting illness (ACT/RCPCH 2003). Palliative care may sometimes be most appropriate from the time of the child's diagnosis and, at others, treatment may be used alongside palliative therapy, such as in children with cystic fibrosis (Goldman and Schuller 2006; Robinson *et al.* 1997). Furthermore, the need for palliative care may vary throughout the course of the illness, depending on remission or relapses.

Goldman and Schuller (2006) believe that the problems faced by children and young people are dependent on many variables. In traditional approaches to children with complex needs, practitioners have worked separately which has resulted in fragmented service provision. More recently there has been a commitment by many agencies to working collaboratively with families and with each other. For example, ACT has campaigned for many years about the need for services to be coordinated around the individual needs of each family, taking account of their views and recognising the central role and expertise that parents have in the care of their children.

In 2005 Al Aynsley Green, the Children's Commissioner for England, acknowledged that top level managers and those charged with governance and strategic decision-making have in the past failed sick children by perceiving them as 'small adults needing small beds'. Aynsley Green expressed a commitment towards extending and developing the historical success and efficacy of social reformers such as Barnardo, Rowntree and Dickens. He believes that the new role of Children's Commissioner must support a transformation of children's services.

Families are often overwhelmed by the number of professionals involved with them (Neill 1996). The DfES (2005) document *Professional Guidance for Children with Additional Needs* recommends that parents and carers should have one practitioner who acts as a single point of contact for them and supports them in making informed choices about the care they need; who ensures they receive appropriate help at the right time, delivered by skilled and appropriate practitioners; and who makes sure that professional duplication and inconsistency are avoided. Such a person can make a real difference to the quality of experience families enjoy, especially if the paediatrician remains involved in caring for the child and works alongside a range of service providers.

There is evidence that provision for adolescents and young people with life-limiting illnesses diminishes as they grow older. Indeed, young people who survive to adulthood and make the transition to adult services find that service providers do not have as much experience of caring for patients with non-malignant illness as their paediatric counterparts.

Each family's needs are individual and will change over a period of time. Therefore, a wide range of services will be required in order to provide flexible care that complements each family's own skills and the contribution of Primary Care Teams. In many cases the needs of children with life-limiting conditions are closely allied with the needs of families of children who have disabilities.

Since the early 1980s, a tremendous amount has been written about working with parents who have a child with a disability. Authors such as Carpenter (1997), Brown (2001) and Hornby (1998) have described the importance of working collaboratively in practice. However, it was not until 1999 that Hornby developed a theoretical model that recognised the collaborative relationship between parents and professionals (see Figure 2.1). Although Hornby's model was originally deigned for educational settings, it has relevance, with some adaptations, to working in children's hospices.

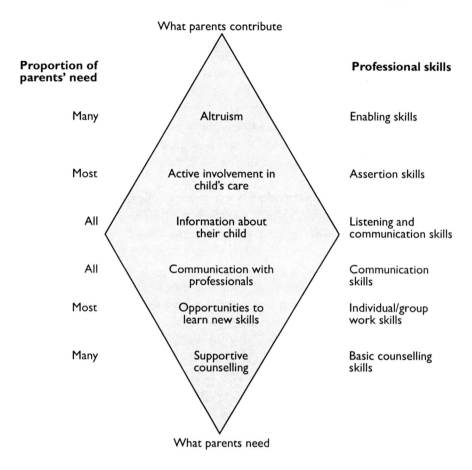

Figure 2.1 Meeting parents' needs – the supportive role of professionals (based on Hornby 1999)

The diamond represents parental needs and the contributions that parents are able to make to their child's care. The model also demonstrates how some parents will need greater guidance, whilst others are able to make extensive contributions. For example, all parents need professionals who are able to communicate with them, and some may need individual counselling.

Information about their child

All parents have a wealth of knowledge about their child. Indeed, they *are* the experts about their child's behaviour, likes and dislikes and daily care, including medical care. Professionals need to work collaboratively with parents in order to be able to tap into this knowledge. They will also need to possess excellent communication and listening skills, in order to enter into meaningful conversations with families.

Involvement in their child's care

Many parents develop complex skills in their child's care, including medical procedures, symptom control and pain management. Professionals are often astounded by the expertise of parents. They need to encourage and empower parents to make decisions on behalf of or with their child, whilst also being available to give advice and support when it is needed. A flexible working partnership involves listening to parents' needs and helping them to be assertive, in order to communicate their ideas, needs and concerns, so that they are able to gain the best care for their child. Professionals also need to be assertive with colleagues from within and outside their own service, in order to act as advocates for families.

Altruism

Many families with a life-limited child seem to possess the capacity to reach out and support other parents. At Acorns, this is lived out in practice in groups such as Fathers' Groups, Asian Mothers' Groups and Grandparent Groups. Other parents, both bereaved and non-bereaved, speak at professional conferences and open days or write in hospice journals and newsletters. It should be recognised however that parents should *never* be exploited, but enabled by professionals to make the contribution that is right for them.

Opportunities to learn new skills

Most parents welcome opportunities to learn new skills in caring for their child. Sometimes parents prefer to develop new capacities through attending groups, but, more often, skills are acquired through modelling care and medical procedures carried out by professionals. Whatever the setting, in addition to learning, parents will benefit from being able to share their own ideas and to raise their concerns, a process that can be facilitated by professionals who have developed teaching and group-work skills.

Hain (2002) says that the early assumption that all aspects of care of children were the paediatrician's domain has, in more recent times, given way to appreciation of the skills of other members of a multi-disciplinary team. The numbers of home-based palliative care teams are increasing, together with Specialist Children's Palliative Care posts in nursing and medicine. Community Care Teams usually include children's community nurses, social workers, psychologists, occupational therapists and speech and language therapists.

Children's hospices and the voluntary sector make an increasingly important contribution, frequently filling the gaps in statutory provision.

The ACT/RCPCH (2003) document makes the following recommendations:

- a named person in each district to monitor and coordinate services to families
- Provision of flexible holistic palliative care services in each district
- a Key Worker assigned to each family with a life-limited child
- development and extension of paediatric community nursing services
- provision of respite care, both in children's hospices and in the community
- education and professional development opportunities for professions allied to medicine
- a network of tertiary consultants with specialisms in paediatric palliative care.

Children's hospices provide the majority of care in respite services and they employ a multi-disciplinary team including staff nurses trained in paediatric work, nursery nurses, occupational therapists and physiotherapists, play and activity workers/therapists, teachers, adolescent workers, social workers and care assistants. Many also employ Key Workers and some, such as Acorns, have staff dedicated to coordinating and supporting care for families from minority ethnic communities.

Because each children's hospice service is unique, it is difficult to generalise concerning cooperation with outside agencies, and most continue to have to work very hard to gain collaboration. In the early days of children's hospice services some hospices sought expertise from local and national voluntary organisations, but with limited success. The founding trustees of Acorns Children's Hospice were so disappointed with the lack of cooperation, help and advice offered that two paragraphs were included in the Memorandum and Articles of the Association stating the objectives of the service would include research and assisting in the teaching and training of personnel in other like-minded organisations. As the work of Acorns has developed, the organisation receives an increasing number of requests for partnerships. Most children's hospices can disseminate their knowledge and expertise through professional development and training courses. Requests from adult services which are beginning to extend their outreach to patients with life-limiting illnesses other than cancer are increasingly looking to children's hospices for information and partnership opportunities.

In 2002, the RCPCH created a special interest group to further professional development programmes for paediatricians, GPs and others committed to expertise in palliative care. Today, increasing numbers of Paediatric Community Nursing Teams such as Diana Teams, and individual paediatricians from hospitals and the community, are undergoing training. Links are also being made with children's hospices and there appears to be a genuine commitment to demonstrate collaborative partnership.

A number of recent policy initiatives affect the lives of children with disabilities and, in some cases, those with life-limiting illnesses. The 2003 ACT/RCPCH document identifies a number of factors that will contribute to the type and level of services commissioned or purchased for children with life-limiting conditions, and their families:

- identification of children in their home district with coordinated care from diagnosis onwards

- symptom management and knowledgeable reliable support in the case of emergencies through local medical and nursing services

- encouragement to attend appropriate play and recreational facilities and programmes provided by health, social services and education

- psychological and spiritual support from the NHS and outside agencies as appropriate

- assistance with practical and financial concerns to help families receive their entitlements

- short-term regular respite care, both within and outside the home

- care and emotional support, comfort and guidance during the end stages of the child's life and at the time of the child's death

- bereavement care for the parents, siblings and the extended family.

The DfES (2004a) document *Every Child Matters – Change for Children* sets the context for the Government's commitment towards every child having the support they need. Although *Every Child Matters* has little specific information about developing services in response to the needs of children with disabilities and their families, the following five outcomes provide a foundation for the development of service provision:

1. Be healthy.

2. Stay safe.

3.   Enjoy and achieve.

4.   Make a positive contribution.

5.   Achieve economic wellbeing.

The National Service Framework

The National Service Framework for Children, Young People and Maternity Services (NSF) was published in the latter part of 2004. It aims to ensure fair, high-quality and integrated health and social care for children from pre-birth to adulthood.

The framework incorporates 11 National Standards including five standards that are matched to the health and social wellbeing of all children. A further six standards are specifically matched to sick children and those with disbilities. It was anticipated in 2004 that the NSF would take up to a decade to implement the standards fully, but the NHS and local authorities are already undergoing an assessment on the quality of service provision in relation to the standards.

Standard 8 of the NSF confirmed a commitment to improving services for life-limited and life-threatened children and their families: 'High quality palliative care services should be available for all children and young people who need them.'

Furthermore, Standard 8 also identifies a number of service providers of palliative care including children's hospices and other voluntary agencies, the NHS and education and social care and recommends that these agencies work together to provide an integrated service. The standard also makes it a requirement for children's palliative care to be prioritised in Local Development Plans.

Children's Trusts

The development of the Children's Trust model for delivery of local services has been at the forefront of taking forward the duties of the Children Act 2004 (DfES 2004b) and *Every Child Matters*, with 35 Pathfinder Children's Trusts established in Local Authorities. The brief of these Pathfinder Trusts was to improve partnership working, matched to local needs, in order to develop high-quality, responsive and flexible service delivery for children with disabilities and medical conditions. By 2008, Local Authorities are required to have in place arrangements that produce integrated working at all levels from planning through to delivery.

The creation of Children's Trusts has presented authorities with a huge challenge, not least because it demands a strong strategy and a commitment from all agencies, together with the inclusion of service users and strategic and operational changes within all partner agencies.

At the time of writing, many of the 35 Children's Trusts have made progress in budget sharing and agreeing joint funding. Not withstanding, for voluntary agencies such as children's hospices, there are dilemmas, not least concerning agreement on who pays for what. Furthermore, there is still a lack of robust evidence concerning the number of children requiring palliative care services in a Health Authority or PCT. In reality, by and large, children's hospice services are not fully integrated into the work of Children's Trusts but are involved where appropriate.

National mapping of life-limited children and children's palliative care services

Many existing registers of children with special needs or disabilities do not identify children with long-term needs, particularly those who have less contact with secondary and specialist services. Services for children with palliative care needs have often evolved in a piecemeal fashion, with little or no local or national strategic planning. Even with the increase in services through pump-priming from The Big Lottery Fund, it is likely that more children's palliative care services are still needed. Ideally, further development of services will be guided by robust needs-based assessment and delivered as part of a clear local and national strategy. However, without accurate information on existing services, together with solid epidemiological data, the needs of the population of children with life-limiting conditions cannot be correlated within current service provision. Therefore, there is likely to be unmet needs and inequity of service provision.

The need for mapping of children's palliative care services has been recognised as a priority for many years. Mapping is essential to ensure that there is solid evidence of the number of children who need palliative care and to determine where the gaps are in service provision. Only then can service development be strategically planned to meet the needs of children and families. Work is already underway in The Wirral on developing a methodology for capturing the number of children in need of palliative care, and for developing a mapping process for children's palliative care services. It is planned to implement the model of data collection across the whole of the Merseyside/Cheshire region and then to carry out an evaluation to see if it will be feasible to roll out a national model. Once the register has been compiled, ACT recommends a paediatrician (who works both in hospital and community settings), a community children's nurse and a therapist, who should be appointed to each district. These persons should have direct responsibility for life-limited children, assessment and review of the child's needs and those of the child's family. They will also need time to develop and plan services. Family Key Workers will play a vital role in the coordination of services to meet individual family needs. Families appreciate continuity of support from a dedicated Key Worker and, wherever possible, changes in Key Worker should be avoided to safeguard seamless care.

Over the last two decades, Central Government has promised financial support to children's hospices but delivered little. Local Health Authorities have constantly been reorganised, demanding new negotiation and new responses. Overall funding to date by the statutory sector has been minimal and, in part, some fault must lie with children's hospices which were often *in situ* before negotiations were instigated. In some cases, the skill mix of trustees and staff fell short of someone with expertise in negotiating contracts with Local Authorities. Where partnerships were formed, Health Authorities or PCTs were often struggling to make ends meet.

To secure the future of children's hospices, Primary Care Trusts need to determine the needs of families in the communities they serve. To do so, they must establish a genuine relationship with the voluntary sector and there needs to be informed discussion at local level that relates to funding decisions. Above all, it means thinking globally about the needs that a child and family may have. There is an urgent need for professionals and services to work collaboratively in order to enhance the quality of client experience and the effectiveness of support to life-limited children and their families. Working together is a continuum that incorporates multi-disciplinary, inter-disciplinary and trans-disciplinary cooperation. At each point along the trajectory of the child's illness, there is scope for professionals and service providers to work together to enhance the quality of experience for families.

Key points

- The care of children with life-limiting illnesses is holistic and multi-disciplinary, requiring a range of services and skills.
- Each family's needs are individual and will change over a period of time.
- Seamless care follows the child from one environment to another, and recognises the skills and expertise of the multi-professional team.
- There is a lack of robust evidence concerning the number of children requiring palliative care services in Health Authorities and PCTs. Many existing registers do not identify children with long-term needs.

- Children's hospices and the voluntary sector make an increasingly important contribution to palliative care, frequently filling gaps in statutory provision.

- There is evidence that provision for adolescents and young people with life-limiting illnesses diminishes as they grow older.

- In order to provide flexible, comprehensive support to all members of a child's family, services must be coordinated so that a wide range of agencies across health, social and voluntary sectors are able to make a valid contribution.

- Working together is a continuum that incorporates multi-disciplinary, inter-disciplinary and trans-disciplinary cooperation.

Implications for practice

- A range of services will be required in order to provide flexible care that complements each family's skills and recognises the contribution of Primary Care Teams.

- Mapping of children's palliative care services is essential to ensure that there is robust evidence of the number of children who need palliative care, and to determine gaps in service provision.

- Organisations need to ensure effective networking, cooperation and a commitment to collaborative partnership in practice.

- Families should have one practitioner who acts as a single point of contact for them and supports them in making informed choices about their needs.

- Further development of services should be guided by robust needs-based assessment and delivered as part of a clear local and national strategy.

Part 2

Responding to Holistic Needs from Diagnosis through to Terminal Care and Bereavement

Assessment of Needs
and Models of Care

Ann Smallman

The Children's National Service Framework (NSF) expects high quality palliative care to be available to all children and young people who need it and
requires consideration of the child's and family's physical, emotional, cultural
and practical needs in a way that promotes choice, independence, creativity
and quality of life (DoH 2004).

Palliative care services for children have been defined as:

> an active and total approach to care, embracing physical, emotional,
> social and spiritual elements. It focuses on enhancements of quality of
> life for the child and support for the family and includes the manage-
> ment of distressing symptoms, provision of respite and care through
> death and bereavement. (ACT/RCPCH 2003, p.6)

Palliative care services are frequently described as needs-led services, but it is
necessary to identify and understand those needs.

Identifying need
The historical perspective
Assessment of need has generally been based around the medical model of care
and traditional nursing models have reflected this. Historically nursing was
based on the biomedical model of care with an emphasis on the physical
aspects. This philosophy was further supported by a view that the mind and
soul was the province of clerics, while the body became the province of the
doctor (Pearson-Vaughan and Fitzgerald 1994). Over time, as medical knowledge and nursing expertise progressed, nursing models were increasingly
focused around individual body systems, for example the gastrointestinal system and cardiovascular system. Models were developed that linked the systems
together in different ways.

In 1976, Roy looked at how external influences impacted on the different body systems, for example the impact of stress. Roy's Model of Nursing Care has been revised and developed over the years (Roy and Andrews 1999). In her Model of Care, Roper (1980) used activities of daily living (movement, breathing, eating and so on) as a framework to assess the patient and to plan and evaluate practice.

Many nursing teams have built their own assessment documentation on the back of these principles. Most have been designed around body systems and activities of daily living, but have broadened to encompass more detail and incorporate further micro-assessments within the wider process. This might include specific assessments such as pain assessment, respiratory function assessment, postural assessment etc. While attempting to include the needs of the whole patient, most of these models remain very medically orientated and fail to consider the many facets of need the patient (child) may have.

Other assessment tools were built around the needs of professionals such as physiotherapists or speech therapists, but without any links to the overall assessment process. This has led to duplication of information and causes frustration to the patient and their family.

Additionally, models are built around a process or expected progression, for example child development assessments comparing individual progress against the expected norms or Pathways of Care, that score deviation from an expected recovery, such as following surgery.

Family-centred care

With recognition of the importance of the family in caring for the sick child came the introduction of models of care and assessment, based around the family. Family-centred care was implemented in major teaching hospitals from the late 1970s, and in 1988 Casey introduced a family-centred nursing model. Together with other models developed from the Casey principles, existing nursing models were revised and the family's need to be involved in the care of their child was taken into account. Built upon the principles of partnership and negotiation, these models encourage family members to participate in assessment, planning and delivery of care.

Many practitioners consider family-centred care to be a cornerstone of paediatric practice, yet there is no single definition of family-centred care in existence. One definition is 'negotiation between health professionals and the family, which results in shared decision-making about what the child's care will be and who will provide it' (Corlett and Twycross 2006, p.35). Others interpret the concept as a list of elements of care. Thus, whilst family-centred care considers the wider needs of the child and family, in practice this may be at a relatively superficial level depending on the depth of the assessment and the interpretation and communication of the information received from individual families.

Assessment will also depend on a definition of 'family'. Who does the child consider as core members of their 'family'? For some children, their grandparents may be the main carers, for others their parent's partner may be a crucial support and influence, even though they are not related. The situation may be further complicated by former partner's relatives, step-siblings, foster carers, home-care teams etc.

Family-centred care is grounded in the participation and involvement of the family, but there is much evidence to suggest that this is not always a reality and in many cases mere lip service is paid to the process. It is well-recognised that experienced nursing staff are generally confident in enabling decision-making, but negotiation of care and the assessment of need may be affected by the expectations of both staff and parents, issues of control and the lack or quality of information (Corlett and Twycross 2006). Family-centred care may also be less successful where family involvement in care is influenced by resource issues such as staff shortages or poor facilities. Success is also determined by the family's previous experience of healthcare.

All families need to achieve a balance between stability and change, but roles and relationships may need to alter to accommodate developments in the physical, social or emotional life of family members (Down and Simons 2006). This means that the assessment of care must be constantly revisited to deal not only with changes in the child's condition, but also on the impact of this on the family.

Family-centred care and the adolescent

A model of family-centred care does not always meet the needs of adolescents who may wish to develop the capacity for self-care and making their own decisions. Models may also fail to consider issues such as body image, sexuality or the importance of peers to this group of young people.

Parents who have acted as carers and advocates for their child for many years may find it difficult to enable their child to make decisions or choices for themselves, particularly if it means that they have to step back and are less involved or informed. Young people may feel strongly about consenting or otherwise to treatments and care options and family members may feel excluded. They may become frightened and marginalised and see it as failure to protect their child or become angry by their lack of involvement. This may be particularly pertinent around the time of transition to adult services. Adolescents may also view their friends and peers as their 'family' and wish them to be factored into the arrangements for their care. (See Chapter 18, 'Transition from Paediatric Palliative Care to Adult Services'.)

Child-centred care

The child should be at the heart of any planning process. The Social Care Institute for Excellence's) *Blueprint Project* (SCIE 2004) defines child-centred care as:

- respecting and valuing children as individuals in their own right
- respecting children's rights under the United Nations Convention on the Rights of the Child (UNCRC)
- seeing each child as an individual with their own interests and abilities
- focusing on children's needs and interests now and in the future
- respecting children's competence and their ability to make decisions.

A child-centred approach requires professionals to consider the child first and their condition second. While traditional nursing models, such as Roper, are easily adapted to focus on the physical and health needs of the child, they frequently fail to address other necessities for children, such as development, education and play. They also neglect to recognise that children with palliative care needs may require care over many years. Such children are still developing and they will need constant reassessment, even if their health needs do not change. A child-centred model also needs to consider factors such as the availability of age-appropriate surroundings, activities, language and the child's cultural norms.

The Assessment Framework

The DoH describes:

> those children whose vulnerability is such that they are unlikely to reach or maintain a satisfactory level of health or development, or their health and development will be significantly impaired without the provision of services, as 'in need'. (DoH 2000a, p.5)

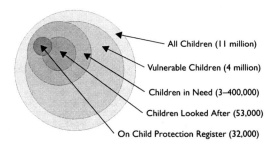

Figure 3.1 An Assessment Framework (DoH 2000b). Reprinted with permission from the Department of Health.

An Assessment Framework (DoH 2000b) was designed as a comprehensive tool for the multi-professional assessment of 'children in need', with the aim of both safeguarding the child and promoting their welfare. The framework is built on, and around, the standards of the Children Act (1989) and applies to children with and without disabilities. It acknowledges that in addition to identifying services or care for the child, 'providing services which meet the needs of the child are often the most effective way of promoting welfare of children, in particular disabled children'. The framework requires that the child is central to the assessment, but that care is also considered within the context of the child's family and of the community and culture in which the child is growing up.

The core assessment is developed around three main areas: the child's developmental needs; parenting capacity; and family and environmental factors. Greater detail is shown on the assessment triangle in Figure 3.2.

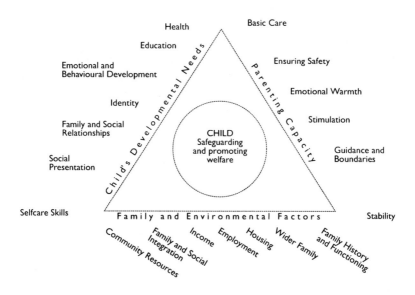

Figure 3.2 Safeguarding and promoting welfare

However, while the model provides the breadth of assessment required for holistic care, there is a lack of focus concerning the assessment of sick children and their families.

A suggested model for paediatric palliative care

It is clear from the research that no single model of care completely meets the needs of the child, family and extended family on their journey through palliative care. Each model provides some elements of care, yet none completely provides the depth of assessment that would give a family confidence to leave their child in the care of others. Neither does any single recognised model of care provide continuity and familiarity for a child who is severely sensory deprived or describes in detail the expertise and clinical skills required to alleviate symptoms. Nor do existing models help to identify the information required to support the entire family through the emotional journey that takes them from diagnosis to the death of their child.

Many factors contribute to palliative care and, where care is worthy of being called 'excellent', this is down to the depth of information obtained as part of the assessment, together with the way that information is incorporated into the delivery of care. As the child and family are conjoined, each is dependent on the other. A holistic approach to care is required that embraces the physical, emotional, spiritual and social needs of the child, their family and significant others in their lives.

The Mercer Model

In 2005, Brown and Mercer described a model of care, based loosely upon Roper's activities of daily living (Figure 3.3). The model is built on the broad philosophy of Acorns Children's Hospice – 'Care for the Child and Support for the Family'. The model, which is used across the Acorns multi-disciplinary team, ensures the child is central and that the needs of the family, local influences and national influences are considered.

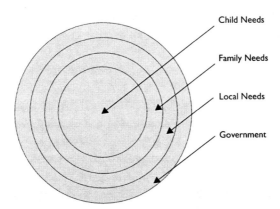

Child Needs

Family Needs

Local Needs

Government

Figure 3.3 The Mercer Model of Care (2005)

The model is based on four key principles:

1. Each child and family is unique and should be treated and respected as such.

2. The family and child are, or will become, the experts in care.

3. Active listening is critical in understanding the needs of the child and family.

4. Sharing information and good communication enables decision-making and informed choices.

Mercer's Model also recognises the need for the child's care to be considered in relation to their developmental needs and that care will need to be age-appropriate, particularly when caring for adolescents.

However, the existing Mercer Model does not totally explore the depth of assessment required to fully meet the needs and expectations of children and families.

The majority of parents are experts in interpreting their child's needs and know intuitively whether they are happy or sad, comfortable, uncomfortable, frightened, uncertain, hungry or tired. Parents and carers of children with complex and palliative care needs are often the *only* people who are able to fully comprehend and meet their child's holistic care. They become experts in their child's condition and treatment options and frequently know more than the professionals caring for them, particularly when that condition is very rare. They become experts in their child's reaction to medication. They are also expert in observing their child's behaviours and how to respond to them especially where the child has difficulties in communication. Their exposure to the minutiae of their child's life means that their attention to detail is second to none. For parents of children with life-limiting conditions, their fear of the future means that no detail of care is too small to bother about or too insignificant to dismiss. Their child's needs often become central to their own needs and those of the extended family.

An effective model of care needs to listen to and observe parental expertise, recognising what is of significance to the family and to the child, in addition to identifying more basic needs. The 'drilling down' into the detail of each and every action is also critical in recognising and utilising parental expertise and in replicating the care at home. 'Layering' of detail in assessment gives the family confidence to trust (Figures 3.4 and 3.5). It also gives the child the reassurance of familiar actions and activities and enables continuity of care from one professional to another. Brown and Mercer (2005) suggest the assessment process of the individual child's needs can also be used as a learning aid for members of the multidisciplinary team.

Child's basic need
Added detail
Micro detail
Underpinning related needs

Figure 3.4 Layering of assessment and care

Child's basic need	Sleep.
Added detail	Child usually sleeps from 7 pm until 6 am, waking once for a drink.
Micro detail	Child settles at 7 pm following bath and story. Child sleeps in a cot with Disney quilt from home. Child prefers to be settled on her back. Child has two dummies – sucks the pink one, holds the yellow one. Blue and white teddy is tucked into the quilt to the child's right. Brown teddy is tucked under child's left arm. Night light is left on. Curtains are shut. Child wakes for a drink between 11pm and midnight – drinks water from red teacher cup. Child wakes at 6.30 am but lies quietly in cot 'chattering' for at least 15 minutes.
Underpinning related needs	Routine has been developed over the last 6 months. 7 pm bedtime allows Mum time to do homework with the older siblings. 15 minutes in the morning is crucial time for Mum to grab her shower before the day begins.

Figure 3.5 Example of layering detail of assessment

Recording a high level of detail enables staff to become familiar with the normal behaviour and responses of the child. For example, a child may regularly become hot and sweaty at night, but this could be interpreted by hospice staff as pyrexia, if the child's normal variation in temperature is not known. The depth of assessment also allows for swift recognition of any abnormal behaviour that may indicate pain or discomfort, thus enabling relevant actions to be taken. This is of particular relevance where children are unable, or too young, to communicate themselves. Layering of assessment gives scope for expertise from other professionals to be easily added to the care plan, enhancing collaboration of care and enriching the care for the child and family.

Assessment may take place in the home, hospital, hospice or school. Privacy and comfort are important and potential sources of distraction should be minimised. It is important that questions are asked that use appropriate levels of language and with interpreter support if required. A generous allocation of time should be allowed for the assessment so that questions can be re-framed to capture the detail needed.

A detailed assessment framework may need to be revised on several occasions before it is complete so that the contributions of different family members, carers, professionals and the child can be included. Thus the depth of assessment enables the identification of significant gaps or misinformation, allowing the expertise of staff to be used to inform or negotiate change with the family. This is of significance as the child deteriorates and the family may have difficulty in coming to terms with loss of function or an increase in symptoms. Understandably, families may cling to old behaviours to try and normalise or 'hold' the situation. Obviously, times like this need to be handled sensitively to avoid a 'we know best', patriarchal approach.

Detailed and layered assessment can be repeated for every aspect of care for the child and family, from basic activities such as feeding and personal care, through a child's health needs and emotional support to their spiritual care, play and education. Additionally the assessment can include discussion about areas such as the use of complementary therapies, the child's likes and dislikes, favourite food, activities and colours. Detail can be sought about the intricacies of equipment, such as sleep systems, new wheelchairs or new medications. Changes in behaviour, bruising and skin marks and sleeping patterns are equally explored in a non-threatening manner. Families and young people can also use these as opportunities to seek answers of their own – their disease process, the availability of other resources or perhaps the supplier for a particular piece of equipment. Discussion around resuscitation status may lead on to more in-depth discussion regarding the disease progression and answering parents' and children's questions about their own illness.

Assessments need to be updated at every opportunity to reflect current detail. The detail of information recorded ensures that changes to the family structure, routines, child development and interests are treated with as much consideration as changes in medications, positioning, symptom management or feeding regimes.

Regardless of the framework used to assess the child's needs, the quality of information will be dependent on the experience and expertise of the assessor. The NSF core skills (DoH 2005) identifies that staff caring for children require skills in six key areas:

1. Communication and engagement

2. Child (young person) development

3. Safeguarding and promoting welfare

4. Supporting transitions

5. Multi-agency working

6. Sharing information.

Less experienced staff may need to be supported in order to gain experience and confidence in using a chosen model of care. They may also need guidance about how to record the complexity of information. They may feel threatened by the knowledge of both the child and family which may outstrip their own and they may need support in dealing with this. Families used to contributing to care assessments in this way will also welcome opportunities to share experiences and feedback, whether as part of evaluation of services or a larger piece of research.

Key points

- There are many models of care in existence – all have both strengths and weaknesses.

- Assessment of need has traditionally been based around medical models of care. Past practice may have failed to consider the holistic needs of the child and the family.

- Family-centred care was introduced to major teaching hospitals from the late 1970s, but there is no single definition of family-centred care.

- Holistic care embraces the physical, emotional, cultural, spiritual and social needs of the child, their family and significant others in the lives of family members.

- Parents and carers of children with complex and palliative care needs are often the *only* people who are able to fully comprehend and meet the child's holistic care.

- Young people require assessment of need matched to their age, developmental level and personal, social and cultural needs.

Implications for practice

- In-depth assessment is essential in order to identify the holistic needs of the life-limited child and their family.

- Regardless of the framework used to assess the child's needs, the quality of information will be dependent on the experience and expertise of the assessor.

- Assessment records need to be documented in ways that provide clarity of content and ease of access.

- Assessment should contain sufficient detail to ensure that care at home is replicated. This 'layering' of assessment should contain a high level of detail to enable all staff to become familiar with the normal behaviour and responses of the child.

- Ways should be sought that enable families and children to contribute to the assessment.

- Assessment should take into account the child in the context of their environment, family and local community.

- Detailed models of assessment provide a learning tool for less experienced staff and students.

- Professionals need to listen to and observe parental expertise, recognising what is significant to the child and the family, in addition to identifying more basic needs.

Managing Children's Pain

Erica Brown

Children vary greatly in their cognitive and emotional development, medical conditions, responses to pain and personal preferences for their care. Symptom control, including pharmacological and alternative management of pain, has been given considerable attention in recent literature. The chapter discusses responses of non-verbal children to pain and discomfort based on recent research findings and the literature. Experience of nurses and care staff at Acorns are also described.

There have been many attempts at reaching a definition of pain. McCaffery (1992) says that 'pain is whatever a person says it is, existing wherever they say that it does' (p.1).

Pain in children and young people with life-limiting illnesses may have many origins and, during the course of their illness, children may experience several types of pain. If pain is untreated, the discomfort that children feel can have serious physical and psychological consequences. Many children with profound and complex disabilities receive excellent care, but professionals may struggle to understand how their behaviour communicates their needs.

Myths surrounding children and pain

Several well-known misconceptions surround childhood pain. These include:

- Children are able to tolerate pain more readily than adults.
- Babies are unable to feel pain due to incomplete mylenation of nerve pathways.
- Children tell the truth about pain.
- Children who play cannot be in pain.
- Children who are given opiate-based medication will become addicted (Collier 1997).

Views such as the above are, however, refuted by some professional bodies. The Royal College of Surgeons and College of Anaesthetists (1990) concluded that although children's experience of pain is different from that of adults, it is no less severe. However, some children use distraction techniques more effectively than adults, and therefore their pain threshold may appear greater.

Children's developmental understanding and response to pain

Children's concept of pain changes as they mature. The following bullet lists, based on the work of Hurley and Whelan (1988), summarise life-limited children's developmental understanding and response to discomfort. It should be remembered, however, that many children and young people will have learning disabilities in addition to their life-limiting condition, and their responses may vary accordingly.

Early years to about seven years, children may:

- think about pain as a physical experience
- consider that pain magically disappears
- be confused about the cause of their pain
- feel that they are in some way responsible for the pain they are experiencing
- feel that someone else is responsible for their pain
- demonstrate aggressive or challenging behaviour
- fight against interventions for pain relief
- experience difficulty locating their pain.

Eight to eleven years, children generally:

- are able to locate the area where they feel discomfort
- regard their pain as an internal experience although they may believe that the cause of their pain is external
- begin to fear that the pain is symptomatic of a serious medical condition
- regress to immature behaviour
- demonstrate anger, frustration or aggressive/challenging behaviour.

Twelve years to late adolescence, young people may:

- describe their discomfort/pain in terms of their body malfunctioning
- struggle with describing their coping strategies
- deny their pain in an attempt to get on with living their lives.

Children communicating their pain

Even very premature babies communicate through crying and altered facial expression that they feel pain, and that they experience distress (Porter 2001). Furthermore, contrary to the views of many psychologists, life-limited children seem to use a variety of ways to communicate their discomfort. Where they have verbal language, some may use adjectives to describe the extent and location of their pain.

> My tummy has a headache.

> My pain goes back to its corner sometimes and it hides. Then it comes out of its corner and it growls at me.

Where children experience receptive, expressive and articulatory and interaction problems, the recognition of pain may present carers with particular challenges, because in addition to adjusting to living with life-limiting conditions, children may experience discomfort from a variety of disabilities (Nolan *et al.* 2000).

Anecdotal evidence suggests that until Hunt's 2003 *Paediatric Pain Profile*, the assessment of pain and discomfort was somewhat ad hoc and problematic. Kenny (1998) says that if children are unable to communicate, they may become 'depersonalised and dehumanised'. More recently, Hamers (1996) reported that children with cerebral palsy received less pain assessment and pain relief than a normative group of children. Children with communication difficulties may:

- lack the ability to communicate in a meaningful way
- have a distorted perception of their world
- lack the ability to anticipate future events
- have additional medical problems which lead to serious developmental delay.

Despite communication problems such as those above, children and young people with severe learning disabilities *are* able to demonstrate how they feel through non-verbal signs and behaviours. However, there is a paucity of published research on augmentative and alternative communication in the case of children and young adults with life-limited conditions (Hunt 2001; Tuffrey-Wijne 2003). Hunt's exploration of the context in which the behaviour displayed by a child is occurring is particularly valuable if physical pain and emotional distress are to be differentiated. Of course, it should be acknowledged that there are many different types of pain (Twycross and Wilcock 2001).

Behavioural indicators of pain

Children in pain will often exhibit changes in behaviour. Commonly accepted indicators of pain are shown in the bullet list below. However, children in continuous pain may adapt, and physiological indicators such as raised pulse rate and blood pressure, sweating or pupil dilation may be absent or erratic. Children of any age may deny pain, especially if they are fearful of injections or aggressive interventions (McCaffery and Wong 1993).

Behavioural indicators of pain include:

- irritability
- frowning or furrowed brow/grimace
- restlessness
- moaning
- changed sleeping patterns
- changed feeding patterns
- inconsolability – crying, with variation in crying patterns/screaming
- self-injury, e.g. biting
- repetitive movements, e.g. rocking, head banging or immobility
- postural changes, e.g. spasm, stiffening, extending body, arching back.

Often the recognition of the child's distressed behaviour is an intuitive rather than a conscious act, a fact reflected in the view that parents and professional carers 'sense' children's feelings. Therefore, identifying a child's distress requires knowledge of the child, information about the context in which the distress occurs, and knowledge about how non-impaired children respond.

Children's pain threshold

It is thought children may be able to develop and use some coping strategies better than adults. For example, when a child is engaged in play, their involvement in what they are doing may be a distraction and as a result they may tolerate pain better. However, adults generally have more control over situations than children do, and they are more knowledgeable about pain relief.

When parents know that their child is experiencing pain, they are naturally extremely distressed. Most parents advocate that symptom control, and ensuring their child's comfort, is of paramount importance. A concern expressed by parents is the effect that pain and discomfort can have on their child, not just in terms of suffering, but also in terms of physical assault caused to their child's already vulnerable state. Parents often see their child decline over a number of years.

> I feel that she has had to live with a lot of discomfort a lot of the time. Because she had a jejunostomy formed when she was born, there is a lot that she accepts. She only really expresses her distress if there are changes in her routine or if for any reason the tube becomes displaced.

Research into non-impaired children's pain threshold indicates that parental assessment is generally more accurate than those of nurses (Craig, Lilley and Gilbert 1996). There is increasing evidence that parents are best qualified to assess behavioural changes that indicate their child is unwell (Callery 1997; McGrath et al. 1998). This is largely because parental caring skills have been learnt over the years and parents often describe knowing their own child 'upside down, inside out and back to front'.

Comfort remains central to effective care. Distress can be caused by many different factors including psychological, social and spiritual issues. When parents know that their child is free of pain this can be a huge source of help to them.

The personal beliefs, attitudes and values of healthcare professionals can affect their perceptions of other people's pain. There is an expectation that health workers take children's views into account (Children Act 1989; Children (Northern Ireland) Order 1995; Children (Scotland) Act 1995). However, it is recognised that children's descriptions of pain may be unreliable (Collier 1997). Furthermore, carers may inadvertently draw their own conclusions rather than observing the child carefully, and taking into account what parents say.

Pain pathways

When treating a child's pain, it is important that nurses and carers understand the activity of pain fibres in the human body and how analgesic drugs react on specific pain receptors. Pain pathways have been described comprehensively in other publications (Anand and Craig 1997; Davis 1993a; Goldman, Hain and Liben 2006; Twycross, Moriarty and Betts 1998). Therefore, it is not intended to duplicate the available literature. Experience of working with non-verbal children at Acorns may, however, enhance the evidence-base for practice. This section of the chapter is therefore devoted to a discussion of interpreting and managing pain in this context.

Pain assessment tools

Paediatric pain management often challenges carers because children may find it difficult to express what they are experiencing. Despite the assessment of children's pain using visual analogue scales, numerical scales and 'face' scales with non-impaired children, some groups of children remain vulnerable because they are unable to describe their pain. As recently as 1996, Cummings, Reid and Finley found that children in hospital were enduring unacceptable levels of pain in spite of the efforts of some professionals to dispel myths about childhood discomfort. Misunderstandings about childhood pain still abound, often centring on a belief concerning the incapacity of young children to feel pain and an uncertainty about a baby's past memory of pain.

Terms such as 'signs' and 'symptoms' are still used interchangeably when describing children's pain, yet they are different in both definition and expression. 'Signs' are observable, obvious and quantifiable (Swartz 1989). 'Symptoms', on the other hand, refer to what the individual child feels – they are subjective responses that are not directly observable or measurable by other people.

Reliable and developmentally appropriate methods are now available for the assessment of pain in children, although paediatric nurses do not always use formal pain assessment tools when assessing children's discomfort. Further, it was not until 2003 that Hunt devised an innovative *Pain Assessment Tool*. The tool is designed to help parents and healthcare professionals to work collaboratively in assessing pain and discomfort in children unable to describe how they are feeling.

For a pain assessment tool to be useful it must:

- detect the presence of pain and discriminate pain from other causes of distress
- detect the severity of the pain (i.e. grade it)
- determine the effectiveness of interventions
- be simple to use
- be appropriate to the child's cognitive development.

N.B. It is recommended that readers refer to Hunt's *Pain Assessment Tool* (2005).

Assessing pain in non-verbal children

Children and young people may experience communication difficulties for a variety of reasons. These include very young non-verbal children of normal cognitive ability, those with neuro-degenerative diseases and metabolic disorders and children with profound and multiple learning disabilities. However, little research has been undertaken in relation to assessing profoundly disabled children's pain. Anecdotal evidence suggests that, where pain is assessed, it is on a somewhat ad hoc basis (Fanurik *et al.* 1999).

Vocalisation is often the means of expressing discomfort with children either crying or moaning. Parents describe their child's pain cry as characteristic. It is often high-pitched, but each child's behaviour is individual and unique. Facial expression may be another indicator of distress, with a child's eyes lacking brightness and sparkle. Sometimes their skin takes on a general pallor, with either an increase in bodily 'floppiness' or rigidity. Often children appear less responsive generally and some may turn away from carers and appear 'empty' or 'depressed'. Self-harming, including biting and head banging or hitting limbs against cot sides and walls, is yet another symptom of a child's distress. Physiological responses such as raised temperature, increased pulse rate and sweating are other indicators.

Parents, carers and professionals who work with children with severe communication difficulties often describe a 'language' of distress, although the interpretation of this distress is often implicit rather than explicit. In other words, distress is often noted as an impression rather than a conscious observation of behaviours, and in many cases it is not documented. The scenario below describes the kind of situation that may be encountered in practice.

> An 11-year-old boy with Batten disease (also Statemented as having severe learning difficulties) had had a tracheotomy nine months previously. His mother noticed that he would intermittently giggle and laugh in a way similar to previous occasions when he had been in pain. Advice was sought, but the paediatrician did not consider the boy was distressed. His mother did not feel confident enough to challenge the paediatrician's opinion until her son experienced breathing difficulties. Further investigations showed a lesion had formed in the boy's throat which, almost certainly, caused his distress.

In this case, increased confidence in the mother's existing skills may have led to better patient care, although distinguishing cues of physical pain from other sources of emotional or physical distress can be difficult.

Parental roles in assessing their child's needs seem to involve three broad processes:

- guessing about the pain
- working out what is wrong with their child

- instinctively or intuitively knowing what is wrong (Carter, McArthur and Cunliffe 2001).

Guesses are nearly always contextualised and based on the intimate knowledge that parents have of their child. Parents also use a systematic approach to working out what is causing their child's discomfort. Often they refer to going through a mental checklist, which may involve holding or talking to their child and gaining feedback through their cues and responses. Frequently they report that they instinctively know that something is wrong with their child, and they feel that their sense of this is extremely highly developed and generally accurate.

Assessing non-verbal children's pain – some principles

These principles include:

- continuous assessment of the frequency, duration and intensity of discomfort
- involving parents
- finding a way of helping the child to communicate
- observing the child's non-verbal cues.

McGrath et al.'s (1998) helpful checklist below provides indicators of pain behaviour exhibited by non-verbal cognitively impaired children.

Features of distress

- Absence of contentment, changed habitual behaviour and mannerisms, tense facial expression
- general bodily tension
- increased body movement
- repetitive vocalisation
- aggression
- withdrawal
- noisy breathing
- sweating
- changes in skin colour
- moaning
- twitching
- rigidity
- restlessness.

(McGrath 1998)

Complementary and alternative medicine

Complementary and alternative medicine has been used for centuries. In 2001, the World Health Organization published a report documenting examples of complementary and alternative therapy worldwide. Little attention has been paid, however, to the practice of using complementary and alternative medicine to alleviate pain and distressing symptoms experienced by children with life-limited illness.

It is beyond the scope of this book to write comprehensively about the benefits of complementary and alternative medicine in paediatric palliative care. Readers are referred to the website addresses after the References, which may be of help.

In order to manage children's pain, it is essential that a reliable assessment of their discomfort is used. Matching an appropriate assessment to the individual needs of life-limited children, who may be in the very early stages of communication, is extremely challenging. Each child will respond individually to pain and develop coping strategies (Adler 1990). A number of influences also impact on a child's capacity to cope. These include the child's cognitive and emotional stage of development, their gender, the culture and ethnicity of the child, faith (if appropriate), family coping strategies and the child's previous experience of pain. Where possible, children should be involved in their pain management, since it is thought that this may increase their self-esteem and encourage the development of coping strategies.

Remarkable progress in medicine has resulted in the ability of medical science to diagnose and treat symptoms of children with life-limited illnesses. Assessment of children's pain has also advanced considerably, and there have been a number of excellent publications that cover up-to-date symptom control and pain relief, including several produced by children's hospices. Readers seeking a more comprehensive account of the management of children's pain may like to refer to the following: Davies and de Vlaming 2006; Hunt *et al.* 2003; Rainbows Children's Hospice 2006; Wolfe, Grier and Klar 2000. (See References for full bibliographic details.)

Key points

- Pain felt by children with life-limited illnesses may have many origins. During the trajectory of the illness, a child may experience several types of pain.
- The way in which children cope with pain is individual.
- As children mature, their concept of pain changes.
- Life-limited children who experience receptive, expressive, articulatory and interactive problems present carers with

challenges because, in addition to their illness, they may also experience discomfort from a variety of disabilities.

- Children of all abilities exhibit changed behaviour in relation to discomfort and wellbeing.

- Most parents advocate that symptom control and ensuring their child's comfort is of paramount importance.

- The influence of culture, ethnicity, faith, gender, cognitive ability, developmental stage and previous experience of pain will all impact on how well a child copes.

Implications for practice

- Nursing and care staff need knowledge about children's developmental understanding concerning pain and how they communicate their discomfort.

- The successful management of pain requires reliable, valid, measurable and frequent assessment.

- Assessing and recording pain at frequent intervals, using observation of physiological indicators and a valid pain assessment tool, is essential.

- Parents are a valuable asset in assessing their child's pain and they generally judge pain more accurately than medical staff.

- Observation of children's normal behaviour and vigilance in observing indicators of pain (or changes in behaviour) is essential.

- Obtaining a pain history from parents and knowing how a child communicates discomfort and distress are hallmarks of effective pain relief.

The End of Life Phase of Care

Erica Brown

The onset of the end of life or terminal phase of a child's care begins at the point in the illness when care is primarily to make the child comfortable. Making decisions at this stage of their child's life will be extremely difficult for parents, and nursing and medical staff may also grapple with the knowledge that nothing more can be done to prevent the child's death. Heath (2000) writes that 'the welcome success of scientific medicine carries dangers. The chief of these is the implication, and the false promise, that science offers a cure for every ill and the indefinite postponement of death' (p.11).

According to Glaser and Strauss (1996) terminal care begins at the point in the child's illness trajectory when nothing more can be done to delay the disease process. However, it may be very difficult to determine when the end of life phase begins, particularly when the normal pattern of a child's illness has been to experience periods of relapse, interspersed with periods of remission. Assessment of the child's needs, and those of his or her family, should be constantly reviewed and evaluated. Understanding a family's perception of the end of life phase of their child's illness is tremendously important. Sensitive issues will inevitably arise, and families need to know that the information they receive from carers is trustworthy and honest. Factors such as family relationships, the impact of visitors on the child's wellbeing or the spiritual needs of individual family members should all be considered. Team work is essential, and multi-disciplinary team members should strive towards helping the child and the family to be aware of the available options, empowering them to maintain control of their everyday life.

Generally, carers will observe signs and symptoms that suggest deterioration in the child's condition. Simple explanations of these symptoms need to be given to the child/young person (if appropriate) and their family so that everyone is able to consider the choices that can be incorporated into the child's care plan. Using a systematic approach to care helps to keep the child comfortable and the family supported. Sometimes it may be appropriate to make families aware of complementary or alternative therapies, either in conjunction with, or replacing, orthodox medicine. Assessment of the child's discomfort or pain needs to be reviewed constantly. This is discussed in Chapter 4, 'Managing Children's Pain'.

Although from the beginnings of palliative care the aim was to achieve a 'good death', Thomas (2003) believes that the medicalisation of dying has meant that some elements of care may have been compromised. Most adults, when asked the question 'Where would you like to die?', express a preference to die at home, yet only just over a quarter of all people achieve this. Home plays a special part in our affections. Home is both a state and a place. We talk about feeling at home somewhere, as well as a place where we live and belong.

Before the services of children's hospices were available to families, most children were nursed within the hospital setting. However, it is now widely acknowledged that end of life care should take place in the child's home wherever possible, even though this will make tremendous emotional and physical demands on the family (Katz, Baker and Osborn 1991). Indeed, there is evidence that most children and young people would prefer to die at home.

Lauer et al. (1993) advocates that parents who care for their child at home during the end of life phase are likely to experience fewer symptoms of pathological grief after their death. This view is supported by research that has shown many parents have to change their parenting role when their child is cared for in a hospital.

Many parents who care for their child at home become adept at performing complex care tasks (Teague et al. 1993) and in recent years it has become widely recognised that parents are skilled partners with professionals in caring for their child. Totterdell (1990) makes a plea for doctors and staff in all paediatric palliative care settings to allow parents to manage the quality of their own child's life.

> I was terrified at first by the prospect of him dying at home. I didn't think I could cope. But in the end it enabled us to carry on being a family and knowing that helped a great deal. Although the whole thing was so sad, the entire experience is etched in my memory and it was the best thing about such a dreadful time.

In cases where home care does not prove beneficial for families, this may be due in part to a lack of community or family resources, or where families become emotionally and physically exhausted. Martinson (1980) identified several factors that contributed to successful end-stage care in the child's home:

- withdrawal of curative care with an emphasis on comfort care
- the child and the parents expressing a wish to be at home
- access to 24-hour support from professionals
- recognition by the family of the role they play in caring for their sick child
- acknowledgement by the child's consultant that home is the preferred place by the family for end of life care.

Supporting/involving families

The death of a child is a frightening experience for families where parents are robbed of a uniquely significant relationship (Rubin 1993). Even when parents witness their child's deterioration, it may still be a tremendous shock to hear someone say they are going to die. However, many parents want full and honest facts, so that they are not left confused about the situation. Vague ambivalent messages and soothing reassurances may sell parents short, giving them hope that their child will survive. There is such evidence in Sweeting and Gilhooly's (1990) study of collusion between healthcare professionals. Parents developed false hope that their child would recover, and were prevented from anticipatory grief and the opportunity to prepare to say their goodbyes, leaving them with feelings of guilt and remorse.

Professionals who are knowledgeable about the child's medical condition act as a valuable source of information to parents:

> She'd worked in the community with children with special needs for a long time so she knew about Richard's condition. Often she was able to suggest ways that would allow Richard to be more comfortable and once she put us in touch with another family whose son also had muscular dystrophy.

The type of support that families find helpful varies greatly, although many parents say that communication skills and interpersonal skills demonstrated by professionals are equally as important as having confidence that care is matched to their child's physical and medical needs:

> The Community Team Worker was worth his weight in gold. He always had time to listen and he seemed to know exactly when we needed support most. He knew we didn't want to stop being parents even when our son was admitted to the hospice the week before he died. He also knew that other children wanted to be there when he died so that they could say goodbye in their own way.

Families generally look to Care Teams for support in the end stages of their child's life, although they may also welcome the presence of a religious or cultural leader, or representative from their community. In the community, Health Visitors and Community Nurses and GPs also play an important role. McHaffie (2001) cites three major categories of support, namely emotional, informational and practical.

Understandably, parents may be feeling confused, exhausted, frightened, angry, or even relieved that their child's suffering is coming to an end. Families will value and acknowledge the commitment shown by staff. They speak about 'a calm and caring approach', 'someone who gives you confidence', 'skill and personal involvement'. Where they are involved as members of the Care Team, and are able to make decisions about what they want for their child, families feel empowered after their child has died, and they seek solace and comfort in this.

For some parents, there may be a feeling of intense loneliness, even though they are surrounded by caring professionals and accompanied by their partner. The reactions of family members may add to parents' emotional burden, especially if they are unavailable to give support because they are absorbed in their own grief.

Parents value open and honest information from staff, especially where they feel that they are able to ask the same questions over and over again, so that they are able to assimilate what is happening:

> I was terrified when I asked the question, 'Is this nearly the end?' I suppose I knew the answer already because he had gradually slept more and more. When the nurse told me that he wasn't in pain, but his body wasn't getting enough oxygen, I really valued that. Nobody tried to make things sound better than they were.

Experience in caring for families at Acorns has shown that it is generally helpful if the staff caring for the child know of individual family wishes. When parents are burdened with emotional pain about the inevitable death of their child, it is important that, where possible, they do not have additional anxieties. Having meals, a telephone or help with transport can make all the difference.

The final hours

Parents are likely to remember events associated with their child's death very clearly (Laakso and Paunonen Ilmonen 2001). There are several anecdotal accounts regarding the care of children in the last stages of their life, written by both parents and professionals (Brown 2002; Perrens 1996).

Families generally fall into two main categories: those whose child's end of life care was planned or had a definable period, and those whose child did not have a definable or anticipated phase of care, generally because the child deteriorated very rapidly and died unexpectedly. These children may appear to be relatively well until immediately before their death, showing few symptoms of being about to die.

Almost without exception, parents experience shock when their child dies, even though they are aware of the life-limiting nature of the illness. This may be particularly so if the child has survived periods of illness that parents consider to have been worse. The pain of parting can be devastating:

> We felt wide open and raw emotionally.

If parents are absent when their child dies, they may be left feeling guilty, blaming themselves that they should have been there. Where death is expected, care needs to be compassionate, with changed priorities that ensure dignity for the child and their parents, keeping distress to a minimum. Families are likely to look to professionals to support them in making important decisions regarding the care of their child in the final phases of their life (Riches and Dawson 2000).

Many parents derive some comfort if their child dies in their arms or, if this is not possible, lying next to them or sitting very close. For the dying child, the familiar sound of parents' or siblings' voices will bring reassurance.

> Our son was born on 2 July and he died just 25½ days later. Please God, it is the worst thing that will ever happen to us because I am not sure that we have the strength to survive anything like that again. The whole experience brought home with a vengeance that life is precious and fragile and that we should value a life, not simply in terms of its length, but more by the quality of it.
>
> From very early in the pregnancy, I felt that all was not well. Once he was born, it was blatantly obvious that he had a number of problems and I knew, without any doubt, that he would not survive very long. From that moment, all I wanted to do was to take him home and shower him with love.
>
> He had been at the local hospital just about a week when I felt he was deteriorating. Physically, there was nothing to confirm this suspicion. Medically, I was told, there was no change. By the second evening of concern, I knew that he would die very soon. At 2 am on 28 July I brought our son home. At five minutes to seven the same morning he died quietly, and oh! so peacefully in my arms.
>
> Those last hours were wonderful, precious – almost idyllic. I had had a picture, almost a vision, as to how I wanted his end to be but feared I was being naïve in the detail of that hope. I knew that he was

at high risk of choking and dying suddenly in my absence, yet I was clear that I did not want him home to play 'happy families'.

There will always be sadness, but for me it is bearable because the end was all that I had hoped for. The house was quiet as we snuggled up in bed together and there were no distractions as I poured my love over and into him. His passing was not ugly or frightening; he seemed literally just to 'let go' and I felt inner peace and tranquillity as I, too, let him go.

If I look at the events of his life as a journey to that final time together, then I can live with them. There is nothing I can do to change the facts of his tragic life but I thank God for the miracle of bringing him home, and for the loveliness of our last hours together. (Liz Johnson, personal communication with author).

Involvement

Dominica (1997) asserts that ongoing involvement by parents in their child's care is crucial. Parents often like to feel that they are involved, because time spent with their child is very precious. Parents' knowledge that they did so and did not 'give up' on their child will bring comfort. Generally, families who are able to care for their child's body are more likely to accept the reality of their child's death and to say 'goodbye' in ways that they choose for themselves.

After the child's death

There should be no rush attached to the time immediately after a child's death. Where families experience a calm environment, this will help them make the most of the precious time they have left with their child's body. Some parents will wish to be alone – others will prefer someone to be available to offer them support and guidance. Families need professionals who possess practical skills, combined with the knowledge of the ethical and legal factors that are intrinsic to holistic after life care. Caring for children and families requires special skills and sensitivities. Identifying and meeting individual cultural or religious needs and wishes is an important part of that care. The spiritual needs of families when their child's death is very near are broadly similar, regardless of faith or culture. Privacy, dignity, a peaceful environment and good symptom control are always important. Religious ceremonies vary. In some religions they are carried out by faith leaders, in others by the family or members of the religious community.

Having opportunities to perform caring tasks for their child after their death does not necessarily mean that all parents will want to be involved. Some parents will stay with their child for a few minutes after their death, others for hours or even days. Choices are very individual between and within families, with some family members needing to adjust very quickly to a situation where time is running out.

> I was welcomed to the parent accommodation and we stayed there until her funeral. Nothing was too much trouble for the staff and often I popped down to the bedroom where she was just to check on her and give her one more cuddle.

> She was in her own little room with her teddy and her books. Our youngest son made a card and put it on the pillow beside her. It was really beautiful and peaceful.

Stewart and Dent (1994) write about the 'healing and therapeutic' experience of parents washing and dressing their child. Touching their child's body will also help them to experience the physical changes of death and realise what has happened.

Laying out dead bodies can be traced back over 50,000 years and, for many thousands of years, caring for a person after their death has been regarded as a mark of respect (Amene and Treves 2000). Nurses may perform the task for families and the NMC Code of Professional Conduct (2002) gives guidance, underpinned by the expectation that the child's and the child's family's interest and dignity are protected at all times.

Some parents may not want anyone else to touch their child's body after death, taking the child home or to the funeral director's themselves. Memories of their child will be very precious to parents and tangible mementos such as photographs, handprints, locks of hair, footprints, toys or clothing will bring comfort and a sense of reality of their child's existence in the years ahead:

> We have pictures of Robert everywhere around the house. We also have a memory box with special things. We take them out on his birthday and at Christmas and talk about the times we shared together.

In their discussion regarding things that help bereaved parents, Riches and Dawson (2000) express the importance of parents being able to acknowledge their child's end of life as a 'good death'. Chapter 12, 'Continuing Bonds', describes some of Acorns' experience of helping parents to continue parenting their child after they die.

Research suggests that when parents feel that their needs have been taken into account, this is likely to influence their grief later on (Clark and Jacinta 1995; Speck 1992).

Key points

- Parents need support in the day-to-day management of their child's end of life.

- End of life care should take place in the child's home wherever possible, even though this will make tremendous emotional and physical demands on the family.

- When parents have felt empowered as partners in caring for their child, they are likely to feel comforted in the knowledge of this after their child has died.

- The spiritual needs of families when their child's death is near are broadly similar, regardless of faith or culture.

- When professionals are absorbed in their own grief, they may find it difficult to give parents comfort and support.

- Parents generally welcome tangible mementos of their child, such as locks of hair, handprints or footprints, and these may bring comfort to the family in the years to come.

Implications for practice

- Checking out what parents and the child (if appropriate) know and understand about the closeness of death is important.

- Checking out parents' hopes, fears and needs is important. These should be constantly reviewed and evaluated.

- As far as possible, parents should be allowed and encouraged to manage the quality of their child's end of life care.

- Facilitating 24-hour access for parents to professional support should be a priority.

- Good communication skills, interpersonal skills and practical support are as important to parents as the care their child receives.

- Knowledge of ethical and legal facets of care is intrinsic to after life care. Safeguarding the child's and the family's interests and dignity are important parts of this care.

- Many parents derive comfort from being physically close to their child at the time the child dies. There should be no rush attached to the time after the child dies.

- Identifying cultural, religious and spiritual needs is important.

- Parents generally welcome tangible mementos of their child, such as locks of hair, handprints or footprints, and these may bring comfort in the years to come.

Administrative and Practical Requirements when a Child Dies

Brian Warr

When parents are aware their child is going to die, it is advisable that, as well as planning where the child will die, they are helped to make some other important decisions. This chapter outlines the administrative and practical requirements after the child's death. For ease of reference, questions are asked at the end of some sections.

Death in hospital

When a child is admitted to hospital, a relative will be identified and recorded as the next of kin or as the person identified as having parental responsibility. When the child dies, the hospital will inform the next of kin or the person with parental responsibility. The hospital will arrange for a doctor to sign the 'Medical Certificate of Cause of Death'. This will state the cause of the child's death and when a doctor last saw the child.

Once the 'Medical Certificate of Cause of Death' is obtained, the child's body can be removed from the hospital. Some hospitals will ask the next of kin/the person with parental responsibility, to sign a Release Form. The family must decide where the child's body is to be cared for and who will move the body from the hospital. In most cases the family will arrange this with a local funeral director. However, it is possible for families to transport their own child. Obviously this will depend on individual family circumstances and the age and size of the child.

It is important to recognise that different cultures may require different procedures after a child has died, for example the body may need to be washed by the family and certain items may need to be left on the child. It is important to clarify what the wishes of the family are (see Chapter 15, 'Religious, Cultural, Secular and Spiritual Aspects of Care').

The hospital may prohibit the removal of the child's body if the circumstances of the death are such that a Coroner is involved, or if the child died from a notifiable disease (see DoH 1984, Sec. 43–45; Public Health [Infectious Diseases] Regulations 1988).

The hospital may ask permission from the next of kin/the person with parental responsibility to carry out a post mortem (autopsy). A post mortem should not be carried out without the permission of the next of kin/the person with parental responsibility, unless a Coroner has made an order (see Chapter 16, 'Post Mortem, Organ Donation and Tissue Retention'). Staff at the hospital may also suggest organ donation. This should be discussed with the next of kin/the person with parental responsibility.

Considerations

- Who is the named person as the child's next of kin/person with parental responsibility?
- Will the family allow a post mortem if the hospital requests this?
- Has the young person or family expressed a wish for organ donation?
- Will the child's body be buried or cremated?
- Which funeral director will the family use?
- Where will the child's body be cared for between the death and the funeral?
- Where will the child's death be registered?
- Does the family wish for religious or spiritual leaders to be contacted?
- Will interpreters need to be engaged?

Death at home

If a family member or person caring for the child dials 999, then the ambulance crew and the police are required to follow strict procedures, which may conflict with the planned wishes of the family (see Sudden death).

When a child dies at home, the child's general practitioner should be contacted and a 'Medical Certificate of Cause of Death' can be issued by the relevant doctor. This may be the GP or hospital community paediatrician. If the GP/medical practitioner has not treated the child within 14 days of death, they may ring the Coroner to discuss whether a post mortem is required. (A Coroner is a qualified doctor or lawyer, sometimes both.)

The family will have to make arrangements about where the child's body is to be cared for until the funeral. It is possible for a child to stay at home if the family wishes and if this is practical. The appropriateness of this will need to be discussed with individual families.

Considerations

- Who will be contacted and informed of the child's death, e.g. GP/medical practitioner?
- Which funeral director will be contacted?
- Where will the child's body be cared for between death and the funeral?
- Will the child be buried or cremated?
- Do the family wish any of the child's organs to be donated?

Death in a children's hospice

When a child is first accepted for care at a children's hospice, it should be established who is next of kin/the person with parental responsibility.

When a child dies, it is essential that everyone who has 'parental responsibility' is informed. In some cases Social Services will also need to be informed.

Staff can arrange for a 'Medical Certificate of Cause of Death' to be signed by the doctor who saw the child most recently. (The medical practitioner needs to state when they last saw the child.) The child's body can be cared for either in a special air-conditioned room, or be taken to an appropriate place by the family or funeral director. The child's body must not be taken away until a doctor has signed the 'Medical Certificate of Cause of Death'. All hospices have a legal right to prohibit the removal of the body if the circumstances of the death mean that the body is the responsibility of the Coroner, or if the child has died from a notifiable disease (see DoH 1984, Sec. 43–45, Public Health [Infectious Diseases] Regulations 1988).

If a conflict occurs within the family concerning where the child's body is kept, or about the funeral arrangements, a hospice would seek a decision from the persons who are responsible for the body. Therefore, unless the child's body is the responsibility of the Coroner or qualifies under the Control of Diseases Act, a hospice has no legal right to keep the body. Indeed, staff are obliged to respect the wishes of the next of kin/person with parental responsibility in possession of a 'Medical Certificate of Cause of Death'. Conflicts which cannot be resolved may exceptionally have to be heard in the High Court (see Conflicts).

If cremation is preferred, staff can arrange for the appropriate forms to be signed by independent doctors. (The body cannot be cremated unless the cause of death is determined.)

Sudden death

Doctors, hospital staff, police, ambulance crews and coroners may be professional, caring and sensitive when a child dies, but they are governed by laws, procedures and protocols. If a child dies suddenly, their responsibilities may bring them into conflict with the family's wishes.

A 999 call for an ambulance will almost certainly result in an attempt to resuscitate the child who will be taken to the nearest hospital Accident and Emergency Department. The police will be notified, and without prior knowledge of the situation they may well be obliged to investigate the cause of death.

Most doctors will inform the Coroner if they have not seen the child within 14 days. The Coroner can order a post mortem (autopsy) or decide that there is no need for investigation, being satisfied that the cause of death is known to be natural.

Conflicts

Conflicts may arise when a child dies. Most are settled within families, but in extreme cases the Courts will become involved, for example Fessi vs. Whitmore (1999).

Conflict may potentially arise over a number of decisions:

- the choice of funeral director
- funeral arrangements
- burial or cremation of the child's body
- permission for a post mortem
- organ donation
- place of burial
- sending the body overseas for the funeral.

Where conflicts are not resolved, the dispute may be taken to the High Court via the family's legal representative.

Caring for the child's body

When a 'Medical Certificate of Cause of Death' is obtained or the Coroner has released the child's body, the family has a choice as to where their child's body is cared for. This may include:

- funeral director
- a special temperature-controlled bedroom at a children's hospice
- an appropriate place agreed by the family, e.g. child's home, religious premises, such as a place of worship.

If it is considered that a child's body is being cared for in an unsuitable environment and constitutes a health risk, the Medical Officer of Health should be contacted and would adjudicate.

Many families will have cared for their child for a long time. The period of separation between the child's death and the funeral is very significant. In order for families to make informed choices, they will need to be aware of practical aspects of caring for their child's body. Some families may wish to visit their dead child a number of times during this period. Others will seek comfort in the knowledge that their child is in a safe place, receiving respect and care. One of the practical issues families need to consider is whether their child needs to be embalmed.

Modern embalming is very different from the procedure used by the ancient Egyptians. It is a means of hygienically treating the body in order to temporarily preserve the appearance, reduce the risk of infection by eliminating natural bacteria, and slow down the natural process of deterioration. Embalming involves injecting a preserving and disinfecting chemical through the arterial system of the body. The solution is carried to tiny blood vessels called capillaries in order to preserve the tissues. Any remaining solution is released through a vein. The treatment is usually carried out through two small hidden incisions and may be likened to keyhole surgery. Embalming should not involve any mutilation of the body.

Registering the death

When a child dies, the death must be registered by the Registrar for the sub-district in which the child died. This must be done within five days (unless the Registrar has agreed to extend the period). For Jewish and Muslim families (and most Hindus and Sikhs), the funeral will need to be within 24 hours, therefore the registering of the death needs to be done within hours. Specialist funeral directors will have phone numbers of the Registrar for weekends (e.g. Asian funeral directors). Rabbis can also arrange this for members of the Jewish community.

If the child dies at home, registration needs to be at the Registry Office for that area. If the child dies in a hospice or hospital, their death needs to be at the Registry Office local to the hospice or hospital.

In order for a child's death to be registered, it is necessary to take the Medical Certificate of Cause of Death to the Registry Office (note – appointments can be made with the office to prevent families waiting).

The Medical Certificate of Cause of Death

The Registrar will require the following information (this can be given verbally):

- the date and place where the death occurred
- the child's name, date of birth and home address
- the town and county where the child was born
- the names of the parents, their home address(es) and occupation(s).

There will be a charge for the issue of the death certificate. Further copies can be issued at an extra cost.

If the person registering the death is able to provide the Registrar with the following documents, this will be helpful:

- the child's birth certificate
- the child's medical card.

The person registering the death will be asked:

- their relationship to the deceased child
- whether they were present at the time of the child's death
- whether the child's body is to be cremated or buried
- about the cause of death (occasionally).

In addition to the child's parents, a number of people are able to register the child's death. Persons qualified to act as informants include: a person present at the death, a matron/head nurse, a relative residing in the sub-district where the child died. (The full list of people who act as informants is on the Medical Certificate of Cause of Death form.)

The Registrar will give the person who registers the death:

- The Certificate for Burial or Cremation (Certificate E, a green form, to be given to the funeral director). If a Coroner's post mortem has taken place and the child's body is to be cremated, the Coroner sends a signed yellow Form E to the funeral director.

- The Certificate for Registration of Death (Form BD8) which may be necessary for Social Security purposes.

- A death certificate (this is a certified copy of the entry in the register which can be obtained on payment of a statutory fee).

- In the case of a Coroner's inquest, an 'Order for Burial' may be issued by the Coroner if the right to cremate the child's body is refused.

Cremation

A child cannot be cremated unless the cause of death has been definitely ascertained. A number of forms supplied by the crematorium or funeral directors have to be completed.

Form A is the application for cremation and is signed by the next of kin or person with parental responsibility.

Two doctors, one who attended the child during the last illness, and one who has seen the child's body, sign Forms B and C. N.B. Forms B and C are not required when a Coroner has issued a Certificate for Cremation.

Another doctor who is the medical referee of the crematorium signs Form F.

Regulations concerning what is allowed in the coffin at cremation

It is not possible to cremate some items that families may wish to place in the coffin, for example items with a high rubber or plastic content such as shoes or toys (Cremation (Amendment) Regulations 2006; Environmental Protection Act 1999; Pollution Prevention and Control Act 1999). Crematoria are fairly stringent on these rules and the wishes of families need to be discussed with the funeral director or crematorium if plastic or rubber is to be left in the coffin. These rules do not apply to burials.

Special arrangements for moving a body

Only a Coroner can give permission for a body to be taken out of England or Wales.

The Coroner issues a Removal Notice, Form 104. This applies even when a death was not reported to the Coroner. The funeral director may assist with this.

Death of a child being looked after
by Local Authorities

When a child dies who is being looked after by the Local Authority, the Local Authority must notify the Secretary of State and, as far as is reasonably practicable, the child's parents and any other person who has parental responsibility. The Local Authority may also arrange for burial or cremation in accordance with the child's religious persuasion (Children Act 1989, Schedule 2, Para. 20[1]).

The Local Authority may make payment for travelling or subsistence incurred by parents attending the funeral. They may also exercise their powers to recover the cost of the funeral (Children Act 1989, Schedule 2, Para. 20[4]) from the child's parents.

Inquests

An inquest is a factual inquiry into the medical causes and circumstances of a death. It is open to the public and press and sometimes has a jury. The Coroner will hold an inquest when the death of a child was:

- violent or unnatural
- sudden and the cause is unknown
- inconclusive, after a post mortem.

The inquest has to determine who the child was, when and where the child died and how they died.

A person with 'a proper interest' (including the parents of the child, or their legal representative) may ask questions relevant to the purpose of the inquest. This includes questions about the medical cause and circumstances of the death.

Professional persons who have been involved with the care of the child may, at the Coroner's discretion, be allowed to ask questions.

Key points

- When a child dies at home the child's GP should be contacted so that a 'Medical Certificate of Cause of Death' can be issued.
- If a child's family or carer dials 999, then the ambulance crew and the police have to follow strict procedures that may conflict with the parents' wishes.
- Hospices have a legal right to prohibit the removal of a child's body if the circumstances of their death means that the body is the responsibility of the Coroner.

- The period of separation between the child's death and the funeral is very significant for families.

- When a child dies, the death must be registered with the Registrar for the sub-district in which the child died. A number of people are able to register a child's death.

- The Registrar issues a Certificate for Burial or Cremation. This is given to the funeral director.

- A death certificate is a copy of the entry of death in the Register.

- Cremation cannot take place unless the cause of the child's death has been ascertained.

- A Coroner has to give permission if a child's body is to be taken outside England or Wales.

N.B. The information in this chapter is accurate as of May 2007.

The Child's Funeral

Erica Brown

For many parents, seeing their child's body is an affirmation that they have died and a powerful first step in the journey of grief. Seeing, touching, holding and talking to their child has special significance to parents and usually there is no reason why they are not able to care for their child's body after death and before the funeral.

Most families with a life-limited child will have thought about their child's funeral before the child has died (Goldman 2002). Often this accompanies other thoughts which form part of what has become known as 'anticipatory grief'. Parents may need help and support to talk about their fears, wishes and beliefs about cremation or burial so that they are able to make an informed choice. Some young people may have expressed wishes about their funeral and how they would like this to be.

Arranging a child's funeral is an extremely distressing time, especially when many parents are already physically and emotionally exhausted. Phoning the funeral director, and hearing themselves ask for the services available, is likely to be one of the most difficult tasks that families face immediately after their child's death. Hospice staff can play an extremely important role by being present at this time, so that in the weeks and months ahead parents can look back on their child's funeral and feel it is what they wanted.

Some of the legal and financial aspects of funerals are discussed elsewhere in the book. This section of the book is designed to help professionals to support parents in making the choices which are best for them. Religious and cultural requirements vary greatly. Most funeral directors will be willing to make the arrangements but, if they take complete charge, plans may suit the funeral director's agenda rather than the parents.

The choice of place for the service is likely to be determined by the locality of the family home and factors such as the cultural or faith background of the family, or the person who is chosen to officiate at the service. Families will remember the place and it is therefore important that they are made to feel as comfortable as possible. Although visiting the chosen place beforehand may not be possible, parents who know what the place is like, and what is going to happen and where, generally find that this helps on the funeral day itself.

Viewing the child's body at the chapel of rest

If parents and relatives are planning to visit the chapel of rest before the funeral, it may be helpful to them if the coffin is still open. Liaising with the funeral director after speaking to the family first will ensure that the visit will be as the family would like it to be. There may be a charge for viewing a child's body at the funeral director's, and this should be explained to parents.

It is generally possible to choose where the funeral will depart from. Some parents prefer to start from home, others from the funeral director's or perhaps from the children's hospice, if the child's body has been looked after there between their death and the funeral. Other alternatives include asking the funeral director to arrange for the child's body to be taken directly to the crematorium, burial place or religious place of worship, enabling the family to gather there before the ceremony takes place.

If the funeral director is providing transport for the immediate family, then it is important to establish the colour of the limousine. Generally cars are black, but some funeral services have their own company colour and they will be able to meet parents' needs, although this may incur an extra charge. Likewise, it may be culturally important for some families to choose a funeral director where staff wear a particular kind of uniform.

Costs

The funeral director's fees usually include:

- removal of the child's body from the place of death (if the family wish)
- supply of the coffin (of the family's choice) and a shroud or gown (if the family are not dressing the child themselves)
- funeral car and driver
- pallbearers
- travel to the place of cremation or burial.

Extra charges may be made for:

- night-time removal of the child's body from the place of death
- viewing of the child's body at the funeral director's
- embalming

- cars to follow the funeral hearse
- additional travel, for example from a church to a burial place
- flowers
- memorials, for example a headstone
- announcement of the child's death in the local press
- order of service.

The prices charged for funerals vary considerably between funeral directors. Some funeral directors will not make a charge for a child's simple funeral, but the charges for burial or cremation are outside the control of the funeral director.

Choice of coffin

The coffin containing the child's body will be the visible focus for the funeral. Many parents will feel their choice of coffin is their last gift to their child. Although the range of coffins may have much in common, the price differences are likely to be enormous and the price families pay may bear little relationship to actual value.

There are strict regulations about materials for coffins to be cremated, and funeral directors should be familiar with current guidelines. All coffins will have a name plate carrying the child's name, which may also be inscribed with the child's date of birth and the date of their death.

Flowers

Some funeral directors have their own florists. Others will have information to enable families to choose their own tributes. Increasingly at Acorns, we are finding that families prefer to have family flowers only, with donations of money in lieu of floral tributes. Families can choose whether flowers are placed in the hearse with the coffin, on top of the hearse or perhaps in another car. Likewise, they may prefer that the flowers are taken to the cemetery or graveyard or place of worship in time for the funeral cortege to arrive. There are cultural and religious traditions about whether flowers are appropriate at all, and also concerning colours. Families will be aware of these, but where professionals liaise with people who may be arranging the funeral, it is important that they are able to convey what the family would like.

Order of service

It is not necessary to have a special order of service printed, but many families like to mark the occasion with a personal tribute, perhaps including a picture of their child. The funeral director can make arrangements for printing and, of course, families may like to include readings, music, songs or hymns of their choice.

Ceremony and rituals

There are two main elements to the funeral service – the celebration and remembrance of the child's life, and the committal or leave-taking of the child's body for cremation or burial. The celebration usually involves remembering the child's life and special memories that people have. The leave-taking usually centres on the placing of the coffin in the grave or conveying the coffin for cremation. Where the funeral is a religious one, the child's body will be commended to God for safe-keeping. There are of course different rituals and ceremonies specific to faith communities. These are discussed in Chapter 15, 'Religious, Cultural, Secular and Spiritual Aspects of Care'.

Most crematoria or religious places of worship will have prepared orders of service which can provide the framework for the ceremony. However, there are no regulations about how funerals should be arranged and conducted. Usually, the ceremony begins with people gathering together with the coffin at the focal point of the occasion. The religious leader, or the person responsible for this ceremony, will welcome people and briefly explain the purpose of the gathering.

Some families will prefer to lead the ceremony themselves or ask a friend to do it for them, rather than relying on an officiate they do not know. Prayers or readings may follow with time for reflection and perhaps a song, hymn or a piece of music. Readings from religious texts or poems may be read, and often there will be a short eulogy or tribute to the child and the family.

Some families will have traditions that they would like followed. Rituals may be very individual to families and, if they can be included in the funeral, this can bring a sense of comfort or familiarity at a very stressful time. However, family members should never be expected to play a part in the proceedings.

Religious communities conduct funerals according to their own beliefs and practices. When young parents plan something less traditional for their child, preparing grandparents in advance can be helpful.

> I hadn't realised that they had chosen windmills and shining stars to put on the grave. It was a real shock when I got to the cemetery. It's OK, but it wasn't what I expected because I brought up my son to be a Christian.

Walking away from their child's coffin is one of the most harrowing tasks parents will ever face. Ideally, they should be able to take their time, but in many crematoria funerals are booked for frequent services throughout the day. Even when the ceremony takes place in a religious building, there are still likely to be time restrictions.

When friends and family are able to gather together, they have an opportunity to offer each other comfort. Parents will look back on the occasion with a sense of gratitude that people cared enough to attend the funeral. However, they are unlikely to remember everyone who attended, and asking people to sign their name as they enter or leave the place where the ceremony is held will provide a permanent record for the future.

Burial

Most of the regulations for burial have been drawn up locally in line with Acts of Parliament if the burial is in a public cemetery. Churchyards are under the jurisdiction of the church and burial land always remains the property of the cemetery or church. In other words, the right is granted to use the land for a burial in exchange for a fee. The regulations and fees vary from place to place. Everyone with a permanent address has the right in law to be buried in their local parish churchyard. However, many churchyards no longer have space and responsibility for burials may be handed over to the local council.

Whether or not families are on the electoral role of their parish church and worship there, they may still want their child to be buried in the parish churchyard. Sometimes, families have connections with a church outside their parish and they may be able to bury their child's body on that land, if clergy are in agreement.

There are some single denomination cemeteries, for example Roman Catholic, Jewish and Muslim. There may also be sections of public cemeteries set aside for members of communities such as Polish, Irish and African Caribbean.

Although parents have a right to bury their child in their parish churchyard, this right does not extend to erecting a headstone or any other type of permanent memorial. There may be strict restrictions and families need to know what is allowed before they choose a churchyard burial. A church service is not compulsory before churchyard burial, and some families may choose to have a very simple ceremony at the graveside.

Clergy fees in Church of England churches are set annually by the Church Commissioners and there is no variation in costs. Fees for digging the grave may, however, vary and there will be extra charges incurred for an organist, bell ringers and possibly for heating the church during the winter months.

Cremation

It is not necessary to have any form of service at a crematorium, though a period of time will still have to be booked to formally receive the coffin, check details regarding the body and usher the coffin to the crematory.

Fees paid to the crematorium for use of the facilities are usually paid by the funeral director and passed on to the family. Generally, these will include the total cost of cremation and a container for ashes. There may, however, be extra charges made by the person who officiates at the ceremony, organist (if used), or for the signing of forms.

The cremation process

There are different methods of moving a coffin into the crematory (place of cremation). In some crematoria, the coffin is moved mechanically through a panel opening in the wall. Others provide a catafalque that can be lowered through the floor and, in others, the coffin remains on the catafalque but is obscured from the mourners by a curtain. Once the coffin has been removed from the chapel, it will either be pushed manually into the crematory off a trolley, adjusted to the height of the cremator door, or be transported mechanically from a platform into the crematory.

The cremation process for a child/young person usually takes up to three-quarters of an hour. For a young adult this is about half an hour longer, depending on body weight. All that remains after the cremation process is completed is calcified bone, which is carefully processed into cremation remains, usually known as ashes. The ashes are placed in a container and labelled with the identity card which accompanied the coffin from the beginning of the day, as far as the door of the crematory.

The child's ashes will probably be placed in a plastic or cardboard container by the crematorium staff. The container is usually sent to the funeral director a few days after the cremation or collected by them. The ashes can be transferred by the funeral director into a casket or an urn of the family's choice. If a family has considered spreading the ashes themselves, they may choose not to incur the extra expense of an urn or casket. When the ashes are to be sprinkled at the crematorium or buried at a cemetery, either crematorium staff or a member of a religious or secular community may undertake to do this if the family prefer.

Headstones and memorials

A headstone or memorial may be placed in the grounds of the crematorium, graveyard or churchyard, but there will often be strict rules about what is allowed. The style, shape, position and even wording on a memorial may have to conform to a locally agreed format and rules can change over time.

When a family has paid for a memorial, they own it. However, they do not own the land on which it is placed, even in the churchyard, graveyard or crematoria. The time that elapses between the burial of the body and the erection of the gravestone or the memorial varies between monumental masons or providers of the memorial.

In churchyards, a request has to be made to the incumbent before plans are made to erect a memorial. This almost always applies to planting anything on the grave. Church councils set their own regulations in conjunction with the diocese and many churches will stipulate what is allowed in the way of an inscription on a headstone or the style of the headstone including height, width, shape and the material from which it is made.

In civic cemeteries, each authority sets down what is allowed and the personal opinions and preferences of committee members are likely to lead to restrictions. Families should be encouraged to find out what is allowed well in advance of approaching the supplier of a headstone or a memorial.

Books of remembrance

At crematoria, some churches or places of worship and virtually all children's hospices, books of remembrance are provided in which the names and dates of children's births and deaths are inscribed. In hospices, there may be room for parents, siblings and other family members to add their thoughts and tributes. In churches and crematoria, the book is usually kept safe in a display cabinet, open at an appropriate anniversary page each day.

Anniversaries

Anniversaries and special times will always be poignant for families. Encouraging them to maintain rituals and celebrations can be a great comfort. Significant dates will always bring to mind the grief which parents feel, but marking occasions such as having a birthday cake or a shared family occasion will help to keep the child's memory alive.

> The first year after the boys died I remember dreading both their birthday and the anniversary of their deaths. There were three dates in all. I was afraid people would forget, but equally scared a card might arrive from somebody who hadn't heard the tragic news. In the end I was pleased that people sent cards remembering the dates, because it meant that their brief lives had counted for something. Over the years I kept every single memento anyone has ever sent.

Key points

- If parents wish, they should be able to look after their dead child's body up to the funeral.

- Parents who have visited the venue of the funeral before it takes place will generally find that this is helpful.

- There are two main elements to the funeral – the celebration and remembrance of the child's life, and the committal or leave-taking of the child's body for burial or cremation.

- Most religious places of worship and crematoria will have a prepared order of funeral service which can provide a framework for the ceremony. A service is not mandatory at a crematorium.

- Rituals and ceremonies associated with funerals vary greatly between religious and secular communities. Families will have individual wishes.

- When a family pay for a memorial they own it. However, they do not own the land on which the memorial is placed, whether the land is in a churchyard, burial ground or crematorium.

Implications for practice

- Families can be supported by professionals who enable them to talk about their fears, wishes and beliefs, so that they are able to make informed choices about their child's funeral.

- Professionals, who liaise with people responsible for carrying out funeral arrangements, can incorporate the wishes of the family into the occasion.

- Many parents will feel that their child's coffin is their last gift to their child. They will need to be helped to make their choice of coffin according to their financial means.

- Families need to be clear about what is included in the funeral director's costs and what extra charges might be incurred, e.g. viewing their child's body at the funeral director's. Costs vary considerably between funeral directors.

- Parents should be helped to choose what is culturally acceptable to them.

- Families should be made aware of what is included in the burial or cremation fee, and if any family preferences will incur extra charges.

- Families should be encouraged to find out what is permitted in the way of a memorial well in advance of approaching a memorial supplier.

- Arranging for someone to record people who attended the child's funeral can bring parents a sense of comfort in their grief.

Counselling Support

Erica Brown

The bond between parents and their child is biologically and emotionally unique, existing from conception and birth to the present time. Parenting is perceived as a future-orientated role, with both immediate and anticipated rewards. When a child is diagnosed with a life-limited illness, the family system is understandably thrown off balance, because each family member has to develop coping strategies.

Some parents describe the grief they feel as a palpable, almost weighty presence. Others speak of the experience of grieving as an ever-changing emotion which may be very difficult to describe in isolation from other feelings. Rosenblatt (2000) describes a number of kinds of grief. Grief which 'drains' is associated with loss of physical energy and purpose. Feelings of emptiness and isolation, physically, socially and environmentally, in the present time and, in some cases, for many years after the child's death, are common. Parents may liken this 'emptiness' as having a hole cut in themselves, as if a piece has been pulled out or amputated. Others speak of living a partial existence after their child has died because, in a sense, part of them has died. The metaphor of being out of control is used frequently by parents at Acorns and is often associated with feeling powerless. Fear of 'going crazy' or 'losing it' may be used to describe the sense of helplessness and despair.

There is no way of dressing up the harsh facts of a child's diagnosis of life-limiting illness or their death. However, with skilled support, family members can develop strategies that help them to deal with problems and to function as an integrated team, supporting one another.

All professionals who work with families should have a sound knowledge of how parents are likely to respond to having a child with a life-limiting illness. They should also have an understanding of factors from within and outside the family unit that are likely to influence how parents cope. Circumstances such as the family situation and the composition of the family (including siblings and grandparents) should be taken into account. (See Chapter 11, 'The Impact of Life-limiting Illness on the Family'.)

In order to provide effective support, professionals also need to possess knowledge, attitudes and skills appropriate to their roles.

Knowledge

A good understanding of human development and behaviour is extremely important to enable supportive carers to recognise when families are experiencing difficulties. Carers need to be in touch with their own strengths, weaknesses and values and, in particular, any prejudices they may hold. Finally, they need to have a sound knowledge and experience of counselling practice and how the counselling experience may impact on families.

Attitudes

Supportive-carers need the capacity to be emotionally detached from families without appearing to be uncaring and remote. This is sometimes referred to as an ability to be 'a calm and stable facilitator, who is able to listen, accept and understand' (Brown 1999, p.94). Arguably the most important attitudes for supportive-carers to possess are those of respect, empathy and genuineness (Rogers 1980). It is also important that people who work with families are committed to the view that individuals have resources within them that enable them to work through problems. Unconditional respect for another person, regardless of their social class, gender, age or race, is one of the core principles for a helping relationship. Understanding other people's grief demands an insight into human tragedy, and a willingness to accept how this may be at odds with theoretical models of grief.

Counselling is emotionally draining, and those who support families in a therapeutic role often carry a great deal of their client's personal and private information, with the result that counsellors may be rendered vulnerable. (See Chapter 19, 'Acknowledging Staff Stress and Providing Support'.)

How parents cope in the long term with their child's life-limiting illness depends on many factors, including whether the illness was diagnosed at birth or later on, the support available to parents and the demands made upon them. Counselling support should ideally be offered from the time of the child's diagnosis, throughout their illness and after their death. Supporting family members is crucial to the care of the child. Panke and Farrell (2005) acknowledge that, where families receive appropriate support, it is possible, even in the face of adversity, for families to become closer through the experience. Hindmarch (2000) says that, regardless of the client's situation, it is important for counsellors to listen to what people say, rather than to presume what they need.

During the past decade there have been some interesting research findings concerning gender and bereavement. A study undertaken in 1997 by the Centre for Bereavement Research and Intervention concluded that men generally benefit most from emotion-focused interventions, since males have a tendency to develop problem-focused coping strategies when dealing with their personal grief. Conversely, women, who have a tendency to respond emotionally in their personal grief responses, benefit from problem-focused interventions.

Walter, Pickering and Littlewood (1995) have argued that images of grieving women used to highlight calamitous events has fuelled opinion about how people should express grief in public. It is also interesting to note that models of grief in adult life, such as those advocated by Parkes *et al.* (1996), are largely based on studies of women and, in particular, widows. However, it is dangerous to stereotype people, since life-experience, including past experiences of loss, is likely to impact on individuals. Recognising each bereaved person as an individual and avoiding comparison with others' experiences underpin the philosophy of supportive counselling.

Families often benefit from regular opportunities to talk through their anxieties, problems and coping strategies. They speak of the relationship as 'our lifeline', or 'a lifebelt when you feel you are drowning'.

Group work

Group work can help to ease the isolation felt by families. Groups may provide opportunities for altruistic support, a safe place to express emotions and a forum to offer support, as well as to receive it. Groups may also contribute to parent support through:

- promoting grief as a 'normal' emotional response
- facilitating the expression of a range of feelings.

Practice at Acorns combines the use of experiential and psycho-dynamic support. The former endeavours to use client life-experience to set the agenda for discussions. In psycho-dynamic support, facilitators plan activities and lead discussions, having carefully evaluated the needs of group members. In general, it appears that the more group members share in common, the more likely individuals are to benefit. Acorns' experience is that common bonds often act as a catalyst for enduring friendships. Conversely, other people may find groups threatening, especially if members express very intense feelings. Understandably, having empathy with how others feel may be too much to consider in the midst of emotional turmoil.

There have been innumerable attempts to describe the word 'counselling'. The British Association for Counselling (BAC) uses the following definition:

> People become engaged in counselling when a person occupying regularly or temporarily the role of counsellor, offers or agrees explicitly to offer time, attention and respect to another person or persons. (Cook 1999, p.99)

The role of the bereavement counsellor is a demanding one and requires more than the use of everyday counselling skills. Counsellors should have opportunities to work through some of their own personal losses so that they are aware of the impact of their life-experiences on their counselling. Experienced counsellors should also have:

- knowledge and understanding of attachment and loss, grief responses and the tasks of mourning
- information so that they can advise clients where they can access additional support
- regular supervision to talk through their personal experiences.

There is often an underlying assumption that counselling provides people with help to enable them to overcome problems. Indeed, in some contexts, counselling includes problem-solving activities with the counsellor encouraging the client to develop strategies towards resolution of the problem. For bereaved families, this view may appear extremely confusing and irrelevant because, quite simply, the counsellor is unable to reverse the fact that their child has died. A more helpful aim of bereavement counselling might be that the counsellor works with the client to facilitate expression of the client's grief and works through some of the tasks of mourning. Hindmarch (2000) likens bereavement counselling with parents whose child has died as 'touching base in a frightening, changed world' (p.159).

Counselling involves listening, supporting, empowering and befriending and, in these respects, it is a central feature of many professionals who work in health, social and educational settings. It is important to differentiate between professional counselling and counselling skills that may be used in a variety of roles and professions. Those who practise as counsellors should have undergone an accredited course of training that incorporates theory and practice, together with experience of being counselled. Most professionals working in palliative care settings will use counselling skills, without overtly offering counselling.

Counselling methods

Counselling methods will depend on the preference of individual counsellors and there are a large number of counselling models and styles. However, the overriding objective is to encourage clients to develop strategies to help themselves. However, **parents do not adapt** to having a life-limited child, or to their child dying, in relation to psychological theories of grief. Staff working in children's hospices will often play a number of roles in supporting families, and they may encounter individual family members in different contexts. Therefore, a variety of supportive models and caring strategies will be used in a flexible way, matched to individual needs. It is beyond the scope of this chapter to describe models of counselling. Readers should however familiarise themselves with the work of Carl Rogers' (1980) person-centred approach.

Counselling skills

Because counselling is concerned with the therapeutic relationship, it should come as no surprise that many of the skills used by the counsellor are concerned with listening and responding.

Listening is an extremely complex activity which includes many aspects, such as paying attention, being receptive to emotional responses, interpreting behaviour, receiving information, relating key points and themes and clarifying what a person has said through reflecting back or paraphrasing. Good listening skills, with appropriate responses, are the fundamental elements of helping children and their families (Cook 1999).

Remaining focused on what a person is saying, and communicating interest, encourages trust. Responding appropriately demands suspending personal views and prejudices and conveying respect. However, Burnard (1994) notes that:

> Counselling is not one set of skills to be used in a narrow range of situations, but a differing and often idiosyncratic mixture of personal qualities, practical skills and interpersonal verbal and non-verbal behaviours, that combine to make up a particularly caring aspect of the Health Professional's job.

However, supporting bereaved parents is never confined to learning a range of skills which will provide a 'quick fix' that can be applied to individual family circumstances. Fundamentally, it is about standing alongside parents, listening to them, and supporting them.

Sometimes when parents approach staff, it is because they hope the person will be able to alleviate some of the anguish they feel. This hope, combined with the vulnerability of the bereaved parent, renders carers in an extremely powerful position. Therefore, it is imperative that supporters are able to maintain a balance between sensitivity and objectivity. A skilled member of care-staff is aware that, whilst they may strive to alleviate parents' pain, they are never able to eliminate it. The importance of establishing clear boundaries within the client–counsellor relationship cannot be over-emphasised. In children's hospices where families may be well-known to staff for many years, it is inevitable that families perceive the supportive-carer/counsellor as a companion.

There are several questions that staff should ask themselves:

- Am I the right person for the client or the family?
- Am I able to give sufficient time to act in a supportive role?
- Does the client or family feel OK about the supportive-carer relationship?

The culture in which parents grew up themselves seems to influence their view about the potential help that counselling may provide. Where parents of either sex are brought up to feel that they should deal with their problems themselves, they are likely to be resistant to the idea of either one-to-one or group support. Those who are open to counselling seem to value opportunities to meet with someone who is a non-judgmental listener.

Inevitably, there will be times where clients need specialised support which is beyond the expertise of the counsellor or the resources of the support service. There are many national and local organisations that offer support and professionals should feel confident to signpost clients to these agencies. It is, however, imperative that contact lists are regularly updated.

There are myriads of expressions and forms of mourning. Rosenblatt (2000) describes grief as being fluid, changing and socially defined. He also advises that grief should be described in different terms according to the context, for example individual grief, family grief and community grief.

The losses that parents of life-limited children experience are manifold and may include loss of role, responsibility and self-worth. Cook (1999) describes several types of loss which parents of life-limited children may experience:

- loss of parental roles as sole carers
- loss of full responsibility for the child
- loss of control over everyday life and events
- loss of parental identity
- loss of self-esteem
- loss of hopes and dreams for their child.

Grieving is a normal response to loss, and most families do not require sustained bereavement support or specialist intervention (ACT/RCPCH 2003 document). However, some family members will experience abnormal grief reactions, and counselling support from a person such as a family support worker, counsellor, clinical psychologist or psychiatrist may be helpful.

Counselling aims to:

- reduce parents' isolation
- facilitate communication between partners and other family members
- encourage expression of feelings
- recall happy memories
- foster self-acceptance of the unique grief felt by parents.

Supportive caring

The term 'supportive-carer' may be more relevant in children's hospices, rather than the term 'counsellor'. Carers listen to families in a purposeful way which, in turn, enables families to feel valued and respected and to make sense of their experiences. Sharing also helps to remove feelings of isolation and reduces anxiety and fear.

In other words, through the relationship which exists between the supportive-carer and the family, individuals are helped to 'tell their story' and to share their experiences in the knowledge that the carer will support them. The first contact between the supportive-carer and families is very important. It will influence the future success of the relationship. The partnership is dependent on the way in which the supportive-carer is able to 'connect' with individual family members and to perceive their experiences. This relationship is founded on trust, and should have a quality that helps each individual to feel understood and safe enough to share very personal thoughts and experiences.

Families meet a large number of professional people and, therefore, it is extremely important that supportive-carers clarify their role, even if their professional title appears to make this self-evident. Hindmarch (2000) recommends supportive care should include:

- being available and present for the family
- listening more than talking
- clarifying professional roles
- respecting the individual views of family members
- encouraging the family to tell their stories

- avoiding platitudes
- acknowledging the uniqueness of the family's experience
- enabling the family to make informed choices and share decisions.

Breaking bad news

Being told that their child has a life-limiting illness is a point at which parents' lives are changed for ever (Davis 1993b). However, during the span of the child's illness, families are often subjected to many occasions when they are the recipients of bad news. Whatever the context of the news, parents are likely to suffer trauma. Notwithstanding, if the news is given in a sympathetic way, it is likely that this will enhance the relationship that parents have with professionals in the future. Lloyd Williams (2002) has likened the ability to communicate bad news effectively as an art form. It is a salutary experience to find that there may be a big difference between what a professional thinks that they have communicated to a family, and what the family has understood. Experience at Acorns suggests that, when professionals need to give parents bad news, it is important that several factors are considered. Parents say that receiving news from someone they know is less stressful. When both partners are able to be present, this often facilitates later communication between couples and other family members. In the absence of one parent, the support of a friend can be helpful. Bad news almost inevitably affects parents' capacity to recall what they have been told. When professionals appear relaxed and unhurried and parents feel that they have a personal interest in the child and the family, parents are more likely to trust and respect what is being said. It is likely that parents have already feared that the meeting will contain bad news. Honest, accurate and balanced information does not protect parents from emotional pain and anxiety, but it does enable them to begin the process of adapting to what they have been told. Where subsequent meetings are planned with parents, these should take place as soon as possible, in order to demonstrate ongoing care and support. Meeting again may also enable information to be repeated, and give scope for parents to ask questions.

Anticipatory grief

At the time of their child's diagnosis, many families experience intense anticipatory grief. Waechter (1981) describes anticipatory grief as the state where 'grief encompasses the entire family, while the dying child remains an integral part of that family' (p.41). Anticipatory grief seems to accelerate over time, whilst grief after bereavement usually decelerates slowly during the passage of time. There may be many occasions during the child's illness when parents find themselves in a crisis situation. Murgatroyd and Woolfe (1993) have suggested several behavioural patterns that characterise the distress felt:

- physical and psychological symptoms
- panic and the expression of overwhelming loss of control and a feeling of helplessness
- yearning for release from the pain
- impaired ability to function in everyday life.

(See also Chapter 11, 'The Impact of Life-limiting Illness on the Family'.)

Often, parents experiencing stress find themselves in the unenviable position of caring for their child at home, whilst also coordinating the support offered by individuals and service providers in the community. Lewis and Prescott (2006) argue that professionals need to examine their own framework of care with that of the family, and to develop a shared model that places the child and the family as central.

Transition from curative to palliative care

Discussing the transition from curative care to palliative care is a complex task. The way in which the prognosis is given will largely determine the ongoing relationship between professionals caring for the child and families (Brown 2001; Stevens and O'Riordon 1996). Where the relationship between families and the care team has been good in the early stages of a child's illness, families are more likely to feel confident to express how they feel, to ask for information and to ask questions. Increasingly, families seek second opinions beyond the initial diagnosis, and, with access to the Internet, parents may be well-informed about the possibility of treatment or available therapies (Hicks and Lavender 2001; Vickers and Carlisle 2000).

Many stressors will impact on families throughout the trajectory of the child's illness including:

- emotional strain
- physical demands
- fear of the future
- changed roles and life-style
- financial worries
- perceived inadequacies of services
- spiritual distress
- communication problems within, and outside, the family.

Families at risk

Several factors may contribute to families being particularly vulnerable:

- sudden unexpected deterioration in the child's health
- caring demands beyond the immediate family unit, for example sick or elderly parents
- single carers, with little support
- past or current mental health problems
- past loss of a child, or families where there is more than one life-limited child
- lack of practical support, or difficulties in housing or financial concerns
- evidence of drug or alcohol dependency
- conflict with spouse or other family members.

(Based on Oliviere, Hargreaves and Monroe 1998)

The end of life

Bruce and Schultz (2001) used the word 'non-finite' to describe the life-span of grief felt by families who care for a life-limited child, or who mourn the death of a child. The authors describe this grief as having 'a haunting and inescapable quality'. Although families may know that their child is life-limited, and children's hospice teams may have prepared them for the event, families rarely appear to be sufficiently prepared. There may be occasions where parents appear to direct anger towards hospice staff. In most cases, this is not a personal affront – rather, it is an emotional expression borne out of overwhelming circumstances and possibly projection of guilt that parents are unable to stop their child from dying.

Vachon (1993) describes several issues related to how families communicate during the end-of-life phase of care, namely concealed feelings, lack of information and struggling with feelings of helplessness. These are particularly likely when family members withhold information in an attempt to protect each other from difficult issues. Good communication between the child, the family and professionals is never more important than during the end-of-life phase of a child's care. Where families are encouraged to make the decisions that are right for them, they are likely to feel more in control at a very anxious time (Kruijver et al. 2000).

Most people who are involved in bereavement care will feel inadequate in giving support, because there is no way of dressing up the harsh reality of death. Indeed, the only experts in the situation are the family themselves.

Being a supportive-carer is much more about 'being there', rather than 'doing something'. Parents' stories about the last moments of their child's life are often told against a background of immense emotion and emotional helplessness. The language that parents use to tell their stories comes from the cultures and communities to which they belong. However, whatever the circumstances, the story is about dying and its ending is the death of the child.

Most parents will feel overwhelmed by the intensity of the emotions they feel and isolated in the rawness and pain of their grief. Situations like this can put a tremendous strain on relationships, and counselling can provide a safe place to acknowledge and work through these tensions.

Families will feel a sense of shock, which may render them unable to carry out everyday domestic tasks and care at home. Physical and emotional exhaustion will often leave them at a very low ebb and, thus, they may welcome practical help and support. This is not always the case, however. Some people may find that keeping busy and carrying out familiar activities serves as a distraction from the situation.

Talking through events often has a therapeutic effect. When bereaved parents tell their story, it can help them fulfil some of the crucially important tasks of mourning such as accepting the reality of the death, and to name their individual emotions. Most bereaved parents will need to go over and over the events surrounding their child's death. Using the child's name acknowledges the existence of the child and for newly bereaved parents; it may also help them to separate reality from fantasy. When parents talk about their child's death, they often centre on some common themes which include the circumstances and place of the death, the moment of the death, the funeral and ongoing relationships between their family and outside the family unit. Recounting their experience in this way helps them to organise their thoughts and to start the bereavement process. Those who listen to them can often gain an insight into their needs.

Bereaved parents have to learn to accept that the relationship that they had with their living child has ended, and that the continuing bond with their child in the future will be very different. The death of their child may also end relationships with others who were linked to them by their child.

The chasm between the life which bereaved parents believe they live in, and the world of non-bereaved parents, is enormous and one which is central in parents' thoughts.

> My life is an emotional rollercoaster that never stops. Everyone else gets on with living in their world.

Attig (1996) describes parents as having to 'relearn' how to live in a world that no longer makes sense, and every action is a 'first time one'. For many parents, the process of bridging the chasm is made easier by people who acknowledge their child's death.

Families will need different support during each phase of their grief; there are two main phases.

Phase one or the impact phase

This phase lasts from the time of the death and the funeral, to the time immediately afterwards. It is important that families are familiar with the people who will support them at this time of crisis. In many cases, this will include their own extended family members and professional people, such as hospice staff. The overriding aim will be to prevent further distress.

Phase two or adjustment phase

After the shock of the child's death and the funeral is over, and the pace of life has returned to 'normal', many adults and children will begin to experience intense grief. The role of supportive-carer is to:

- establish a relationship with individual family members
- support families through the pain of loss, change and grief, and to convey a sensitive understanding of their needs
- help individual family members to identify and to express their feelings, and to be in touch with their own emotions
- provide continuing and reliable support.

Key points

- Supporting family members is crucial to the care of the child.
- When a child is diagnosed with a life-limiting illness, the family system is thrown off balance because each family member has to develop coping strategies.
- Many factors determine how parents cope with their child's life-limiting illness. These include when the illness was diagnosed, the support available to parents and the demands made on them.
- During the span of their child's illness, families are often subjected to many occasions when they hear bad news.
- At the time of their child's diagnosis, many families will experience intense anticipatory grief.

- Differentiating between professional counselling and counselling skills is important. The overriding objective is to encourage clients to help themselves.
- Families are rarely sufficiently prepared for their child's death. Most will need to go over the events surrounding the death many times.
- One of the core principles of the counselling relationship is unconditional respect for another person, regardless of their social class, gender, age or race.

Implications for practice

- All professionals who work with families should have a sound knowledge of how parents are likely to respond to having a child with a life-limiting illness.
- Professionals should have a sound knowledge of counselling skills, and how counselling may impact on families.
- Factors from within and outside the family unit should be taken into account when determining the support a family is likely to need.
- Professionals who find themselves in caring roles need to be able to maintain a balance between sensitivity and objectivity.
- The first contact between the supportive-carer and families will influence the success of the future relationship.
- Helping families to make decisions that are right for them is likely to make them feel more in control.
- Families need different support during each phase of their grief. After the child's funeral is over many families will experience intense grief.
- Even when professional titles appear to make their role self-evident, it is important that carers clarify these with families.
- Groups may provide a safe place to express emotions through altruistic support.

The Financial Impact of Caring

Erica Brown

Having a very sick family member inevitably leads to extra costs (Smyth and Robus 1999). It is far more difficult for parents with a life-limited child to manage on the same income as families where people enjoy good health, yet most families with a life-limited child have fewer opportunities to earn, and despite the range of benefits and other help available, they may struggle to find their way through the maze and claim their full financial entitlements. Often the impact of life-threatening illness is greatest for families with the lowest income. To obtain benefits families need to be proactive in discovering what is available to them. According to Simons (2002), parents may glean information in a piece-meal way from voluntary organisations, or well-informed friends.

Research has been extensive in respect of the financial implications for families caring for a chronically sick or disabled child (Bennet and Abrahams 1994; Beresford 1995; Dobson and Middleton 1998; While, Citrone and Cornish 1996). Many parents (especially mothers), caring for a disabled child, face financial hardship as the result of not being able to work. Although the benefit system recognises the potential implications of financial hardship for families, there is evidence that the benefits currently available do not always match the additional costs incurred. Furthermore, when a child dies, financial assistance rapidly decreases and some children's hospices report that, in addition to experiencing intense grief at this time, families may also face significant financial hardship (While *et al.* 1996).

Those working with families who have a life-limited child will already be aware of the financial constraints that such families may face. There are a number of reasons why earning potential is reduced or denied to people living in these circumstances. Often the care needs of life-limited children mean that at least one parent needs to be on hand at all times, and therefore they are unable to work. For single parents there may be no opportunity to work. Sometimes, care is best met by both parents remaining out of paid employment, and in some cases this may be determined by the fact there is more than one life limited-child in a family.

The cumulative effect of caring

With improvements in medical science and treatment, life expectancy for many medical conditions has improved dramatically (ACT 2001). Therefore, some families are caring for many years, and the cumulative effect of exhaustion can seriously damage parents' health. Under the Carers and Disabled Children Act (2000), carers are entitled to an assessment of their own needs, and may be given financial support to enable them to receive help. Where paid employment is an option, true working potential may be reduced by a need to respond very quickly to any call regarding the child's health. Promotion prospects may be curtailed if managers are unsympathetic to an employee's needs, such as attending hospital or clinic appointments with their child. During the end of life stages of their child's life, a parent may be unable to work due to heightened emotional stress felt at this time.

Although some families using a children's hospice know that their child is going to die, in many cases they do not know *when* this will be. Therefore, they often have to make decisions based on their child's current state of health. Kagan, Lewis and Heaton (1998) reported that an increased number of children with life-limiting conditions were being cared for in the community. As a result, parents who become full-time carers face increased demands on their time. Indeed, it is not unusual for both adults to be dependent on out-of-work income (Rowntree Foundation 2001), because they are unable to secure care for their child whilst they work (Kirk 1999). For those parents who are able to continue either part-time or full-time employment, it is unlikely that they will gain an enhanced income through promotion.

Parental entitlement to benefits

Information about Income Support to which parents are entitled isn't always forthcoming from statutory services and this may lead to delay in families receiving the support to which they are entitled. Having to prove the case is discouraging and exhausting, and there are times when parents fail to apply for help because of the bureaucracy involved.

> It seems as if no-one coordinated the kind of help that was available to us. Sometimes we heard about support by chance from the battery of people who came into the house. The Internet is helpful, but the law changes so quickly it is impossible to keep up with what we are entitled to.

Some benefits and grants available to parents are means tested. Therefore, whilst their child is still alive, parents may be reluctant to seek employment because of the benefits that they would lose.

Disability Living Allowance

This is an allowance paid to parents whose child has an illness or disability and need help or supervision with personal care, mobility or both.

Carers' Allowance

Parents whose earnings are under a certain threshold may receive Carers' Allowance if they are looking after a child who is receiving Disability Living Allowance. Other benefits and grants such as Income Support and Housing Benefit may also be paid depending on the individual circumstances of a family. Where specialist adaptations have been made to the family home, some families may qualify for a reduction in Council Tax.

Support from voluntary agencies

Despite the relative rarity of life-limiting illnesses, there are an increasing number of voluntary organisations who are able to provide support and guidance to families. A small-scale study (Brown 2004) suggests that being able to access this support as soon as possible after a child is diagnosed is a vital component in how well parents cope psychologically and financially.

The cost of care

Several studies have focused on the financial implications of caring for a disabled or very sick child, and concluded that parents encounter tremendous difficulties in their endeavour to combine paid employment with caring. Indeed, many parents who look after a sick child experience reduced earning capacity and may leave paid work altogether (Dobson and Middleton 1998; Kagan *et al.* 1998). In some cases, many years may elapse between the onset of a child's illness and the diagnosis of their life-limiting condition and the end of life stage of their care and death. During this time, the child may undergo prolonged hospital stays and intense investigatory procedures or treatments, and for many wage earners the disruption to their lives and periods of absence from work have a severe effect on their self-esteem, professional reputation and promotion prospects. Hospital visits often incur additional expenses such as parking and refreshments. Employers may be unsympathetic even if the family's GP is prepared to give the parent a sickness certificate. Even when employers are willing to allow short-term leave of absence on compassionate grounds early in a child's illness, employees may find that their contracts are not renewed and their opportunities for overtime are greatly reduced.

The child's personal needs

Clothing a child whose weight fluctuates with medical treatments means greater expenditure. Even where a child's weight remains relatively static, constant washing means that clothes are subjected to additional wear and tear. For children who experience skin allergies or conditions, providing bedding and clothing can be costly, with no cheaper options available. Mothers may find it particularly important to be able to dress their child in attractive clothes as a public demonstration of their love and care.

Diet

Ready-cooked meals save time and effort and, although these are expensive to buy, there may be times when a child has a crisis in their illness, and bought meals may prove to be an everyday essential, rather than a preferred option.

Equipment

Many children will not be comfortable in standard equipment such as buggies, cots or beds, and the materials they are made of may cause allergies or an increased risk of infection. Furthermore, Kirk's (1999) study showed a lack of clarity over funding arrangements for equipment for use in children's homes. In some cases, families wait so long for equipment that it is inappropriate when it is finally delivered.

> His new wheelchair was too small for him when it arrived. We never did manage to get one the right size before he died.

Housing

The need for accommodation suited to a child's needs sometimes leads families to move house during the period of their child's illness, entailing removal costs and start-up expenses for a new home. The most common adaptations to a family home are alterations to the bathroom and the child's bedroom.

> The worst thing was deciding to borrow the money from our parents to build the extension so that he had a big enough turning circle for his wheelchair, and then being told by Social Services that they would fund the work. After 18 months of making the best of what we already had, while the plans for the adaptations were approved, we heard that Social Services' budget had been cut and they couldn't help us after all. We'd

told our parents to spend the money on themselves, which they had done, so we just had to muddle along. It looks as if my son's life is coming to an end now so it is not worth fighting any more about money. But it would have helped him (and us) a great deal if the promises had worked.

Leisure

Acorns' research (2003) provides evidence that families with a life-limited child are less likely to be able to enjoy social activities and family outings. However, where opportunities are made available, spending enjoyable time as a family is highly valued, and helps all family members to enjoy a sense of 'normality'. Outings are expensive, and although some families receive financial help from charitable sources, many are unable to take holidays because of the cost.

Additional costs

The costs of maintaining sophisticated technological support for a child (e.g. suction pumps, monitors, alarms, feeding pumps, recharging electric wheelchairs) are substantial, and household utility bills may be high. At Acorns, parents cite having a telephone in the house as tremendously important, and the large majority consider a mobile phone as essential if they are going to keep in touch while they are away from home. Indeed, many carers rely on the telephone as a means of advice and support from medical and social workers, and for maintaining contact with family members. For a significant number of ethnic minority families a phone is the only way of speaking to distant relatives, but this often incurs extremely high bills both during the child's life and after their death (Brown 2004).

Having access to a reliable vehicle adapted to transport a sick child may incur expensive running and maintenance costs (Roberts and Lawton 1999).

The child's funeral

Funerals are tremendously important to parents. The cost of funeral expenses varies widely, largely due to charges made by the funeral profession. Generally, however, parents seem to feel that they receive sympathy from funeral directors and, in some cases, their child's funeral is charged at 'cost' or no request for payment is made. Where costs are incurred, they seem to represent a real source of possible debt. Even when the service is free, families will still have to pay cemetery or cremation fees and, perhaps, for the services of the religious leader to conduct the service. The use of cars to accompany the hearse and floral tributes cost more. When a child is buried and a headstone is required, this is obtained later on and the cost is not included in any free services.

Parents may find it very hard to make decisions concerning expensive floral tributes or an elaborate headstone, fearing that their choice is based on cost rather than on what they would really like. Those who are supporting families play an important part in helping them plan within their means.

Where a family receives Income Support, Income-Based Job Seekers' Allowance, Housing Benefit, Council Tax Benefit, Pension Credit, Working Tax Credit or Child Tax Credit, a parent may be able to obtain payment from the Social Fund for their child's funeral. The Social Fund is a government fund that makes payment to people in need.

After the child's funeral

Some benefits continue for eight weeks after a child dies. These include Carer's Allowance, Child Benefit and Child Tax Credit, as well as child allowances paid in Income Support, Income-Based Job Seekers' Allowance, Housing Benefit and Council Tax Benefit.

Administrative procedures

Understandably, families suffer acute anxiety about receiving standardised letters and forms from benefit agencies requesting that Order Books are returned, although they do value being informed that entitlements may decrease or be withdrawn. Where phone calls are made, or a letter mentions the child's name and expresses sympathy, this is highly regarded.

> I know it is a really small thing, but I was really pleased when the letter arrived from the Benefit Agency and the person had crossed out 'your child's death' and put his name in.

It is evident that all bereaved families experience changed financial circumstances. Many parents experience a reduction in benefit income following their child's death. Where families have received Income Support over a period of years, they may have learnt to depend on it and may not have planned for what would happen when their child died. Entitlement to some benefits cease when the child dies and, understandably, parents may suffer extreme anxiety at a time when they are often at a very low ebb personally. This anxiety is likely to create psychological pain, since withdrawal of financial support may be perceived as the signal that it is the end of their caring role. Where families have previously used benefits to pay bills, they may find that they have insufficient resources, which leads to mounting debt. There are some instances where families have had their houses adapted to make it suitable for caring for their child, and they are no longer perceived as needing this specialist accommodation after their child dies.

Where families have been caring for a young adult who has been involved in decisions about spending money, cessation of regular income following the young person's death may compound parents' pain and increase their sense of loss of the young person's hopes and dreams for the future.

Returning to employment after a child's death

All aspects of life are difficult for parents encountering the grief of losing their child. In families where paid employment has been curtailed to care for their life-limited child, making the decision to seek employment may be extremely difficult. However, where a parent has been employed at the time of their child's death, the general trend appears to be to go back to work after a period of paid sick leave. Indeed, 'normality' of the work place, distractions from thoughts about their child's death and good relationships with work colleagues may be a very positive experience in an otherwise desperate situation. The exception to this is mothers who have young surviving children, and may want to look after them rather than going back to work quickly. Whether they are able to do this is often dependent on the general financial circumstances of the family, and the amount of debt incurred during their child's life.

In Acorns' experience (2003), mothers who do not need to work may want to devote a significant amount of their time to volunteering for the caring services that supported them during their child's illness. Understandably, a variety of circumstances may impact on whether mothers return to work or not, and for those who have to fill long empty hours, this may be a catalyst for heavy spending following their child's death.

The impact of previous spending patterns on the legacy of debt

We have seen that caring for a life-limited child may incur increased expenditure on items such as providing special equipment, high heating costs, adaptations to the home, and transport costs. Over a period of time, savings may be eroded to meet additional costs and, in some circumstances, it may result in a legacy of debt after the child dies. Some parents defer payment of bills or borrow money and they may also face additional costs paying for their child's funeral. A study of one children's hospice in 1999 suggested that parents were under threat of having their homes repossessed through mortgage arrears (Kirk 1999).

Where families have savings, they often have to access these in the period leading up to their child's death. Where parents do not have savings, relatives may contribute to finances and, in Acorns' experience, grandparents are often as generous as their own financial situation allows. Bank overdrafts and high spending on credit cards are often the ways in which families cope with the expenditure they incur on behalf of their child.

Corden, Sainsbury and Sloper (2001) cite the following factors as helpful in enabling parents to avoid financial problems while caring for their life-limited child:

- stability of family income
- supportive employers and work colleagues
- supportive GPs prepared to issue sick certificates to enable time off work
- full take up of Social Security entitlements
- stability/suitability of accommodation
- financial support from family/friends
- availability of aids/equipment from care services
- access to charitable/trust money
- aptitude for careful budgeting/home management
- shared family views about financial arrangements
- good health of parents/other children
- active avoidance of debt.

Key points

- Many families with a life-limited child have limited opportunities to earn and, in spite of benefits, they may struggle to claim their full financial entitlements.
- Being able to access financial support from voluntary organisations and benefit agencies are vital components in how well families cope.
- When a child dies, financial assistance rapidly decreases and entitlement to some benefits cease almost immediately.
- Some parents care for their child for many years and the accumulative effect of exhaustion can seriously damage parents' health.
- The disruption to parents' lives and periods of absence from work is likely to have a severe effect on parents' self-esteem, professional reputation and promotion prospects.

- The costs of maintaining sophisticated technological support for a child are substantial and household utility bills may be high. Likewise, phone bills and running and maintenance costs of adapted vehicles are usually high.

- The cost of funerals varies enormously and families may find it very difficult to make informed choices.

Implications for practice

- There are an increasing number of voluntary organisations able to provide support and guidance to families with a life-limited child. Professionals should help families to liaise with possible sources of support.

- Professionals play a vitally important role in helping families with a life-limited child claim their financial entitlement.

- Providing opportunities for families to spend enjoyable times together helps families retain a sense of 'normality'.

- Professionals working with individual families play an important role in helping the family plan their child's funeral within their financial means.

- Families appreciate acknowledgement of their child's death from benefit agencies and support services who have worked with them.

Part 3

Meeting Individual Needs

Children's Developmental Understanding and Emotional Response to Death and Dying

Erica Brown

Children do not live long before they encounter loss and change. Every year thousands of children face bereavement through the death of a grandparent, parent, sibling or friend. When someone dies, adults are understandably so engrossed in their own grief that children's grief may be unnoticed. However, the way in which children are helped when sad things happen may have a profound effect on how they are able to adapt to loss and change throughout their lives. Before we explore the impact of life-limiting illness on children who are sick, it is helpful to consider healthy children's developmental understanding of death and their responses to it.

Children's understanding of death

Early years

Because children mature at different rates, their understanding of death may vary. Knowledge comes through experience. Therefore, what a child understands may depend as much on past experience as it does on their chronological age. From as early as six months old, a baby may respond to the absence of a primary carer by showing irritability and changes in their feeding, sleeping or crying patterns. This is sometimes called separation anxiety.

In the early years, children begin to develop strategies to help them deal with the world around them. They may attempt to make dangerous or threatening situations seem safer, so, in games about monsters or 'scary' people, the 'bad' character is dealt with by removing them, for example shouting, 'Bang! Bang! You are dead.' Few children will understand the permanence of death and they may believe that dead means being asleep (see Figure 10.1). They think in literal terms, so euphemisms and metaphors such as 'lost' or 'gone away' may be confusing. If children ask questions, these are usually to gain more facts. It is unusual for children to ask more than one question at a time. However, children may need to ask the same questions over and over again, in order to make sense of them in different ways.

Figure 10.1 'My cat is dead' (Sophie, aged 4½)

By the time most children are seven years old they begin to understand death as having a cause, as being permanent and as being something that can happen to anyone, including themselves. Therefore, they may show signs of fear, although some children as young as seven may demonstrate a denial of their feelings and appear to be unaffected by a sad event. Generally, children will expect adults to be sad when someone dies. Where families are members of faith communities, children's understanding of what happens after death will reflect the teachings and beliefs of the community. Nicola, aged nine, belonged to a Christian family. When her brother died she told her grandma, 'Don't be sad granny, Sam has gone to heaven. It's a lovely place.'

Middle years

Gradually, a young person's understanding of the finality of death becomes more mature, although in the early stages abstract concepts may still not be fully grasped. Young adolescents are likely to ask questions about funeral arrangements or cremation or burial practices, and they have often formed their own opinions about what happens at death and beyond (see Figure 10.2). It is not unusual for children to 'idealise' a person who has died.

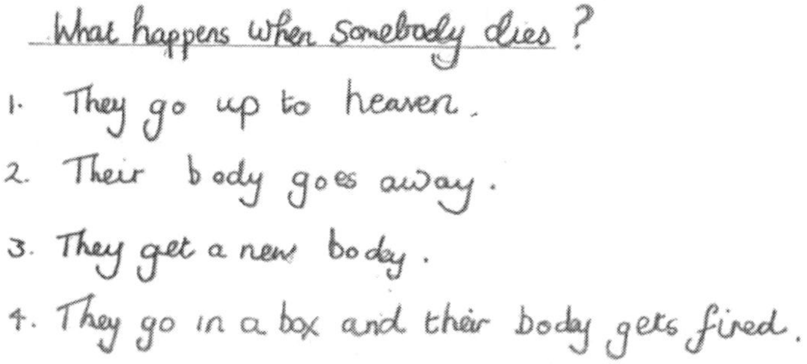

What happens when somebody dies?
1. They go up to heaven.
2. Their body goes away.
3. They get a new body.
4. They go in a box and their body gets fired.

Figure 10.2 'What happens when somebody dies?'

Young adulthood involves independence and psychological, physical and social changes. The death of a family member may result in guilt-feelings or self-reproach, or it may be perceived as a stigma or something to be ashamed of. Many young men suppress their emotions and denial of death is common. Some youngsters will seek out dangerous experiences in an attempt to gain control over death.

Children's grief responses

One dictionary definition of grief is a 'deep and violent sorrow'. Like adults, children react to the news that someone has died in a variety of ways, but it is important to understand that bereavement in a child is just as painful as it is for an adult (see Figure 10.3). The results may be devastating and last for years, because children are less in control of their circumstances.

Figure 10.3 'The hurt of the pain inside me splits my heart in two'

Whilst it is important to realise that not all children will experience the following grief reactions, the most usual responses are:

- 'searching' for the person who has died
- crying, yearning or anxiety at being separated from primary carers
- school refusal
- role-playing the dead person
- denial of grief in an attempt to protect adults
- anger, self-reproach or guilt
- sadness, withdrawal or depression
- overeating or loss of appetite
- psychosomatic symptoms such as tummy-ache or headache
- phobias about hospitals or doctors
- sleep disorders
- loss of self-esteem
- inability to concentrate or to study
- regression in academic performance.

The presence of any of these responses *over a period of time* may give cause for concern and indicate a need for specialist support. However, most children will reach an acceptance of the death of a person, and learn to live with the loss, providing they are given:

- information
- reassurance
- opportunities to express feelings.

In order for older children to understand the significance and permanence of death, they will need information and opportunities to respond to what they have been told. So often children become 'the forgotten mourners'.

If a death has been sudden, children may have limited access to accurate information. They may even have to live apart from their family for a while. Most young people find it helpful when they are given facts in an open and accurate way. In the case of young children, adults may need to explain the finality of death. If insufficient information is given, it is likely they may make up their own explanations in an attempt to make sense of what has happened.

Children are very perceptive to the emotional responses of adults. No amount of silence or secrecy can hide the fact that something is wrong. Overheard conversations, glimpses of adults in tears and changed routines can make children fearful. By giving children concrete information, fantasies and confusion can be avoided. Often adults hold back from telling children the truth because the task is such a difficult one.

Sick children's understanding of life-limiting illness

Some researchers (Judd 1993) conclude that, although children may not have reached a conceptual understanding of death, most are aware that something is physically wrong with their body. Whatever the circumstances, most professionals would agree that, even when children are life-limited, it is important to maintain a sense of hope, not only for the children but also for the people who love and care for them.

Bluebond-Langner (1995) says children who are life-limited have a more mature understanding of death than their healthy peers. It is a process that builds on their experience of illness and the changes they have in their self-perception. First, the child understands they are seriously ill and then they gradually move towards a realisation of acute, chronic and fatal sickness (see Figure 10.4). It is important to recognise, however, that these phases are not clear-cut. The stages may overlap and, in some cases, be delayed by pathological grief (Herbert 1996) or, where children have complex learning difficulties, by their lack of understanding.

Stage One	Stage Two	Stage Three	Stage Four	Stage Five
My illness is serious	I am taking powerful drugs and they have side-effects	I know why I am having the treatment	I am suffering relapses and remissions	The pattern of relapses and remissions will end in death

Figure 10.4 Stages in child's awareness of severity of illness (based on Herbert 1996)

Stage one is dependent on the child observing how other people respond and hearing what they say. After receiving treatment and visiting hospitals/clinics, the child reaches Stage two which may include a period of remission in the illness. After the first relapse, Stage three is reached and, as a result of several more relapses and remissions, the child realises at Stage four this is the pattern in their life. When the child realises that someone else has died from the same illness, they parallel their own experience and Stage five is achieved. Whether a child should be told of the seriousness of their illness is open to debate. Kubler-Ross (1983) says, 'Although all patients have the right to know, not all patients have the need to know' (pp.80–1). Generally it is believed parents' wishes should be respected regarding how much information should be given to the child. Herbert (1996) believes:

- Parents are important as role models in determining a child's response to their illness and inevitable death.

- Where parents are able to break the news calmly, the child will cope better.
- Many children are resilient to stress and they may cope better than their parents.
- Children need to know the truth.

How children communicate their awareness of the seriousness of their illness will be considered later in the chapter.

Life-limited children's experience of illness

The impact of life-limiting illness on the everyday life of a child is difficult to evaluate fully. However, they experience a number of events, which are unlikely to be experienced to the same extent by their 'healthy' peer group. These include:

- repeated GP, clinic and hospital visits and possible admission to hospital
- repeated absences from school
- long-term treatment/palliative care
- distress and discomfort of medical procedures and possible side-effects of treatment
- chronic or continual episodes of pain
- separation from family and friends
- restricted social interaction or social isolation from their peer group.

Infant

Serious illness in the first year of a baby's life may alter the development of the child's self-awareness. Parents usually find this particularly distressing because they may be unable to offer the baby reassurance. Babies learn primarily through motor activity and sensory stimulation, and the daily care tasks performed by parents encourage sensory-motor development. Where possible, parents should remain the main carers of their child and continue familiar tasks such as bathing and feeding. Invasive procedures should *never* be undertaken in the child's bedroom, which should be a safe, comforting environment.

Toddler

During the toddler stage, the major developmental tasks include gaining a sense of autonomy and self-control, factors that may be severely jeopardised when a small child is very ill. Because the child does not possess the capacity to understand the concept of death, they will not experience anxiety about death. The most frightening aspects of life-limited illness are likely to include pain and separation anxiety, and trauma if invasive procedures have to be carried out. Even though the toddler does not suffer anticipatory grief about their own death, they are likely to be very aware of parental anxiety.

Most toddlers are likely to show regression in previously mastered skills. These may include toilet training and speech. Many will withdraw from primary carers and become easily agitated and angry. It is extremely important to maintain familiar routines as far as possible, and to encourage parents to be consistent in their expectations of their child's behaviour.

Early years

In the early years, the major developmental tasks are mastering skills such as walking, talking, toilet training and being separated from primary carers. Many young children are able to think about 'bad' things and they may assume that their illness is a punishment for something they have done wrong, or for a bad thought about someone else. A child needs constant reassurance that nothing they have done caused their illness.

Typically, children in the early years of development react angrily to the impact of their illness. This may include breaking toys, lashing out or biting other people, and refusing to cooperate. Because the child's security is derived from routines, it is extremely important to maintain these as far as possible.

Middle years

In the middle years, children increase their autonomy, independence and self-esteem. If their illness interferes with their achievements, they may experience repeated frustration and failure. Peer group approval and support are extremely important to children at this age. Separation from their peer group is often a significant consequence of illness. Maintaining contact with friends is usually a priority. Many children in this age group will have an increased awareness of the significance of serious illness, and they will be developing an understanding of the permanence of death. Life-limited children are often aware of the fatal prognosis of their illness, even though they may not have been told. They are acutely aware of adult behaviour and they will need opportunities to talk about their fears and apprehensions.

Play is an important aspect of childhood and a child may use play to maintain a sense of control and predictability as well as a temporary escape from the stress they are feeling.

Adolescence

Adolescence is a period of rapid physical, cognitive and emotional development. Physical health and psychological wellbeing are important for all young people (Vessey and Swanson 1996). The societal perception of adolescence and adult status varies between cultures. In Western society, there is no accepted age that defines adult status in all aspects of life. For example, there are differences between when a young person may marry, hold a driving licence, and vote.

Adolescence is a journey of discovery, turmoil, challenge, experimentation, ambivalence, egocentricity, confidence and self-doubt, combined with unfolding changes physically, emotionally and intellectually. Coping with a life-threatening illness is a monumental undertaking. Unlike young children, adolescents generally perceive death as irreversible. Therefore, acceptance of personal death is particularly difficult, because for many young people their lives are orientated towards the future.

Adolescence demands that a young person is able to master a number of tasks, including the development of body image; building self-esteem and identity through socialisation; the establishment of meaningful relationships; establishing sexual identity; and reaching emotional independence (Cooper 1999). Peer relationships play an important part in adolescent development.

The effect of life-limiting illness will have different consequences for social interaction depending on the specifics of the condition and its limitations, together with factors such as gender and age (Coleman and Hendry 1993). Generally it is accepted that conditions which limit physical capacity and daily activities, or alter a young person's physical appearance, are likely to have a greater impact on social adjustment. Strax (1991) writes about the significant factor that friendship plays in the development of social skills. Where young people rely on transport to take them to school, they may miss out on opportunities for social interaction with their peers. Furthermore, Emery (1994) believes that wheelchair users may suffer from changed body image and lowered self-esteem.

For young people with life-limiting illnesses, concerns about physical attractiveness and sexual competence and sexual expression may be particularly troubling, and they may feel that they are set apart from their peers. In some cases, the illness may interfere with 'normal' physiological processes. Besides concern for their own welfare, life-limited adolescents are usually concerned about the wellbeing of their family and this may extend to aspects of the mental health of their parents and siblings.

Involving young adults in life experiences that encourage independence and autonomy are vital components of their care. Enabling adolescents to make their own decisions and to consider options open to them is important. Professionals working with adolescents and young adults should:

- take account of how life-limiting illness may disrupt and interfere with the mastery of developmental tasks
- help the young person to develop strategies to adjust to differences they may experience in their physical, intellectual and social development.

Life-limited adolescents with 'normal' cognitive ability know that they are dying (Armstrong Dailey and Zarbock 2001), but they may fluctuate between awareness and denial. Knowing that death is a reality does not mean that young people accept the inevitability. They may often have great anxiety about the process of dying. Many adolescents will withdraw emotionally as death approaches in order to conserve energy and to protect them from the reality of painful separation. Some young people will strive to achieve major accomplishments in an effort to maintain a sense of purpose in the face of impending death.

> Keith was 18 when he went to his local hospice for respite care during the end of life phase of his illness. Although he had spent many hours researching the likely prognosis of his illness on the Internet, he told a member of staff that he planned to take part in a sponsored walk of The Great Wall of China the following year.

This young adult was expressing his hopes and dreams, although he knew he was unlikely to live more than a few weeks. Conversely, a young lady debilitated by the end stage of cystic fibrosis became distressed when her parents expressed no recognition of the fact that she was dying. She told her nurses that she knew her life was running out. Staff validated her feelings by reassuring her she would not be left alone, and asking her whether she would like to tell her parents she knew her life was coming to an end. Sally agreed, and asked that her family came to the hospice the following day so that she could say 'goodbye' to them. Through gathering her family together before she died, Sally was dealing with unfinished business and maintained a sense of control.

Life-limited children with learning disabilities

Oswin (1991), writing a decade and a half ago, says that, in spite of the empowerment of children with learning disabilities, 'it appears in the area of loss and bereavement they are still not receiving enough consideration, or the appropriate support they require'. First the author argues that this shortfall is due to an assumption that children with learning disabilities do not experience the emotional response to loss and grief as others do. Second the combination of a 'double taboo' of learning disabilities and 'death' has challenged society to the extent that they have been swept under the carpet. Finally, grief is often considered as part of abnormal behaviour associated with the learning disability, rather than a normal human response.

Research into how children with learning disabilities respond to bereavement is limited and, in the main, concentrates on children in long-term residential care (O'Brien 1998; Oswin 1991; Strachan 1981). McLoughlin (1986) believes that children and young people with learning disabilities are too often perceived as a homogeneous group, with the result that their needs may be seen to be different from their mainstream peers. Brown (1999) supports this view, saying that problems experienced by children who have learning disabilities are often the direct result of being treated differently from the norm.

The grief experienced by life-limited children with learning difficulties does not appear to progress through straightforward clearly defined stages, beginning at the time of diagnosis and finishing with the end-of-life phase of their illness. The work of Black (1989, 2002) suggests that the way in which children adjust to their illness is largely dependent on how well their primary carers cope, and how open the family is to the expression of grief. Various scholars describe different stages of adult anticipatory grief in non-disabled persons.

Brown (1999) describes work with life-limited children and young people with learning disabilities aged between five and 16 years of age. The findings reveal a huge number of individual responses to impending death. Informal interviews with the young people's parents and teachers also suggest a range of inter-related factors, which impact on the way in which the youngsters respond. These are often described as 'inter-related features of bereavement'. It is interesting to note how many of the life-limited children in Brown and Arens' (2005) study at Acorns demonstrate aspects of the grief reactions described by Parkes, Relf and Couldrick (1996). Furthermore, the children also respond to their illness in ways that have come to be accepted as 'normal' grief responses for children of average cognitive ability, who suffer from a life-limiting condition. The findings of Brown and Arens' (2005) research is summarised below.

Anxiety

Because children are dependent on adults for their wellbeing, they seem to show a tremendous awareness of the anxiety felt by their primary carers. Sometimes adults describe the child as 'looking vulnerable' or 'being withdrawn'. There are instances where children seem to avoid eye contact from adults or refuse to communicate with them, and occasions when young children refuse to go to bed alone, because they want to keep adults in sight. Children's sleep patterns may be disrupted at times when parents are feeling under greatest stress, and parents speak of their child 'being perpetually tired'. Neither the child nor their parents are able to relax. Occasionally, children protest at having to go to school and they are described as 'fretful' on weekdays.

Changed feeding and eating habits prevail. Parents wonder whether their child attempts to maintain some control over their life by either refusing food or 'comfort' eating.

Anger

Anger appears to be a very confusing and frightening emotion (see Figure 10.5). Often anger is accompanied by physical aggression, such as kicking or lashing out at other people. There are instances where children engage in self-harming behaviour. Dyregrov (1994) believes anger is more commonly expressed by boys than girls. However, this is not always the case in Acorns' experience.

> A ten-year-old life-limited girl with autism was so angry, she used a chair to break every mirror in the house, repeating as she did so, 'You won't ever, ever look in here again.'

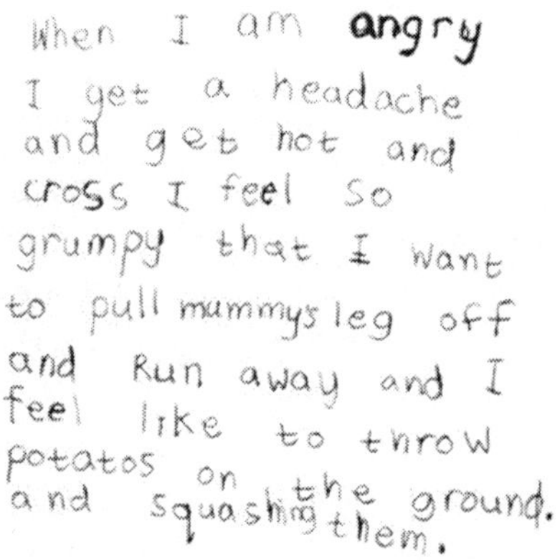

When I am **angry**
I get a headache
and get hot and
cross I feel so
grumpy that I want
to pull mummys leg off
and Run away and I
feel like to throw
potatos on the ground
and squashing them.

Figure 10.5 'When I am angry'

Denial and disbelief

Many children seem to show an awareness of the confusion and turmoil felt by family members, and they may respond adversely if there are changed routines in their everyday care. Instead of being able to relax in the security of their familiar surroundings, they behave as if they are disorientated. It is common for young people who know they are going to die, to deny the reality of the situation and, in some cases, this appears to be in an attempt to protect their family. There are also times when the prospect of an early death is just too much to bear.

> When Kevin, aged 16 (with cerebral palsy and a life-limiting congenital heart condition), learned about his prognosis, he shouted at his

mother, 'No, no.' Later he had to be told again and again how ill he was, and that nothing could be done to save his life.

What is significant about Kevin is that his responses are human ones. They are not specific to a life-limited person with cerebral palsy. He is angry and confused, and he disbelieves what is happening.

Night terrors and disturbed sleep

Disturbed sleep is common, and cognitively-able young people may have heard adults use the euphemism 'sleep' to describe death. Consequently, they may be afraid of falling asleep in case they die.

> Amy, aged five, had heard her parents talking about how laboured her breathing had become. One night she sobbed herself to sleep, telling her mummy she might forget to breathe.

Here the responses are not unlike those described by Brown (2001), in relation to trauma.

Longing for the normality of life

Most children seem to experience a range of emotions. Their anxiety is expressed in different ways which range from bitter outbursts of crying, to quiet withdrawal. Often they need familiar, tangible comfort objects. However, if the presence of the toy reminds them of something uncomfortable or distressing such as a medical intervention, they may hide it. If the toy is out of sight, then the stressful event cannot recur.

Many children remember past family occasions such as birthdays and holidays and they still look forward to future shared events. When the time arrives to celebrate, however, they may appear sad, almost as if they are aware of their parents' thoughts that this might be the last time the child will be able to share in the fun.

However life-limited children with learning disabilities respond, they will need to be supported. Anger, tears and apathy are normal human emotions, and for those children who do not have verbal communication skills, they may need help to express levels of grief.

Anxiety about death is an issue for life-limited children, although it is only during the last three decades that children's conceptual understanding and emotional response to their impending death has been studied. As recently as 1960, clinicians such as Knudson and Natterson advocated that children should be protected from the inevitability of their own death. It was the pioneering work of practitioners such as Bluebond-Langner (1995) that changed this view. She described young children as having a clear understanding of death as the end of life, although many of them utilised a range of defences in order to avoid the reality of the situation. Life-limited adolescents, unlike younger children, may be caught in what Judd (1993) describes as a 'polarised struggle' as they attempt to stake out their identity and independence. Often this determination continues in spite of the restrictions and limitations that their illness imposes upon them.

The psychological effects of children facing a life-limiting illness are dependent on many factors including the child's age, the phase of the illness, the degree to which normal activities can be performed and how body image is affected. Parkes et al. (1996) describe children's reactions as being very like those of adults who are bereaved and suffering grief. Responses include initial shock or numbness on learning the news; denial of the seriousness of the illness; anger about the restrictions the disease imposes on their life; a sense of injustice; depression, sadness and helplessness, associated with being out of control as the illness progresses; bargaining, in an attempt to postpone the inevitable outcome; and finally, acceptance that death will happen. Serious illness during adolescence may cause particularly turbulent emotions. Just as young people are achieving independence and separation from their families, they are cheated by serious health problems and by reminders that their goal of reaching adulthood will never be achieved.

In the past, it was common to withhold information from children concerning their death. Although this view is still held by some parents and health professionals, seriously ill children generally have an awareness of death. If parents or staff avoid talking about the situation, this may increase the child's stress. Brown (1999), writing about children in hospitals or hospices where other young people are dying or who have died, says they seem to show an enhanced awareness of death (and in some cases increased anxiety). As a result of her concern about how to explain death to life-limited children, Kubler-Ross (1983) developed a model for explaining the physical and spiritual process of death and the relationship between death and the individual child. The model describes the physical body as a cocoon that envelops a butterfly waiting to emerge, which is the child's spirit. At the moment of death the cocoon opens up and releases the butterfly, which represents the child. The cocoon is buried or cremated and not the butterfly, which continues its existence elsewhere.

Children who are aware they are having information withheld from them may feel alone, deceived and vulnerable. Often they are battling with fantasies about death. How information is conveyed to the child is important. It needs to be done in an age-appropriate and cognitive-appropriate level. The greatest support to the child is his or her family, but peer group support is also vital. Family responses to a child's life-limiting illness are discussed in more detail later in the book.

Children may communicate their awareness of the severity of their illness verbally or through play writing, drawing or the arts. Kubler-Ross (1983) describes these responses as 'pre-conscious awareness' from the 'inner-spiritual, intuitive quadrant'. Doka (1993) advises that adults should consider how they will give information to children.

Brown (1999) tells of life-limited children in a hospice who were aware of memorial services held for their peers who had already died. The children were angry that the adults who surrounded them were reluctant to help them to express their feelings of anxiety and isolation. She also describes another child who had heard the words 'kill' and 'invade' in relation to the therapy given to treat her illness. Understandably, the child had fantasies about warfare and was constantly checking she was not being attacked.

We have seen that children's perception of death varies according to their age, life experience, cognitive ability, environment, seriousness of their illness and their world of fantasies and dreams. Dying children need to be given age-appropriate opportunities to explore their fears and concerns.

Children's developmental understanding of death provides a reference point for communicating with dying children, but it should not be the sole framework. A child's willingness or need to talk is paramount, as well as their level of understanding. Most children will need repeated opportunities for them to absorb what is happening to them, as well as planned times for further exploration. For young children or those with learning disabilities, their communication may be through symbols or play. Children become very adept at protecting family members and, when they are aware that people find the situation too painful, they may choose to engage in what Riches and Dawson (2000) refer to as 'an unspoken conspiracy of mutual protectiveness'.

Children's questions about death

Questions children ask about death generally fall into four main categories (Brown and Arens 2005). They may be curious about their illness. Questions such as 'Why did I get ill with…?' or 'What happens next?' may be asked. Often young people are very confused by the range of emotions they experience and by the way in which adults respond. Their questions may reflect this confusion as they ask 'Why are you upset?' or 'Why is my head in a muddle?' It is a human response to search for a reason for an illness, and children may feel that they are in some way to blame for what is happening to them. Their questions may include 'What did I do wrong?' or 'Why couldn't the hospital make me better?' Lastly, children may live in families and in communities that reflect religious and cultural beliefs and practices. Some of the questions they ask are very difficult to answer such as 'Why does God take the young ones first?' or 'Is there enough room for everyone in heaven?'

Questions like these may catch adults off their guard. However, children usually phrase questions in a way that lets adults know how much information they require. Therefore, it is very important to listen carefully to what children ask and to observe how they are responding. If they do not understand, it is likely they will return to the question again. But it is not always easy to judge exactly what a child is asking. Reflecting a question back, or re-phrasing it in a way which encourages the child to give more information about their underlying concerns, can be very helpful. For example, the child who asks 'Will I have a pain when I die?' may have a deep-seated fear of his or her own capacity to cope. The adult who asks 'Why do you think you might have a pain?' will help the child to express their anxiety and they will often be able to offer reassurance. Children who have been ill for a long time may be very aware of what is happening to them through conversations they have heard, or observations they have made about the behaviour of the adults around them.

Adults should:

- consider the age and developmental level of the child
- listen carefully to what the child is asking
- clarify any unspoken contexts in a question
- clarify any ideas of confusion or misunderstanding
- respond to questions in straightforward, easily understood language, avoiding clichés, euphemisms and rehearsed answers
- strive to give answers that dispel fantasy and encourage reality
- make distinctions between physical and spiritual aspects of death
- acknowledge that nobody knows all the answers.

Children communicating an awareness of their illness

How children respond to the news of their own life-limitation will determine the way in which they are told the news. Support should include:

- helping children to express their fears and concerns
- helping children to communicate what they already know about their illness
- helping children to express their own preferences and needs.

Many children who are dying show an awareness of what is happening to them before the event happens, but the acquisition and assimilation of the knowledge is a prolonged process. Bluebond-Langner (1995) refers to the process as one of *internalisation*. Where children are not told directly but learn what is happening, the same author refers to this as a process of *discovery*. As children progress through the stages of their illness, their view of self changes as they accumulate more information. It is a process which is dependent on experience rather than on age.

Children may refer less to treatment, and more to how the time that they have left will be spent. Certainly many children at Acorns have an urgent need to achieve ambitions. They may want to be included in social events even though they are too ill to fully participate in their chosen activity. Some young people seem to be intent on what Bluebond-Langner (1995) calls 'disengaging people' in a rehearsal for the final separation of death.

It is amazing how many life-limited children and their families achieve a sense of hopefulness. This may relate to being able to fulfil an achievement, or being able to maintain a good quality of life, right up to the end. For children from families with a strong spiritual or religious belief, hope of an afterlife may bring solace and give tragedy a sense of purpose.

It is a challenging task for those who have to break the news to a child or young person that their life is threatened. Telling must be amongst the most difficult and painful things anyone will ever have to do. Throughout this book, I make a plea for open and honest communication between families facing death and those who care for them.

Box 10.1 and Table 10.1 show how individual needs can be met and children's cognitive, emotional and physical responses to death.

Box 10.1 What Children Need

Baby

Symptom relief and pain management.

Frequent physical contact (or touching) from primary carers.

Frequent awareness of the voices of primary carers.

Normal routines and maintenance of familiar, cultural and religious traditions.

Opportunities to play and to interact with family members.

Pre-school

Symptom relief and pain management.

Reassurance that any separation from primary carers is unavoidable.

Communication in easily understood language.

Explanations about care procedures and administration of medicines.

Constant reassurance about love and care from family members.

Help to indicate levels of pain or distress.

Normal routines and maintenance of familiar cultural and religious traditions.

Opportunities to interact with peers and family members.

5–7 years

Symptom relief and pain management.

Honest responses to questions about life-limiting illness.

Opportunities to communicate preferences, needs, fears and concerns.

Constant reassurance of the love and care of family members, peers and friends.

Help to communicate levels of pain or anxiety.

Access to educational activities and hobbies.

Contact with school.

Opportunities to reflect on achievements and hopes for the future.

Maintenance of familiar routines and cultural or religious traditions.

7–9 years

Open and honest responses to questions about the nature and inevitable outcome of their illness.

Opportunities to express opinions, wishes, anxieties.

Constant reassurance of the love and care of key people.

Freedom to make decisions about pain control, symptom relief and care.

Opportunities to express awareness of how family members are responding.

Maintenance of routines and religious and cultural traditions.

Opportunities to reflect on achievements throughout their life, and hopes for the future.

Adolescents and young adults

Symptom relief and pain management.

Opportunities to express fears and concerns for self and family members.

Privacy, especially when undergoing personal care.

Opportunities to maintain autonomy and independence for as long as possible.

Support from peer groups as well as family members.

Involvement in decisions regarding their care, including symptom control and pain relief.

Maintenance of familiar cultural and religious traditions.

Opportunities to reflect on what they have achieved throughout life.

Acceptance and affirmation of sexuality.

Table 10.1 Children's cognitive, emotional and physical responses to death

	Infant/toddler	5–7 Years	7–11 Years	Adolescent
Cognitive factors	Onset of attachment at about 6 months after birth. Permanence of death not understood. Ability to conceptualise the word 'death' very limited. Children begin to incorporate small 'losses' into their lives. Children are aware of the adult use of the word 'dead'. Fantasies about being reunited with a person after death.	Able to classify, order and quantify events, but unable to give a rationale. Concepts of 'life' and 'death' established, e.g. death equals separation. Understand physical state of death = not breathing, not moving, still, etc. Permanence of death still not established. Stage of 'magical' thinking, e.g. thoughts/actions may be responsible for death.	Able to explain reasoning in a logical way. Realisation of own mortality. Permanence of death established. Death is understood as an ultimate reality. Confusion about metaphors and euphemisms associated with death, e.g. 'gone', 'asleep', 'lost'.	Abstract thought patterns established. Interest in physical characteristics of death and dying. Questions asked How? Why? Own theories about what happens at death. Interest in ethical issues, e.g. abortion, euthanasia.
Emotional responce	Separation anxiety. Yearning and searching for a person who is not there. Expression of sadness short-lived. Blame other people for a person's death. Rejection of affection from primary carers.	Excessive crying. Unable to control emotions. Poor concentration at school and play. School refusal. Illusions/hallucinations about the dead person – night terrors. 'Play out' death and dying.	Anxiety about primary carers dying. Change in normal behaviour. Some control of emotional responses. Inability to organise thoughts and to concentrate. Stealing objects as 'comfort'. Capacity to sustain feelings of sadness for longer.	Wide range of emotional responses. Anxiety about the future, e.g. material possessions/economics. Reluctance to form lasting relationships. Rejection of affection from family members/peers.
Physical responce	• bedwetting • wetting by day • viral infections • disturbed sleep	• restlessness • loss of appetite • 'tummy-ache' – psychosomatic illness • clinging behaviour • night terrors	• aggression • changed behaviour • nail-biting • sleep disturbance • physical illness	• eating disorders • challenging behaviour • physical illness • disturbed sleep • conflict • risk-taking behaviour • increased sexual behaviour

Key points

- A child's understanding of death may depend as much on past experience as it does on their chronological age.

- The way in which children are helped when sad things happen may have a profound effect on how they are able to adapt to loss and change throughout their lives.

- Where children are members of faith communities, their understanding of what happens after death will reflect the teachings and beliefs of the community.

- In order for children to understand the significance and permanence of death, they will need information and opportunities to respond to what they have been told.

- Children react to the news that someone has died in a variety of ways including: crying, yearning, anger, denial, sadness, psychosomatic symptoms and regression in academic performance.

- Life-limited children's perceptions of death vary according to their age, life experience, cognitive ability, the seriousness of the illness, and their world of fantasy and dreams.

- The physical effects of life-limiting illness are dependent on many factors including children's age, the phase of the illness, how body image is affected and the degree to which normal activities can be performed.

- Anxiety about death is an issue for life-limited children and young people. There are conflicting views concerning whether a young person has the right to know.

- Some children and young people may employ strategies to deny the inevitability of their illness ending in death. Others may express a mature and sophisticated understanding of their life-limited condition. Indeed, many show an enhanced awareness of what is happening to them.

- Research into how children with learning disabilities respond to the death of a family member is limited.

- Children may choose to communicate their awareness of the severity of their illness verbally, through play, writing, drawing and the arts.

- Children who know they are having information withheld from them may feel alone, deceived and vulnerable.

- For adolescents and young people, coping with life-limited illness is a monumental undertaking.
- Parents are important role models in affirming their child's response to their illness.
- The greatest support to a child is their family and peer group.

Implications for practice

- Giving children information helps to dispel fantasies and confusion.
- Children should always be given information in an age-appropriate and cognitive-appropriate way.
- Carers should listen carefully to the questions children ask about death and dying.
- Where possible, parents should remain the main carers of their life-limited child.
- Carers should provide opportunities for children and young people to talk about their fears and apprehensions.
- Adolescents and young people should be encouraged to make their own decisions about their care.
- Maintaining familiar routines is important.
- Invasive procedures should never be undertaken in a child's bedroom, which should be a safe, comforting environment.
- Support for life-limited children and young people should include: helping them to express their fears and concerns; helping them to communicate what they know about their illness; and helping them to express their own preferences and needs.
- It is important to maintain a sense of hope in life-limited children and young people.

The Impact of Life-limiting Illness on the Family

Erica Brown

Throughout the Western world lifestyles are changing dramatically. Past research on families tended to focus on the traditional model of a nuclear family and neglected diversity in family composition.

Although the structure of family groups varies, the central purpose of the family is to create and nurture a common culture that encourages the wellbeing of the people concerned, providing physical and emotional support. Many parents view their children as their common life-project (Bjornberg and Buck-Wiklund 1990).

Family members are inter-dependent. Therefore, anything that affects one member will affect the family as a whole. There is extensive literature concerning the way in which parents are first informed of a child's diagnosis of life-limiting illness. Research suggests that the manner in which parents are told about their child's diagnosis affects both the way in which they adjust to the situation and the wellbeing of their child. So often parents are confronted with a diagnosis that is unfamiliar to them (Wendell 1996). This means that they may be left without professional support and with unanswered questions concerning their child's condition (Melander-Mattala 1995; Read 2000).

Diagnosis may well be a watershed between two different lifestyles – the pre-diagnostic life with normal ups and downs, and post-diagnostic life, where parents feel that their future is unknown and everything is at the mercy of their child's illness. The situation may render them confused and in a state of extreme anxiety (Davis 1993a; Knudson and Natterson 1960). Not only do they have to cope with the diagnosis, but they also have to acknowledge that the illness will end in their child's death.

Many parents are able to vividly recall the time when they were told their child was life-limited (Bradford 1997; Woolley *et al.* 1989b). They describe their initial reaction as one of extreme shock, a state likened by Goldman (2002) to being similar to that of bereavement.

One of the first dilemmas of having a child with a life-limiting illness is the shattering experience of how to cope with something which was unexpected and how to accept, as a parent, what is unacceptable (Cooper 1999). Several authors write about the isolation which parents face as they struggle to come to terms with their shock (Carpenter 1997; Hornby 1998). The task of coping is a process in which parents find themselves constantly adjusting to the new demands that their child's illness makes. Murgatroyd and Woolfe (1993) refer to this process as 'recurrent crises'.

Adapting to the diagnosis

How parents deal with the diagnosis of a life-limited child varies. It is thought that the way in which families cope with stress before the diagnosis of the illness may play a critical part in how families cope (Kasak and Nachman 1991).

Gascoigne (1995) says 'parents rarely come to terms with the fact that their child will die'. She goes on to say that they are likely to experience a tremendous number of different emotions. Brown (2002) describes these emotions as follows:

- Disillusionment – parents' hopes for their child's future are shattered.

- Aloneness – bonding and relationships may be more difficult for parents to establish with their child.

- Inequality – parents' perceived unjustness and unfairness of what has happened may lead to a feeling of inequality in relation to other families.

- Insignificance – having a life-limited child may shatter parents' perceptions of rewarding parenthood.

- Past orientation – because the future may be uncertain, parents may focus on the past and look back on the time before diagnosis as one that was more secure.

Family communication patterns

Family communication patterns appear to be critical in determining how well families cope with illness, since the most valuable sources of support are embedded in their relationships, parenting styles and philosophy. Evidence from a number of studies suggests that a family's cultural, social and educational background also influences how they cope (Brown 2001).

Family members communicating with each other

Families who are collectively able to communicate their feelings may adapt better to life-threatening illness. Children look to their family for support, especially when situations are unknown and unexpected. Typically they mirror the coping strategy shown by their parents (Moody and Moody 1991). Indeed, it is thought that parents play a crucial role in mediating the effects of the illness on their child (Greenburg and Meadows 1991). Brown (1999) contrasts closed and open family communication systems. Rigidity and tightly defined roles, together with strict behaviour patterns, characterise closed family systems. Generally the significance or impact of the diagnosis of life-limiting illness is not openly acknowledged or discussed. Conversely, the open family system functions in what Brown calls a 'nurturing' environment, where the impact of the diagnosis is recognised and adults express their thoughts and feelings, encouraging children to do likewise. She describes this as 'parents and children facilitating each other's grieving'.

Within each of the phases of illness experienced by the child, the family will also have to develop strategies for adjusting and coping. These will differ from the diagnostic phase to the end of life phase, but they may include:

- recognising the symptoms, pain and physical changes
- adjusting to medical intervention, treatment and palliative care
- developing strategies to manage stress
- communicating effectively with professional people and carers
- maintaining the family identity
- preserving relationships with partners and friends
- expressing emotions and fears
- preparing for death and saying 'goodbye'
- accepting the finality of death.

Parental relationships

The diagnosis of life-limiting illness may challenge parental ideas of nurturing and protecting their children. Social support and family relationships have been shown to be particularly important for parents with a life-limited child (Mulhern et al. 1992; Speechley and Noh 1992). However, parental worry and distress can result in irritability and tension, which in turn may reduce the support available from family and friends (Olverholser and Fritz 1999).

Whyte (1997) believes that caring for an ill child may jeopardise family stability. Inevitably the focus within the family, especially around periods of illness, will be the sick child. Cooper (1999) argues how well families cope will be influenced by demands such as employment (or lack of it), family problems, the presence of other children, and the quality of support from partners and other family members. It is often assumed that the incidence of family breakdown will be greater in families caring for a life-limited child, although a study by Cooper (1999) showed that this was not the case.

Past research has tended to focus on the effects of chronic illness on mothers, assuming that they have the largest burden of care (Eiser 1993). However, other family members play an important supportive role. Too often fathers' involvement is overlooked, especially if they are the major wage earners. Siblings and grandparents may manage other aspects of care. Gender differences and coping styles may also affect the quality of parental relationships. Views about child rearing, including discipline and education, also play their part. Where partners have negotiated clear boundaries for each partner's role prior to diagnosis, these perceptions and roles may need to be re-negotiated.

Research has provided some interesting insights into the pace at which mothers adapt to their child's life-limiting illness (Martin and Doka 2000). Not surprisingly, mothers of life-limited children are likely to exhibit higher levels of stress than mothers of healthy children. Additionally, they may take responsibility for the majority of domestic tasks (Barnett and Boyce 1995).

Research is conflicting regarding whether fathers experience more or less distress than mothers when their child is life-limited. The study by Affleck, Tennen and Rowe (1991) of mothers and fathers found that, while mothers reported more distress, fathers were reluctant to express their distress outwardly and focused their attention on helping their spouse cope. Murphy (1990) also found that fathers hid their concern about their children in order to provide emotional support to their wives. Continuing to work is often an important means of fathers maintaining control. However, Svavarsdottir and McCubbin (1996) found that fathers viewed providing this emotional support as a great strain. The majority of fathers also expressed fear about becoming attached and interacting with their child because of the child's threat of death. Programmes have been designed to support fathers, and the positive effects have also included diminished stress levels (Bray 1997).

One father, Alistair, whose son Stuart is now in his 30s, said:

> At first we thought that there had been a mistake. Then we kept asking ourselves whether it was our fault. In the end you realise you cannot go through life burying your head in the sand. Reality of that first shock has been renewed so many times as our son's life has started to run out.

We have seen that, for many parents, their family is a great source of support, and this appears to be particularly evident with their adult siblings (McHaffie

2001). Often relationships strengthen, and family members who appeared aloof and undemonstrative before the child's diagnosis may show sympathy and support.

In a small-scale study by Brown (1999), the supportive role of godparents has been noted. This seems to be particularly evident where a child is born with a life-limiting illness and godmothers and godfathers are chosen because of their proven commitment to the family, or because they have professional expertise within the field of medicine or disability.

> When Julie was born I found it hard to be sociable to my friends and family. But Natalie was different. She never once told me that perhaps it wasn't as bad as the diagnosis. Neither did she tell me to pull myself together. The greatest gift she has ever given me is to hold me tight and say, 'It's tough and it hurts, but give me a chance and I will support you every inch of the way.' Five years on she has never let me down.

> As a couple his godparents are fantastic. They have bailed us out again and again. They know we trust them. It's not just Charlie who gets the looking after. Sometimes at the weekend there is a ring at the doorbell and there they are, with dinner for two, ready to put in the oven. Occasionally there is a bottle of wine too!

Adapting to life-limited illness

Strategies which families adopt for dealing with any crisis would generally be an indicator of how they will cope with a life-limiting illness. Families need to witness that their child is cared for, and to experience how their own emotional, psychological and spiritual needs are met. There are several phases which most parents who are caring for a dying child will experience:

- *Numbness* – on hearing the news of the child's prognosis. This may be accompanied by feelings of shock, disbelief and denial.
- *Yearning* – for the normality of life before the news was heard which may be accompanied by acute feelings of searching, crying, reminiscing, anger and guilt.
- *Hopelessness and despair* – this may be accompanied by feelings of loneliness, helplessness, depression and anxiety.

When the diagnosis of life-limiting illness is made, each family has to come to terms with the implication of the news and also to learn strategies which will help them cope emotionally and practically with the demands of care (Altschuler 1997; Brown 1999; see Table 11.1)

Table 11.1 Adapting to life-limited illness

Emotional responses	Behavioural changes	Change in lifestyle	Conflict within family and local community
Sad	Anxiety about own health	Changed emphasis on domestic activities	Spouse or partner
Shocked	Sleep disturbance		Professionals
Scared	Fear of developing illness	Decreased social opportunities	Other family members
Unprepared	Inability to concentrate	Increased dependence on extended family	Neighbours
Angry	Over dependency on employed work as an 'escape'	Decreased time with family members living in the same household	Siblings and school friends/peer group
Disbelief			
	Eating disorders/alcohol or tobacco dependency	Financial worries	
	Over protectiveness of other siblings	Fewer holidays	
	Psychosomatic illness	Trying to provide stability for the future	
	Depression		

A number of frameworks explore the adaptation process (Hornby 1999). Families vary in the ways in which they deal with the stress. Factors that influence family adjustment include:

- The demands of the illness, including onset, progression, severity of symptoms and symptom visibility.
- The impact of the illness.
- The personality of the child and family and their ways of communicating with each other.

Practitioners at Acorns have noted how the demands of care alter and change as the child's illness progresses:

- *Crisis phase* – pre-diagnosis/diagnosis requires the child and the family to come to terms with the implications of the illness and its treatment.
- *Chronic phase* – a time when the family learns to cope with the day-to-day demands of the illness whilst maintaining a sense of normality. During this phase the family coping strategies may stabilise or degenerate.
- *End of life phase* – a phase where the family has to adapt to the progression of the child's illness and the child's eventual death, followed by a period of mourning and adjustment to the loss.

Caring for a life-limited child is exhausting and individual family members are likely to experience care fatigue (Ray and Ritchie 1993). Many parents also experience loss of self-esteem and purpose, believing that they are unable to produce healthy children (Brown 2002; Whyte 1997).

Traditionally there has existed a tension between the coping strategies adopted by parents and those preferred by professionals. Parents need to be encouraged and empowered to develop the coping strategies which are best for them. The challenge to professionals is in helping parents to develop those tactics which will enable the strategies to work (Goldman 2002).

We have seen that mothers and fathers differ in the pace in which they adjust to their life-limited child. Although parents may have lived with the diagnosis or a prognosis for their child for a long time, this does not mean that their original feelings of shock, grief and anxiety are healed. The memories which they have of learning about their child's diagnosis will remain very real and very detailed. Under every stiff upper lip there is a wobbly chin! Most parents who display a calm and controlled exterior will be struggling with turmoil within. Rarely will parents have 'come to terms' with their child's inevitable death. Many will live their lives in the hope that the diagnosis was wrong and it may well be that this hope is what sustains them.

These words speak of a mother's chronic sorrow, still felt 25 years after her life-limited twins died:

> Maybe it seems unreasonable, but all I wanted was for the experts to recognise our rights as parents to receive the very best available for the twins and not to deny us the hope of a miracle.

Professionals who work with parents after their child's diagnosis should not assume that, because a family has been coping for some time, they are no longer in need of constant support. The coping strategies which families learn and the skills they acquire need to be acknowledged.

All parents will need:

- continued support in adjusting to their emotional and psychological reactions
- assistance in seeking professional support
- support in recouping their physical strengths
- assistance in ensuring benefits and resources to meet their needs
- adequate information at each stage of the child's illness.

Sloper (1999) writes about parental reluctance to use support services themselves, which they may perceive as an admission of failure in their parenting skills. Aldred (2001) argues that encouraging parents to maintain their sense of control, and empowering them, is something that is at the heart of children's hospice care.

Whilst emotional support is vital for parents, there is an increasing under-standing of the importance of honest and accurate information at each stage of their child's life. This will include:

- information about their child's illness
- helping parents to understand the information which is given to them
- helping parents to understand the information within the context of their family, culture and lifestyle
- help in contacting parents of children with similar life-limiting illnesses
- knowledge about rights and benefits including medicine, education, respite care and financial support
- helping parents to recognise and celebrate their parenting skills.

Key points

- Family members are inter-dependent. Therefore, anything that affects one member will affect the family as a whole.
- Diagnosis may well be a watershed between two different lifestyles – a pre-diagnostic life with normal ups and downs, and a post-diagnostic life where the future is unknown and everything seems to be at the mercy of the child's illness.
- Parents play a crucial part in mediating the effects of the illness on their child.
- Family communication patterns appear crucial in determining how well families cope with illness, since valuable sources of support are embedded in their relationships and parenting styles.
- Within each phase of their child's illness, the family will have to develop strategies for adjusting and coping.
- The diagnosis of life-limiting illness may challenge parental ideas of nurturing and protecting their children.
- Mothers of life-limited children are likely to exhibit higher levels of stress than mothers of healthy children.

Implications for practice

- Parents need honest and accurate information at each stage of their child's illness.

- Professionals, who work with parents after their child's diagnosis, should provide continuity of support.

- Parents should be encouraged and empowered to develop coping strategies that are best for them.

- Families need to witness their child's care and to experience how their own emotional, psychological, cultural and spiritual needs are met.

Continuing Bonds

Erica Brown

The loss of a child is often considered to be more painful than any other bereavement. Many parents describe the experience as having a part of themselves severed and their loss renders them bereft and vulnerable. Often this can make coping seem even more challenging.

Individual grief does not occur in a vacuum, but in the context of close bonds. Grief is a blend of emotional and cognitive reactions, where feelings and thoughts are not separable. When family members share a loss, they may feel that in some sense they lose one another, since they may become preoccupied and debilitated with their own grief (Rosenblatt 1996).

Bereavement has been linked with emotional distress, relationship problems, lack of self-esteem and mental ill health. However, it may also serve as a catalyst for positive growth if parents can recognise that, although the bond with their child is changed, it can be continued. This part of the book explores how some parents find solace through sustaining a 'continuing bond' with their child. However, the idea of a continuing relationship challenges the view that, when people grieve, they are able to sever the relationships they had with the person who has died, freeing them to make new attachments. Until comparatively recently, the notion of 'continuing bond' relationships has been largely overlooked and undervalued in most scholarly work (Klass, Silverman and Nickman 1996).

Models of grief

Traditionally, there have been two principal schools of thought concerning the grief process. On the one hand, the emotional response to the loss of a person has been considered the normal human outlet for grief and yet, on the other, it has been advocated that the bereaved person's ability to return to 'normal' life indicates a healthy resolution to their grief.

Self-help literature is still published which offers advice to bereaved people, telling them that they should reach a point where they do not grieve

(Rosenblatt 1996). Therefore, it should come as no surprise that the idea of parents being able to sustain a 'continuing bond' with their child may be perceived by some as being symptomatic of deeply rooted psychological problems. Indeed, continued attachment to a person after their death has in the past been referred to as 'unresolved grief' (Parkes et al. 1996).

Cultural and religious variations

Cultures differ enormously in how grief is understood and how much long-term grieving is encouraged. However, most faiths seem to support the notion that, after earthly life, the person's spirit continues to exist and mourners carry out rituals to sustain appropriate relationships. For example, in Shinto and Buddhist communities when people have died, they are still regarded as ancestors with whom communication is possible. Nearly all homes have an altar dedicated to deceased family members. In sharp contrast to Shinto and Buddhist communities, among the Hopi of Arizona contact with dead bodies is considered polluting and mourners are encouraged to forget people who have died as quickly as possible with a return to normal routines, reflecting beliefs about the after world.

Parental grief

Grief is a unique experience for each person involved. Family and community pressure to overcome grief often seems to be based on each individual person's understanding and previous experience of loss. Furthermore, there is huge diversity in the way in which people are encouraged to grieve and the length of time over which grieving is desirable.

When a mother gives birth, she does not abandon the relationship she has developed with the baby during her pregnancy. But the relationship changes and includes other people who are able to form bonds with the child. Staff at Acorns believe that bereaved parents, like a new mother, can be helped to find ways of forming a new relationship with their dead child.

Studies on the effects of parental bereavement are numerous and provide a benchmark against which professionals should endeavour to match the care they provide to the individual needs of families. At Acorns, we are beginning to understand more about the beneficial effects of 'continuing bonds' through bereavement work with parents and other family members whose child has died. Many parents have developed a capacity to retain vivid memories of their child that keep them 'connected'. The connections are not static, however. They develop over time so that the parent–child relationship remains appropriate to present circumstances. Memory is sustained through talking about their child and believing their child is somehow able to watch them as they go about their daily life. Parents and grandparents tell us that, several years after the child's death, they 'talk' to the child or 'connect' with the child's spirit, as if their child has continued to mature after their death. Sometimes visiting a grave or a special place set aside in memory of their child provides a continuing link between the past and present.

Sometimes parents choose mementos and objects which symbolically provide a bridge between them and their child. Often they speak about how the object conjures a sense of the child's presence, especially if it is an item of the child's clothing or an object that they held. Tangible reminders also validate the child's ongoing place in bereaved parents' lives, and in some cases they even provide proof of the child's existence.

> I have a birth certificate, a death certificate and a hand print. The only reminders that Jonathan really was my son.

Significantly, when parents talk about their child, it is almost always in an idyllic sense where the child is remembered as perfect.

> His legacy to us is an example. He was stoic, brave, enthusiastic and funny to the very end, even though this was all wrapped up in a frail body that let him down.

At times when family members are particularly aware of the child's presence in their lives, they describe this as an energy that exists between the child and themselves, a kind of living spiritual existence. This is an idea that transcends many cultures and is found in ancestor worship. Children are immortalised and present in the same world in which their parents lived. Furthermore parents do not only hope that they will be reunited with their children when they themselves die, they expect it.

However connections are sustained, they seem to provide comfort, solace and a way of taking the memories forward to the future. Indeed, many parents tell us that maintaining a continuing bond helps them cope with their loss. Often family members write poetry as a way of helping them to understand their experiences. In many ways they 're-solve' their grief by incorporating the memory of their child into their everyday lives, rather than disengaging and putting events behind them.

Parents cherish the feelings that they have, even if these are painful. They perceive the pain of their loss as equal to the love they had for their child and as a marker of how important their child was to them.

> My friends say time will help me – it will take away the pain. But I don't want to forget – Oh no! I want to remember – plain as plain. I need to remember because if I forget, how will I ever live?

Memories of happy, shared times together are also tremendously important. Remembering the sound of their child's laughter, the tender feelings of holding their child or their child's mischief can help form a link with the past and provide an affirmation of the possibility of an ongoing relationship.

> I remember your steady heartbeat
> As the gentle lapping sound of waves against a rock.
> I remember your smile like the summer sun
> Spreading warmth everywhere.
> I remember your laughter
> Like ripples on a pool.
> I remember your tears
> Like summer showers.
> Unable to dampen those golden hours.
> I remember the calm before the storm.
> I remember your love.
>
> (Glenys Booker, Acorns mother)

Mementos of the child's life become important ways of maintaining links with the past, and sometimes they are used to provide comfort. The child's presence is experienced through parents feeling that they watch over the family, especially on shared occasions such as birthdays and holidays. Reminiscing about happier times also brings solace in the face of despair and loneliness.

Parents often develop individual ways by which they feel connected with their dead child. Sometimes they seem to maintain a relationship in which they 'reach' out to their child's spirit in an interactive way. They talk about their child being in 'heaven', in 'the wind, the stars and the sky'. Being able to locate their child's presence when they visit the place where they are buried, or their ashes have been scattered, is an important activity and seems to serve as a source of comfort. Perhaps the most distinguishing feature of parents' stories is that, almost without exception, they talk to their dead child, sharing their feelings, daily events in their lives, prayers or even jokes. Moreover, mothers and grandmothers in particular feel the child is able to communicate to them in reassuring ways.

> On the first anniversary of his death, I was standing ironing in the kitchen. A feather floated through the window and I remembered how an identical feather had floated onto his coffin before the burial. I just know that he has sent a sign to say that he is OK.

Through experiences such as this, parents are not trying to deny the reality of death but to temper the pain and anguish they feel. Some parents describe the feeling that their child still influences their life as a 'welcome presence'. Sometimes this presence is perceived as a reality in the physical environment in which parents find themselves, like the mother above with the feather. At other times, it is described as the positive influence that the child's life had on them.

> Sometimes I just know she lingers in the wind and the trees. When I sense that she is, it is such a strong feeling, I am 100 per cent sure that it is real.

To say that parental experiences of the ongoing relationship with their child are always positive would be untrue. Some parents have a real sense of unfinished business, and it is not unusual for them to experience dreams and nightmares in which they reach out to their child to discover that they are no longer within their grasp.

> Tumbling, careering, spiralling down,
> Totally out of control I dream that I crash, smash and cascade
> Through the depths of an abysmal black hole
> Reaching out, grasping for you.
> I scream your name but find that I am voiceless
> And wake to find that you are already gone.
>
> (Glenys Booker, Acorns mother)

Death is always traumatic because it cannot be reversed. It robs parents of the present and the future, but it does not mean that they have to forget the past. As parents move on with their lives, they seem to incorporate the past into the present. Memories are probably the most precious gift that parents have. They are accessible links that can be revived. Talking about the child who has died and thinking about them helps to make the death real. Many of the children become immortal to bereaved parents, not only as memories, but also as blueprints for the values that shape the way in which parents continue to live their lives. Thus, bereaved parents do not let go of the ties they have with their children, but create new bonds that are likely to shape their future lives. They adapt to what has happened rather than denying the reality of the event. Therefore, grieving does not entail severing the bond with their dead child, but integrating their memory into a way of living that is different from when the child was alive.

Bereaved parents care whether other people share their loss. People outside the family who are deeply affected by the child's death can validate the enormity of what has happened. Conversely, where parents perceive that the pain they feel is not felt within their community, they often struggle with the social reality of what has happened. (See Chapter 15, 'Religious, Cultural,

Secular and Spiritual Aspects of Care'.) People may refuse to mention the child's name in their presence or, even worse, tell them that their child is better off with God in heaven. In short, when a child dies, it often seems to parents as if their lives have stopped while other people's lives go on.

As parents and other family members begin their bereavement journey, many seem to experience their child's presence. Being bereaved parents will always be part of their identity, but they manage to develop coping strategies. Professionals say that they never cease to be amazed at how families become stronger in their brokenness.

> I shall never forget the moment when I realised that I could let go of the heaviness of my emotional pain without being disloyal to the memory of all she meant to me.

Adjusting to loss demands that individual family members are helped to develop a language for talking about the child who has died. Care staff and Community Team Workers endeavour to help parents to understand that their grief is a physical and emotional response to the pain they feel. The bonds that they have with their child are the most complex of any human relationship, so growing through their grief may be a long and exhausting task. The memories that they have are deeply personal and intensely connected with the unique relationship they had with their child.

Bereavement is a complex process. It demands that parents remember the past yet they are able to live in the present. There is no fixed formula for working through the turmoil of grief. Parents need to make sense of what has happened at their own pace. They need people who are able to share the bonds that they have with their child who has died, and who are prepared to recognise that bond as part of an ongoing relationship.

Key points

- The loss of a child is often considered to be more painful than any other bereavement. Many parents describe the experience as having a part of themselves severed.

- When parents are helped to recognise that, although the bond with their dead child is changed, it can be continued, this can bring comfort.

- The idea of continuing bonds challenges the view that people need to sever the relationship with a person when they have died, freeing them to make new attachments.

- Cultures differ enormously in how grief is understood and how much long-term grieving is encouraged.

Implications for practice

- Studies on the effects of parental bereavement provide a benchmark against which professionals should endeavour to match the care they provide to the individual needs of families.

- Helping parents to keep mementos of their child is an important way of maintaining links with the past and continuing the relationship.

- People outside the family who show they are affected by the child's death can validate the enormity of parental grief.

- Professionals should endeavour to help parents understand that their grief is a physical and emotional response to the pain they feel.

13

Working with Siblings of Life-limited Children

Erica Brown

The dying child is often referred to as 'the victim of illness'. But brothers, sisters and entire families are partners in the same experience. Indeed, the devastation spreads far beyond the child who is affected. Bluebond-Langner (1995) describes siblings as 'living in houses of chronic sorrow'. Many siblings experience a change of role in the family and a change in status. Where a family have struggled to cope with a child's illness for many years, or indeed, where more than one child in the family is very ill, the environment in which well siblings are growing up is far from normal. In some families, well siblings are caretakers of ill siblings or, in extreme cases, they are so affected by their family, they become what Almond, Buckman and Gofman (1979) call *non-persons*, because their parent's attention is elsewhere. As a result they may feel unsupported, neglected and confused about who they are and who they are supposed to be.

Bullard and Dohnal (1994) suggest that children do not work through problems, nor do they 'get over' them. Rather they develop patterns of adjustment and, once established, these coping strategies are often used throughout their lives. Sibling grief is a long journey without time limits and specific paths (Davies 1999). Each child will respond differently.

Many siblings experience intense anticipatory grief before their brother or sister dies, and it is likely that they will continue to grieve for the rest of their lives. Inter-related factors such as children's individuality, the family situation and the home environment shape how siblings grieve (see Figure 13.1). These factors have been previously described in relation to children's grief in general by Brown (1999), and in relation to sibling grief by Davies (1999).

Figure 13.1 'My people at home are frightened'

The chapter describes the findings of a three-year project at Acorns, funded by the Diana Princess of Wales Memorial Fund. The project set out to discover the needs and experiences of siblings with a life-limited brother or sister using Acorns hospices.

The child's individuality

Age, gender, personality, coping strategies, place in the family hierarchy and past encounters with loss, change and death contribute to how siblings cope. The relationship between the ill sibling and well siblings is also important.

> My sister is different from me, but very special, and I love her for that. (Girl age 12)

The family situation

The duration and type of the sibling's illness, and how well siblings are included in the family situation, are important factors in children coping. The culture, values and the family lifestyle, both before and throughout the duration of the sibling's illness, also need to be taken into account.

> We have already planned my brother's funeral. It will be bright with lots of colour and rock and roll because that is what he likes. We have lots of parties in our family. We want to make the most of everything while we can. (Girl age 13)

A question that emerges frequently is not 'Why did my brother or sister die?' but 'Why did it happen to me?' This sense of being different sometimes entails anger directed at God, everyone, or no-one in particular. (See Figure 13.2).

Figure 13.2 'I don't know where my baby brother is now'

The home environment

The physical environment of the family home, family communication styles and parental adaptation to the situation play a large part in sibling experiences, because children are dependent on their families for the information and support they receive.

> She passed away in the hospital but I was not there at the time. I was fast asleep. I was so tired but I was forced to wake up. I was told that my sister was really not well and that she was very bad. So we went to the hospital to see her and it was then that I was told that she had already passed away. Mum and Dad told me. Before we came to the hospital my cousins already knew, but they just didn't tell me because they were told not to. I was so upset about it. (Girl age 14)

Parental preoccupation with their own struggles often creates tension, especially where they are trying to sustain employment to pay for the added expense of a child's illness. Siblings become very dependent on each other.

Some children show greater changes in their behaviour than others. Sometimes siblings use 'acting out' behaviours at home and at school. Parents find this particularly challenging, because their emotional resources are often already stretched to the limit. It appears that some younger siblings respond to grief-stricken parents by behaving badly. They are described as 'argumentative', 'attention-seeking', 'moody' and 'loud'. What they are doing is quite normal. They are displaying their irritability and anger at the way in which their brother or sister's illness is disrupting their lives.

> Sometimes it can be awkward when my sister is ill because any plans that were made are destroyed, and we have to plan around her illness. (Girl age 12)

It is extremely important to encourage parents to set consistent boundaries and to reward positive behaviour from siblings, as well as encouraging safe ways for them to express their anger. Sometimes it seems as if siblings' feelings are so overwhelming that they do not know how to cope and there is some evidence of risk-taking behaviour in older children. Younger children may find it difficult to describe how they feel, and they say that their friends find it hard to understand them. Thus, there are occasions when siblings become isolated from their peer group.

Siblings experience and demonstrate many grief responses, but they do not express emotions in neatly ordered stages. Each sibling responds differently and often they are unable to sustain their emotions for long periods of time, needing to return to 'normal' activities. Sometimes where a brother or sister's illness has lasted a long time, anticipatory grief reactions seem to escalate. If a brother or sister has already died, the siblings continue to think about them.

> I'm writing this letter to let you know that, even though you are not here, you will always be in my heart. Don't worry; God will look after you and everyone with you. Everyone has to die some day. Some people go early and some people go late, but we all go to the same place. Every day I will arrange flowers and clean your headstone. You don't have to worry now because you are in a better place, near to God. No one can tell you what to do or give you injections. Remember no one will ever forget you because you were so special that no one can forget you. You are a part of everyone's heart. (Girl age 14)

Age, gender and home circumstances make each child's experience unique. Boys and girls learn gender roles from a very early age, and the adults who care for them serve as models in the behaviour they demonstrate. Often boys reflect the contemporary Western view of males as independent, assertive, dominant and competitive, compared to girls who have a tendency to be slightly more passive, sensitive and supportive in their social relationships (Hetherington and Parke 1991).

Distinguishing between young people's sadness and depression is important. Children who are sad are generally able to talk or write about their situation, and they sometimes say they long for the equilibrium of life to be restored to how it was before their brother or sister's illness was diagnosed.

> We both wish we could go back to how it was. Unfortunately, that will never happen. (Boy age 16)

There are other children whose sadness is accompanied by feelings of loneliness, depression and low self-esteem. Younger children seem to feel left out of family events, and often they receive less information about their brother or sister's illness, because they are considered too young to be included. Conversely, older siblings, by virtue of being the eldest, are sometimes given more responsibility than they can comfortably manage (Davies 1999). Sometimes the young people are able to describe their feelings.

> My mum is too busy looking after him and fighting for adaptations. I've had enough! Enough of professionals saying they will help: I don't think so. After hearing five years of their excuses, I'm getting very angry. They just push my mum and my brother around. (Girl age 16)

Young people who have grown up with a life-limited sibling are often painfully aware of the huge difference practical help, or lack of it, makes to the whole family. They are often sad about the disadvantages without understanding the bureaucratic and administrative infrastructure and funding anomalies that can get in the way of their needs being met. There are occasions when this sadness is manifested in somatic complaints or through disruptive or competitive behaviour at home or at school.

Many siblings speak about how their situation makes them feel different from their peer group. Sometimes they have fallen foul of sick jokes that have been played on them, often relating to their ill brother or sister. School-related difficulties seem to be an indication of the stress some children experience. These difficulties range from concentration problems to a drop in academic performance. Teachers describe children as 'sad', 'depressed', 'lonely', 'attention-seeking', 'nervous' and 'worried'. However, problems do not always occur, and some of the older siblings attain very high grades in examinations. This appears to be because they impose very high expectations on themselves, in an attempt to spare their parents further distress and disappointment. Where problems are reported, the period of time varies according to how well children are supported. Often this depends on the ethos and pastoral arrangements of their school.

In some cases, brothers and sisters speak of the difficulties they encounter trying to manage their behaviour and building meaningful relationships with their peer group. There is clear evidence that some siblings are bullied because their contemporaries consider them to be 'odd' or 'different'. Young people are emphatic that being stared at when they are out with their sick sibling is one of the things they dislike most. They all have to learn coping strategies.

> I have been bullied. The difference with me is, because I have a sister with severe disabilities, other pupils see this as a weakness and exploit it. (Boy age 15)

Crying is a normal expression of sadness. However, some siblings do not seem to feel the need to cry or they hold back tears, because they do not want to upset people, or they are embarrassed that tears might be construed as 'weaknesses'. Sometimes, whether they cry or not seems to relate to the way emotions are expressed within their family. Providing 'safe' places for siblings to express their sadness is important.

Past research into brother and sister relationships characterises siblings as attachment figures, playmates, protectors and antagonists (Davies 1999). Through shared experience, siblings have the potential for giving each other tremendous emotional support and companionship. Being part of a family where there is a life-limited child can be lonely. For siblings who have already enjoyed shared times with their brother or sister, but are now unable to do this because the illness has progressed, the feelings of loneliness are enormous.

Siblings are often very protective of their ill brother or sister and of their parents. They speak of not wanting to burden them with their own worries. Sometimes they find it exceedingly hard to engage in enjoyable activities, perhaps believing that they do not have a right to enjoy themselves. A sibling speaking about a planned holiday said:

> Over the next few months I began to lose interest. Why? I was scared. What if my brother becomes ill while I am in America? What if he dies and I don't even know about it? Lots of 'what ifs' were going through my head and it was all I could think of. (Girl age 17)

Although the young people do not generally refer to guilty feelings, this does not mean that feelings are absent. Hopes for the early death of a sibling are not unusual, although generally this is because brothers and sisters do not want the sick sibling to experience more pain and suffering. When they talk about guilt, they say that the feelings they have are very difficult for them to handle. Sometimes emotions are so intense they blame other people for how they feel.

Older siblings may develop a sense of responsibility for the wellbeing of the adults in their family in an attempt to alleviate their parents' pain and sadness. It is also apparent that siblings feel a sense of heightened responsibility for younger well brothers and sisters.

Physical aches and pains and broken sleep are described by children and commented on by adults.

> I started having headaches regularly, especially when I had to go to school. (Girl age 12)

Very occasionally the pains they experience are similar to those felt by their sick sibling. Feeling overtired is common, and teachers report that there are occasions when siblings fall asleep in lessons.

Often siblings feel that their ill brother or sister is their parents' favourite child and, therefore, whatever they do will always fall short of their parents' expectations. Some siblings try to be good all the time, constantly endeavouring to do more, trying to prove that they are worthy of love and affection.

Having a child with a life-limited illness turns family life upside down (Davies 1999). Often parents become overwhelmed with their grief and exhausted trying to care for their other well children. Siblings speak of feeling suffocated by the constant flurry of activity in their homes and the intensity of the emotion that surrounds them.

> Sometimes I was jealous of him as he had people coming to see him all the time. (Girl age 14)

Often they feel that they do not know what to do. Sometimes they want to be involved in helping to look after their sick sibling, but they do not feel they have the skills needed. If they try to help, their efforts do not always seem to be appreciated. As a result they begin to feel on the edge of what is happening, and that they are no longer an important part of the family unit. They speak about the lack of emotional and physical energy their parents are able to give them.

> I would love my mum and dad to spend more time with me but they are always so busy. (Girl age 12)

Family life is often disrupted, and it seems significant that fathers often become more involved in their work. Some siblings are aware the relationship between their parents is strained. Sometimes parents turn against each other, or even direct their anger at their well children. If siblings try to talk about the situation, they may feel their parents' response is patronising. They suffer very low self-esteem and may neglect their own needs in an attempt to win adult approval.

Often the relationship between the sick sibling and their well brother or sister is intensified. Some sick siblings have been the well sibling's closest friend. For younger children who have not formed friendships with their peer group, the anticipated loss of their brother or sister means that they will lose the only friend they have (Davies 1999). Memories of past shared times are often centred on shared experiences. The loss of the intimacy experienced is irreconcilable.

> Then there is the ultimate dream,
> The one that won't come true.
> When your ill sibling is normal,
> As normal as me and you.
>
> But suddenly you wake up,
> And remember that one dream,
> The one about your sibling,
> And not about strawberries and cream.
>
> You don't want them to be normal,
> You love them the way they are,
> To you they are very special,
> Your special shining star.

(Girl age 16)

Research on parental grief suggests parents grieve for much longer than was formerly assumed (Wortman and Silver 1999). Many siblings become impatient with their parents' grief and, in particular, the way in which their brother's or sister's memory is preserved as one of perfection. The strategies that the children use to manage their emotions are strongly influenced by the way in which adults interact with them. If well siblings perceive that it is unacceptable to express their emotions, they stifle their feelings.

Young people often feel that, although they are living in the same house as their ill brother or sister, they are kept on the periphery of what is happening. Although being present at critical times in their brother's or sister's illness may be frightening, young people would still rather be present. They may want to know what the dying process will be like. Witnessing their sibling's death as pain-free is important.

Many life-limited children need medical equipment, mobility aids and nutritional and continence supplies. Although siblings often accept the practicalities of living with a family member with complex needs, these impose difficulties and limitations with respect to everyday living. It may also detract from the way in which brothers and sisters view the appearance and 'homeliness' of where they live. Home is no longer a private place for many young people, and this affects them and the way they live. Furthermore, they often feel that their own personal space and activities are always under scrutiny.

Medical staff and other professionals have relationships with the parents of the sick child, but rarely with siblings. If they have not been included in discussions, they may become adept at piecing together bits of information. Younger children describe how they know something is wrong, but that they try not to think about it, especially if the illness seems to be under control. Where parents do try to explain the seriousness of the illness, sometimes it is difficult for children to understand the concept of life-limitation, especially if they have grown up with a sick brother or sister. It is as if they struggle to equate the 'normality' of everyday life with the anguish that surrounds them.

> Coping is not a problem because it is woven into my daily routine. (Boy age 13)

Several brothers and sisters have never known a time when their sick sibling has been able to walk unaided, to swallow solid food or to manage without oxygen therapy.

> My sister has a tube entering her stomach, has a tube entering her nose, has to use a wheelchair, takes countless syringes of medicine a day, and can have violent fits. I believe at 13, I have been through quite a bit. (Boy age 13)

Fears that parents might think that they are being silly, hypochondriac or selfish keeps many siblings from asking questions or talking about the worries they feel. Instead they may keep everything inside, bottling up their fears. Where siblings have a genetic disorder, anxiety is particularly acute. Sometimes well siblings worry whether they might develop the illness or, if they have children of their own later on, that the illness might be passed on.

Sometimes siblings are very knowledgeable about their brother or sister's illness.

> Before you have the disease you are normal, like other kids. First you stop walking, then talking and after that you lose your eyesight. Then you can't do anything and after that you even have fits which you can't stop happening. (Girl age 14)

It is unwise to assume that all siblings of life-limited brothers and sisters will experience complicated grief. To do so disregards the possibility of psychological growth that may happen as well. Some siblings undoubtedly grow up as caring and sensitive as a result of their experiences, and they are able to name tactics they have developed to manage personal stress. Some of these strategies seem to be transferable to other areas of their life. Teachers speak of siblings demonstrating empathy if members of their peer group experience adverse life events.

Although grief may be a long and difficult journey for siblings, it is not one that they must necessarily travel alone, if adults acknowledge the impact of living in a family with a life-limited brother or sister. Acorns' experience seems to suggest that siblings of life-limited brothers or sisters feel less isolated and cope better when they are informed about the illness. Nevertheless, there appears to be an overwhelming need to help and to encourage siblings to express their feelings in a safe environment and to help them to engage in enjoyable activities with their peer group. The benefits of focus groups, therapeutic input and opportunities for social interaction made possible throughout the project are enormous.

Acorns is grateful to the Diana Princess of Wales Memorial Fund for their financial support from 1999 to 2002. Their generosity enabled the Hospice Trust to offer a greater level of support to siblings of life-limited children and to learn from those siblings how best to be alongside them in the life and death of a brother or sister.

Readers interested in planning and introducing sibling support may find a pack on Sibling Support by Brown and Arens (2005) published by Acorns is helpful in the development of their own policy and practice. This chapter is largely based on the publication, and the Acorns training video, 'Speaking Out, Please Hear Us' quotes from it at length.

Key points

- The environment in which brothers and sisters of life-limited children are growing up may be far from normal.
- Sibling grief is without specific paths. Grief is not expressed in neatly ordered stages.
- Inter-related factors such as children's individuality, the family situation and the home environment are likely to impact on how siblings grieve. Culture, family values and lifestyle also need to be taken into account.
- Siblings may take on more responsibility in their family than they can comfortably manage.
- Medical staff and other professionals seldom have supportive relationships with siblings.
- Grief is particularly acute in siblings when their sick sibling is suffering from a genetic disorder.
- Some of the coping strategies employed by siblings are transferable to other areas of their life.

Implications for practice

- It is important to encourage parents to set consistent boundaries for siblings and to reward positive behaviour.

- Professionals should take into account gender differences in the ways young people grieve.

- Distinguishing between young people's sadness and depression is important.

- Schools should determine whether decline in academic performance is related to sibling stress.

- Siblings need 'safe' places to express sadness and anger.

- Staff from support services should consider the impact home visits may have on well brothers and sisters.

- Encouraging family members to communicate with each other may have very beneficial outcomes for the individuals involved.

- Finding ways for brothers and sisters to be present at critical times in the sick child's care may be helpful. Witnessing a pain-free death is important.

14

Grandparent Support

Erica Brown

There are 13 million grandparents in the United Kingdom and one in three people over the age of 50 is a grandparent. When a child is diagnosed with a life-limiting illness, everyone in the family is affected because life-limiting illness puts the child at risk as well as the predictability of the family's future. Hearing the child's diagnosis second hand plunges grandparents into a state of extreme shock and the impact may render them at a complete loss as to what to say and do. Meyer (1997) refers to grandparents experiencing 'dual' or double grief. This double grief may be misunderstood or marginalised by other family members. However, there has been very sparse acknowledgment in the literature concerning grandparent grief (Galinsky 1999; Kolf 1995; Reed 2000).

By virtue of their age and hence, their life experience, the assumption is made that grandparents automatically develop coping strategies. Furthermore, there may even be a societal view that because the child is not the grandparents' child, the grief felt is less intense. However, grandparents often have to cope with their own grief and the grief of their adult child. This dual grief renders grandparents unique in their loss. When a grandchild dies, tasks which have been undertaken by grandparents may change or cease altogether, leaving a huge void in their lives.

> I always took annual leave to give my daughter-in-law a break – now I feel that taking a holiday myself is selfish.

Reed (2000) describes the death of a grandchild as 'perverse, absurd and totally unnatural'. Grandparents appear to experience similar emotions as parents. These emotions may, at times, affect the grandparents' ability to provide support to parents when they need it most.

> There are no words for a bereaved grandparent – you are only what the words say. Time heals, but I feel a 'nothing' as a mother and a grand-mother; I have had no training for this role.

Bereaved grandparent support at Acorns

At Acorns, staff have become increasingly aware of the contribution that grandparents make to families where there is a life-limited child and the enormous sacrifices they often make. The hospice recently carried out research into the needs of bereaved grandparents. The small-scale study was conducted using a qualitative approach to allow an in-depth exploration of the personal circumstances and experiences of the families involved. Initial research provided a sound evidence base for determining the type of support grandparents wanted. Community Team workers from Acorns identified and approached bereaved grandparents and invited them to take part in a Support Group. A venue was chosen away from the hospices and the groups met at monthly intervals over a year. The organisation of the groups was relaxed but sufficiently structured for members to feel safe. There were opportunities for support and to build friendships as people talked about their experiences and engaged in practical activities. At the end of the 12-month period, each group member was interviewed to ascertain whether the support had been helpful. A picture began to emerge which showed inter-related aspects of grief such as the circumstances of the bereavement, age, gender, life experience of loss and employment status. Communication between each grandparent and their adult child (their life-limited child's parent) also seems to play a very important part in the progress of each person's grief journey.

The chapter outlines some of the findings of Acorns' study, with reference to relevant literature on grandparent grief where appropriate.

The role that grandparents play in the lives of their grandchildren depends, at least in part, on the extent to which the parents allow the grandparents access to their grandchildren. Grandparents provide grandchildren with a sense of history in the family. In turn, grandchildren provide grandparents with a legacy for the family's future – a kind of 'generational immortality'. In some families grandchildren may be the last in line to inherit the family name. Grandparents often see their grandchildren as helping them keep 'young at heart'. One of the most significant and poignant losses for grandparents is their loss of dreams. Where the grandchild is an only grandchild, this may be particularly intense.

> It's been like a bad dream. You look forward to seeing your own children grow up and become parents – you have plans for them, and

then it's ended before its begun. All our son and his wife are left with is an empty crib and empty arms.

Grandfathers often comment that they feel they miss 'rough and tumble relationships' with their grandchild, as the child's health deteriorates.

> When my son phoned me from the hospital to tell us James had been born, I knew something was wrong, but I wrongly assumed they had another girl and he was disappointed. Then he told me that James had spina bifida and my whole world fell apart. Selfishly, I wondered how you took a handicapped grandson fishing or to watch the match when the team played at home. I just didn't know what to say except, 'That's hard on you.' Years later, I realised that we had been so bound up in our own loss that we hadn't been able to give my son and daughter-in-law the support that they needed.

There appears to be both gender-related and generation-related differences in the ways in which grandparents grieve.

> My husband hurt so deeply he did not have a clue how to communicate his pain to me.

Often parents are reluctant to talk about their sadness and the grief they feel, a feature of adult bereavement in general which has been noted by authors such as Riches and Dawson (2000). Galinsky (1999) says 'the silence of family and friends can be deafening' (p.15).

Grandparent grief can be exceptionally lonely. Even when grandparents have a partner they may find that communication is difficult and this may result in relationship challenges.

> It always seemed that at the times when I needed John most that he would close down emotionally and become unavailable to me. This was particularly confusing because he was physically present.

It seems significant that those grandparents who have lived through war or other extreme life experiences often have many years of unresolved past losses. They are also most likely to hold the view that 'you just have to get on with things', rather than seeing supportive counselling as an option for themselves. When grandmothers are given opportunities to tell their own life stories, it is remarkable that many talk about the miscarriage, stillbirth or death of a child that occurred a generation ago. Many of these grandmothers may have never had previous opportunities to share their stories and some experience unresolved complex grief. The emotional pain that they feel may become unbearable when friends or work colleagues celebrate pregnancy or the birth of a baby.

Grandparents may rage against God, who has allowed their grandchild to die. Sometimes they question the beliefs and values that they have held all their lives. In some families, differences in culture, religion and personal values and beliefs may become heightened, causing long-term rifts.

Grandparents may suffer a great number of anxiety-related health problems such as chest pains or heaviness or shortness of breath. Unless they are aware of the physical impact of stress and grief, they may find themselves overly concerned about their own health, perhaps fearing that they might be about to suffer a heart attack. In turn, those that are aware of psychosomatic illness and the physical body responses of grief may be in danger of dismissing symptoms of a serious physical problem.

> It's been so hard to know what I feel emotionally and what my body is trying to tell me about the way it is reacting to Jason's illness.

Much of the literature concerning the role of the extended family when a child has a disability has concentrated on the supportive role of grandparents (Hornby and Ashworth 1995; Sandler, Wareen and Raver 1995). Acorns' research suggests, however, that the historical relationship between parents and grandparents is a significant factor that influences how much support grandparents feel able to provide to their adult child. Family members often look to the older generation in the family for care, solace and understanding. Observing their own adult child's grief is immensely painful.

> I know she is my grandchild but Melanie [the child's mother], is my daughter. As her mum, I want so much to take away the pain like I did when she was a little girl. But I can't, and that is one of the hardest things.

Hence, despite all their years of parenting experience, there is little that a grandparent can do to make things better. Hornby and Ashworth (1995) note that the relationship between parental grandmothers and the child's mother may be strained if a mother-in-law implies resentment of her daughter-in-law for not producing a 'normal' child. However, in Acorns' experience, this would appear to be the exception rather than the rule. Indeed, some families grow closer. Grandparents may see their adult child in a new light – as a mature, resilient and responsible adult.

> I would never have coped without Phil's mother [husband's mother]. She was wonderful. Her sense of determination that we would win through supported us greatly. But she never expected too much of us.

She has seen me howling and unable to cope in the morning, and come over and sorted us out while Phil was at work. By the time he has come home, everything has seemed OK on the surface. All the shopping and washing and ironing had been done into the bargain. I would never have dreamt in a million years that I would have grown so close to my mother-in-law.

Mirfin-Veitch and Bray (1997) believe that, when grandparents are able to have regular contact with parents, this is likely to enhance parental coping strategies. The geographical location of the grandparents' home in relation to the life-limited child's home plays a role in the relationship between grandparents and the life-limited child's family. When grandparents are more readily available, it is not unusual for them to be in almost daily face-to-face contact with at least some members of the life-limited child's family.

When grandparents are called upon, or feel the need, to offer support to the child's family, they may find themselves involved in surrogate parenting roles with well siblings. Interestingly, some grandparents may have a greater awareness of the sick child's illness and expected death than parents do.

The relationship between grandchildren and grandparents appears to change as grandchildren get older and they are able to form close bonds. Younger grandparents tend to have more contact with grandchildren and there is some evidence at Acorns to suggest that grandmothers have closer relationships with their grandchildren than grandfathers. This is particularly apparent in maternal grandparent relationships where the bond between first and third generations is very close indeed. Throughout their sick grandchild's life, grandparents speak of the very close bond that develops and often this relationship is particularly strong when the child is very unwell.

When a grandchild dies as a small baby or a young child, grandparents have few memories to comfort them, although, like the child's parents, integrating the memory of their grandchild into daily life is important.

My family are around me. Friends are around me. Lots of people coming and going, yet I feel so isolated, alone. Alone in my thoughts and my feelings and my memories. No-one can take these away from me. I get scared in case I forget his smile, what he looked like, how he felt when he snuggled up to me, even his smell. I don't want to forget him. Why should I? I feel safe and secure in the fact that I can remember these things. I don't want them taken away from me. Life continues like a rollercoaster. Everyday life continues.

In many ways, memories tend to keep relationships 'connected'. Sometimes many years after their grandchild's death, grandparents say that they imagine that they hear the sound of their grandchild's laughter. Some grandparents have a sense that their grandchild continues to communicate with them. This experience is often comforting, although the relationship they describe as having with their grandchild changes as time moves on. In some cases they talk to their grandchild or write letters and poems as if the grandchild is now adult. Whatever the context of these 'continuing bonds', memories and treasured objects help provide a link between the past and the present, and they are a source of comfort (see Figure 14.1).

Figure 14.1 'My gran and grandpa look at photos of my sister a lot. They are sad my sister died'

Family rituals become increasingly important and the child's funeral may provide the catalyst to the future shared times when the family gather together and reminisce. Visiting their child's grave or memorial garden seems to provide a source of comfort. There are occasions when grandparents dedicate a special part of their home or their garden to their grandchild's memory. They may even keep a room untouched in their own home which was used by their grandchild.

> Each morning I go into the room which we called hers and I take her picture from the chest of drawers and I say, 'Wake up my little one, it's a new day.' At night I close the curtains and I say the prayer I always said beside her cot when I was rocking her to sleep.

Many of the emotions experienced by parents who have a life-limited child are also felt by grandparents, but generational attitudes to death and mourning seem to play their part.

> I've always thought that you should try and keep a lid on your emotions. I can't remember ever seeing my own parents cry, and I think that had a huge influence on how I behave.

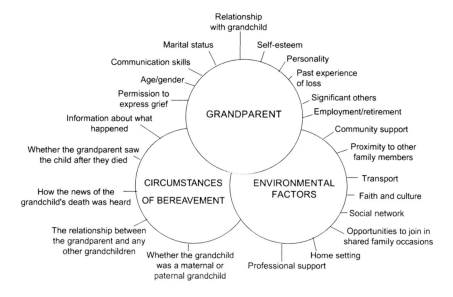

Figure 14.2 Inter-relating aspects of grandparent grief: emerging trends

Furthermore, Acorns' study shows that many grandparents hold back from talking about their own grief to the life-limited child's parents because they do not want to burden their adult child with more worry. If they do express how they feel, this is more likely to be to someone outside the family such as neighbours, older relatives, work colleagues or professionals, such as their GP or spiritual leader.

Many grandparents survive the death of their grandchild at great cost to themselves emotionally, psychologically and physically. They find themselves in a situation where there is the expectation that they will know what to do and that they will be able to offer strength and support. However, they may have had no previous opportunities to guide them in the role that they now play. Professionals working with parents from the time of the child's diagnosis onwards need to be aware of inter-generational relationship and inter-relating aspects of grandparent grief (see Figure 14.2).

Grandparent Support Groups at Acorns are still a relatively new part of service delivery and it is impossible to make informed judgments about the benefits or otherwise of the therapeutic support offered. However, transcripts of interviews with grandparents suggest the following:

- There is likely to be reluctance and apprehension about joining in group work until grandparents experience the benefits of peer support.

- Group work is helpful, although grandparents do not always anticipate the 'rawness' of their grief.

- Grandparents rarely have alternative support systems to draw on.

- Because grandparents have often made huge sacrifices for their own children and grandchildren, they find accepting support for themselves extremely hard.

- Sharing experiences with other bereaved grandparents reduces the isolation grandparents feel.

- Grandparents wish to reserve the right to choose how they pace their grief.

- Grandparents are keen to input to groups as well as to receive support.

Key points

- When a child is diagnosed with a life-limiting illness everyone in the family is affected, because life-limiting illness puts the child at risk, as well as the predictability of the family's future.

- There appears to be gender-related and generation-related differences in the ways in which grandparents grieve.

- Grandparents who have lived through war or other extreme life experiences often have many years of unresolved past losses.

- Grandparents may suffer a great number of anxiety-related health problems.

- The historical relationship between grandparents and parents before the child's death influences how much support grandparents feel able to offer their adult child.

- The geographical location of the grandparents' home from the life-limited child's home plays a role in the relationship between grandparents and the child's parents.

- Grandparents may play a surrogate parenting role to well siblings.

Implications for practice

- Professionals need to be aware of the impact of a grandchild's life-limited illness and death on grandparents.

- Grandparents need to be helped to integrate the memory of their grandchild into daily life.

- Encouraging grandparents to join in family rituals where they have opportunities to reminisce about their grandchild's life is important.

- Professionals working with parents from the time of the child's diagnosis onwards need to be aware of inter-generational relationships.

- Professionals need to be aware that grandparents are likely to be reluctant to seek support for themselves.

- In therapeutic group work situations it is likely that grandparents will welcome opportunities for input as well as to receive support.

15

Religious, Cultural, Secular and Spiritual Aspects of Care

Erica Brown

Birth and death are events experienced by all people. Belief in survival beyond death is perhaps the oldest religious conviction of humankind. As long ago as pre-historic times, bodies were buried together with tools and ornaments for use in the next life. Today there is a great variety of teaching in world religions about death and afterlife, ranging from belief in the resurrection taught by monotheistic faiths, to belief in reincarnation held by the religions of India and beyond.

During the past decade, parental bereavement has received considerable attention and a number of descriptive studies have brought to light the unique needs of life-limited children and their families (Brown 2002; Goldman 2002; Hill 1994). However, while there is a growing amount of literature available on the psychological needs of families with a life-limited child, scant attention has been paid to cultural care (Irish, Lundquist and Nelson 1999).

There is an increasing awareness of the importance of listening to the views of parents of life-limited children and planning services which are sensitive to individual family needs. There has also been corresponding concern about the stereotypes which have been created concerning the level and nature of support which families would welcome. Until fairly recently, it was considered that a family's own spiritual leader or a chaplain had sole responsibility for faith matters (Neuberger 1994). Nowadays, carers need to have knowledge and skills if they are to provide holistic care, but the sensitivity required is enormous.

The United Nations Convention on the Rights of the Child (UNESCO 1991) makes several references to the importance of religious and cultural care. In the United Kingdom, families embrace a wide diversity of religious beliefs, or none. Information for practitioners about different faiths and cultures is only useful if it is relevant to the people concerned, and comes from reliable sources. Therefore, it is essential that practitioners should have access to accurate information and advice.

There is sometimes an assumption that the needs of families from ethnic minority groups are met by resources within their own community (Atkins and Rollings 1998), but evidence shows that, although they often do not come forward for help, their needs may be unmet and they struggle with little support (Brown 2004; Firth 2001; NHS Executive 2000). Therefore, the need to provide appropriate and accessible palliative care to ethnic minority groups has been recognised as a significant service development issue. A report from the National Council for Hospice and Special Palliative Care Services (Hill and Penso 1995) identified, amongst other issues, a need for the provision of culturally sensitive services in relation to the 'spiritual, language and dietary needs of black and ethnic minority service users'.

The chapter is divided into five sections. The first section discusses cultural and ethnic aspects of death and the importance of equal access to care. The second section attempts to define religious needs, including the religious and cultural development of children with life-limiting illness. The third section discusses aspects of religious and cultural care in practice, including the experiences and expectations of a group of Asian mothers with a life-limited child. The four section addresses secular aspects of need, and the fifth section includes spiritual aspects of parental grief.

Effects of ethnicity and culture on bereavement

Many people have multiple ethnic and cultural identities, possessing mixed heritage, with parents, grandparents and great-grandparents from different groups or communities. Ethnicity and culture profoundly affect the way families experience death, dying and bereavement. Furthermore, the way in which society deals with death reveals a great deal about that culture, especially about the way people are valued.

In pre-industrial societies there were high rates of death at the beginning of life. Children did not enter the social world until a naming ceremony had taken place and the baby became recognised as a member of the community. Indeed, babies who died before this time did not receive full funeral rites. Instead of birth and death being viewed as two separate events, they were treated as though one cancelled out the other. Peri-natal deaths were still high in the United Kingdom as recently as Victorian times. Parents saw about a quarter to a third of their children die before they reached ten years of age. Today, many societies see death as a transition for the person who dies. How people prepare for this transition, and how survivors behave after a death has occurred, varies a great deal. There are, however, some common themes. Most societies provide social sanction for the outward expression of this, in the funeral rites and customs that follow death.

Ethnicity

The term 'ethnic' is often misunderstood and discussion about the meaning of ethnicity has been extensive (Hillier 1991; Jenkins 1995; Smaje 1995). For the purposes of this chapter, ethnicity is regarded as referring to a group of people that share distinctive features, such as origin of descent, language, culture, physical appearance, religious affiliation, customs and values.

Literature about death and ethnicity is limited in both its volume and its scope. Little is currently known about family roles in paediatric palliative care settings within different ethnic groups. There is, however, some literature available, giving accounts of death beliefs and funeral rites, focusing on ways of dealing with the body, rather than the experience of death and dying within these groups (Brown 2002, 2005a, 2005b, 2005c, 2005d; Firth 2000). A fundamental weakness of the literature has been its insensitivity to the processes of change which occur as members of minority ethnic communities adapt to their new societies (Jonker 1996). The view that families from minority ethnic groups 'look after their own' has rightly been criticised as a stereotyped over-simplification (Atkins and Rollings 1998). Traditional family structures are changing in Britain and often relatives may live too far away for them to be present at the time of death (Firth 1996). Young people from minority ethnic groups, who have been brought up in Britain, may not have experienced a death in their family until they themselves are adults.

Culture

Numerous definitions of culture abound. In general, they tend to place emphasis on culture as a shared system of meaning, which derives from 'common rituals, values, rules and laws' (Geertz 1993). For the purpose of this chapter, culture is defined as how people do and view things within the groups to which they belong. Culture also includes a set of shared values, expectations, perceptions and life-styles based on common history and language, which enable members of the community to function together.

For many people, it is important for them that they are able to maintain their cultural values and practices, but cultures are not fixed and static. They change in response to new situations and pressures (Ahmad 1996).

Some aspects of culture are visible and obvious (Hofstede 1991). These include dress, written and spoken language, rites of passage, architecture and art. The less obvious aspects of culture consist of the shared norms and values of a group, community or society. They are often invisible but, nevertheless, they define standards of behaviour, how things are organised and events such as birth and death.

Most Western Europeans view physical illness as caused by some combination of bad luck, external factors, heredity and individual behaviour. In other societies, people may consider other possibilities that include bad behaviour, divine punishment, jealousy or another person's ill-will.

It is often assumed that a child inherits the culture into which it is born, but cultural awareness is also nurtured through shared rituals, values, rules and laws. In the opinion of Unger (1999), the word 'culture' is not a noun, but a verb.

The culture of the community in which people grow up has a predominant influence on their world-view and on the way in which they behave. Each culture has its own approaches for dealing with loss, and there may be differences concerning spiritual beliefs, rituals, expectations and etiquette. Research indicates that grief is experienced in similar ways across all cultures but, within cultures, there is a huge range of individual responses (Cowles 1996). Furthermore, micro-cultures exist within cultures, with individual differences.

Throughout the history of humankind, the death of babies and children have continued to be common events. Today in countries where the rates of infant mortality are still high, the death of a child may seem inevitable, with mourning lasting little longer than a few days. In societies where medical and scientific advances have resulted in the decline of infant mortality, childhood death is likely to be perceived as tragic and unfair. Most societies designate the status of bereaved individuals, referring to them as 'widows' or 'widowers' for those losing a spouse, or as 'orphans' for children losing parents. There are no culturally accepted terms to describe the state of the bereaved parent.

Some cultures and communities may attribute unique significance to the death of a child. Individual cultures hold a variety of beliefs about where children come from before they are born, and where they go after they die. Furthermore, the age, gender, family position and cause of death may affect the meaning attributed to the death and determine the rites of passage – the grieving behaviour within a given culture.

Religion

The word 'religion' probably derives from the Latin 'religare', which means 'to bind' (Stoter 1995). Faith is the recognition on the part of humankind of an unseen power, worthy of obedience, reverence and worship. In monotheistic faiths, this power is referred to as 'God', and in polytheistic societies as 'the gods'. All religions teach that their deity, or deities, have control over the destiny of a person's soul after earthly life is over.

The great world religions have evolved in diverse ways under the influences of the cultures into which they have spread. Some religions provide detailed codes of conduct covering aspects of daily life such as diet, modesty, worship or personal hygiene. Others have looser frameworks, within which people make their own decisions. In most but not all religions, there is an orthodox, progressive or liberal wing. There will also be groupings which may relate to the country or area of the faith origin. For example, in Islam there are Ahmadiyya, Sunni and Shi'ite Muslims. Variations need to be borne in mind.

The influence of religion on people's lives varies a great deal. Religion may act as a form of social support, providing companionship and practical help and affirming personal self-esteem through shared values and beliefs. Many people find that their faith is a source of comfort, giving meaning to suffering and providing hope for the future. However, people may also feel angry and let down by their god or gods and lose their faith. People who do not aspire to belonging to a faith may, nevertheless, have strong ethical and moral values and a sustaining spiritual dimension to their lives. It may be tempting to assume that if a family have stated on a form that they have membership of a particular tradition, that they are practising members of that tradition. However, it may be more a matter of labelling. Nevertheless, the label gives carers an insight into what the family's needs may be.

Different generations may hold different views within their own faith, particularly where a second generation has grown up in a different cultural milieu. Children absorb parental attitudes towards religion in the early years of their development without question or analysis. This can influence their thoughts and attitudes in later life.

Sometimes people turn to religion for an explanation of personal tragedy. Most major faiths teach that physical death is not the end. However, the precise form that the continued existence takes varies within different religions and, sometimes, within different denominations. Major themes include:

- belief in the cycle of birth, death and reincarnation
- judgment that results in reward or punishment for past behaviour and thoughts
- existing with God in an afterlife, in heaven or paradise
- being reunited with loved ones who have died earlier
- sleeping or resting until spiritually, or physically, resurrected by God
- exclusion from God in purgatory, or hell.

Ceremonies and rituals

Much of life is made up of rituals, but these are so much part of everyday activity that people do not necessarily think about their origins or their meanings. The ritual is acted out in such a way that there is instant recognition of the event. Indeed, part of the importance of the 'acting out' is that there is little need to explain. Often, a variety of non-verbal ways of expressing feelings come into play. Sometimes, people create their own rituals to give meaning and resonance to what has happened. Others find meaning and comfort in traditional ways of doing things, particularly if they are part of a cultural minority.

Acorns' Medical Officer sees his pronouncement of the child's death to parents as a ritual. Using his stethoscope he takes time to listen to the child's chest, feels for a pulse and looks into the child's eyes before announcing the child is 'dead'. Often it is only when this ritual is concluded that the family begin to understand their child's physical death.

The coming together of family and friends at a funeral is a statement of ongoing love and respect, even though a person has died. Those who watch what takes place are constantly made aware of the fact that what is important, is not so much what is said, but what is implied, by the coming together. The more ceremony and ritual that is present, the more opportunities there are for the expression of feelings.

Death rites

In virtually all religions there are clearly set rules, religious laws and procedures about what is to be done during the dying process and after the death. Periods of mourning last for a clearly defined time in many cultures. This allows the bereaved time to come to terms with what has happened, and to adjust to changes in their lives psychologically, as well as adapting to their changed social status.

The value a culture holds for children, and the significance of their death, is reflected in the care and disposal of the body and in funeral rites. These may be quite different from those performed when an adult dies. In several cultures, children are considered innocent and their premature death affords them heavenly status. Thus, Puerto Ricans dress their child in white and paint the child's face like an angel. Some Orthodox Christians believe death to be particularly traumatic if it occurs before a young person is married, since marriage is viewed as the consummation of earthly happiness. If a young person or a child dies, their body is dressed as if they were wearing wedding clothes, and funeral laments are sung that bear a striking resemblance to wedding songs. In other cultures, such as China, the death of a child is perceived as a 'bad' death and parents and grandparents are not expected to go to the funeral. People avoid talking about the child, because the event is considered to be shameful. Hence, the values, beliefs and practices held by families in Western cultures may clash with those held by families with a different cultural background.

The ways in which families commemorate their child's life demonstrate and reinforce their belief. Individual members may hold differing views about the role of children as participants in funerals and mourning rites. Some parents may not feel able to discuss their own feelings with members of an older generation, who may want to 'protect' children from the pain of death. Hence, the attitudes and practices within families may clash. Funerals will be discussed later in the book.

Religious rituals can also have important spiritual, social and emotional significance, strengthening bonds between members of a group and giving a shared sense of meaning and purpose. Ceremonies surrounding death often stress forgiveness, preparation for the life to come, transcendence and hope. Sometimes, religious rituals offer a person a chance to participate in religious behaviour, without specifying the extent of their beliefs. They may provide comfort and reassurance to the mourners. The ritual dimension of religion encompasses actions and activities, which worshippers do in the practice of their religion. Activities may range from daily ablutions before prayer, to taking part in a once-in-a-lifetime pilgrimage.

Signs and symbols

Symbols may have great significance for families. Religious symbols are inextricably associated with belief and observance. Sometimes symbols are large and displayed in the family home, or they may be small and private, such as a pendant or a sacred thread, worn by Hindu males under clothing. Statues or pictures may be used decoratively, or as a focal point for private worship.

Natural phenomena such as light and darkness also have powerful significance. The crescent moon and stars appears in Muslim countries, representative of light and darkness for persons on a spiritual journey. 'Guru', a word with particular emphasis for Sikhs, may be translated as 'teacher' or 'enlightener' and is derived from the word '*gu*', meaning darkness and '*ru*', meaning light. Thus, a Guru is a spiritual teacher who leads from the darkness, of ignorance to enlightenment.

Worship

The basis of most religious observance is the worship of a deity, or deities. The form which worship takes, and the expression and location of worship, varies between communities, denominations and individual worshippers.

Worship comprises components such as thanksgiving, praise and repentance. Expression may be found through prayer, physical position and movement, reading and reciting sacred scriptures, and silence. In some faiths, music is very important. For example, in Hinduism the sound of a *mantra* or sacred verse reflects deeper meaning, and its repetition acts as a focus to concentrate the mind of the worshipper.

For some people, prayer is essentially a private matter, and it may be silent. For others it may be a corporate activity with family members. Worship at home is important in most faiths. Some religions prescribe set prayers at certain times. Others encourage silent prayer and meditation. In children's hospices, where staff endeavour to create a homely environment, it is important that people have private space set aside for worship.

Most religions identify sites of historical and spiritual significance, particularly where the founder of the faith experienced a revelation. Sacred places may include cities, such as Makkah or Medina for Muslims, or Jerusalem for Jews and Christians. Sometimes, shrines commemorate miraculous events and appearances, and they are the destination of pilgrimages. Muslims, for example, aim to complete the Hajj by visiting Makkah, the birthplace of Mohammed, at least once during their lifetime.

Of course, there is a danger that attempting to describe and to classify beliefs and practices may lead to one-dimensional snapshots. Hence, all guidelines are likely to contain some generalisations and crude stereotyping, that ignores variations and idiosyncrasies. Acorns has produced a series of booklets giving guidance to professionals on how to enhance the quality of care provided for families from different religious groups. Space prohibits comprehensive information. The bullet lists below summarise some of the sensitivities that staff should show families. Readers should refer to the References for details of the series of books written by Erica Brown, *Enhancing the Quality of Experience* (Brown 2005a, 2005b, 2005c, 2005d).

Religious rites and rituals surrounding death

In many faiths life is a preparation for death and the life to come. It is extremely difficult to summarise the most common rituals and ceremonies which occur at the time of death or immediately afterwards. The bullet points below summarise common customs in faith communities.

Christianity

- The dying person may receive Holy Communion and/or The Sacrament of the Sick (or Sacrament of Reconciliation).

- The family may wish to say prayers thanking God for the life of the person and the life to come.
- Prayers may be said on behalf of the family and on behalf of the dying person.
- The family will want to carry out the wishes of the dead person and to be able to make their own decisions with regard to burial or cremation. In some traditions Mass or Communion may be included in the funeral service.

Judaism

- It is usual for someone to be with the person at the time of death. Some Jews would request for a rabbi to be present.
- The body is washed by members of the local burial society (the *chevrah kadisha*).
- The body will be watched over from the time of death to time of burial.
- The body will be buried as soon as possible after death, preferably within 24 hours (but not on the Sabbath or holy days).
- Close family members will mourn for a period of 30 days after the death.
- Immediate family members should refrain from attending celebrations during the first year of mourning.
- Normally the family will arrange for the tombstone to be consecrated within the year.

Islam

- If possible, the declaration of faith (Shahada) will be recited before death.
- A dying person will wish to have somebody with them.
- Family members will try to be together where possible.
- The dead body will be washed three times and dressed in clean clothes. Family members will wish to wash themselves afterwards.
- The head of the deceased is turned onto the right shoulder and then positioned facing Makkah (south-east in the UK).
- The body is covered with a plain clean cloth.
- The next of kin will make the funeral arrangements. Islamic law requires friends and relations to feed mourners for three days after the death.

- Burial will take place as soon as possible.
- The body may be returned to the place of birth. In some cases the body may be embalmed.
- Mourners will avoid bodily contact with persons of the opposite sex (other than blood relatives).
- Relatives may wish to visit the grave regularly on Fridays for up to 40 days after the death. Mourning ends with a meal and Qur'anic reading.

Hinduism

- The dying person will wish to have someone with them. They may wish to lie on the floor and to sip Holy Ganges' water.
- Members of the religious community will wash the body after death.
- The body will be wrapped in a white shroud or white clothes, except in the case of a young woman, who may be wrapped in a red sari.
- A gold coin or leaf from the sacred tulsi plant may be put in the mouth of the deceased person.
- Family members will wish to keep the body close to them or as close to the Hindu community as possible until the funeral.
- The next of kin will make the funeral arrangements. The first part of the ceremony may take place at home.
- The body will be cremated with the exception of children under three years old who will be buried.
- The eldest male in the family will play a key role in the funeral service.
- In Great Britain there may be mourning rituals during the first year after death.

Sikhism

- Sikhs will wish to have somebody with them at the time of their death. They may wish to have portions of the Guru Granth Sahib (holy scriptures) read to them.
- After death the body will be washed before cremation and dressed by members of the family or members of the religious community.

- Sikhs will wish to wear the five K's wherever possible, including a white turban for a man. Young women will be dressed in a red sari or a red shroud.
- The body will be covered with a clean white sheet and money or other gifts may be placed in the coffin.
- Sikhs will wish other people from outside their community to refrain from comforting them or having physical contact with them, e.g. hugging.
- Families may like to listen to readings from the Guru Granth Sahib for about ten days after the funeral.
- If the father of the family has died, the eldest son may be given a turban to signify he is now head of the family.

Buddhism

- Where possible families will wish to be with the person who is dying. A religious teacher may be invited to talk to the person.
- The body will remain untouched until a priest arrives.
- Family members will stay together for as long as possible.
- The body will be washed after death and laid out, sometimes by members of the family or religious community.
- A photograph of the deceased may be placed near the coffin.
- A period of between three and seven days will usually elapse before the funeral.
- Burial or cremation will depend on the school of Buddhism/country of origin.
- Periods of mourning vary according to the country of origin.

Children's experience of death

The context of many children's experience of death has changed. In the past, most deaths occurred at home. Death and illness were witnessed first-hand and children were often present at funerals. The ancient nursery rhyme 'Ring-a-ring o'roses' describes a game played by children during the Great Plague and Black Death of the fourteenth century and seventeenth century in Britain. The 'rosy-ring' refers to the swelling lymph nodes and a 'pocket full of posy' to an amulet worn as a protection from the disease. 'Achoo' describes the flu-like symptoms associated with the plague, and 'all fall down' is the inevitable death of the victim. In the twenty-first century, most people die in hospitals or other care settings. Death will rarely be within most children's everyday experience.

However, in Great Britain, approximately 15,000 children and young people under the age of 20 still die each year. Although Black and Wood (1989) write of the remoteness of childhood death in the twentieth century, to some children and their families, it will still remain a stark reality.

The religious and cultural development of children with life-limiting conditions

A child's age, cognitive ability, anxiety level and home background, will all influence their understanding of what happens at the time of death and beyond. Each family is unique, and the culture or faith in which children are brought up, and the way in which they are taught at home and at school, will influence the way in which they perceive death. Therefore, it is vitally important that life-limited children are given age and developmentally appropriate opportunities to share and explore their fears and concerns. Children often indicate their awareness of serious illness, and communicate their beliefs about what happens after they die, through drawing and painting (see Figure 15.1). In order that carers are able to work effectively with children, it is important that they are aware of what children have been taught by their families and communities. Children's developmental understanding of death in secular society is discussed in chapter 10.

In the early stages of their development, children are egocentric and their understanding of religion is based on their experience within their family. Some children will have engaged in religious practices; some will have had occasional experience of religion; others, none at all. Many may have an awareness of symbolism in religion and they are likely to have heard stories about the lives of key figures and religious leaders. They may also understand that, for some people, places, food and occasions have special importance. At this stage it is important to provide a foundation on which to build children's

Figure 15.1 'My mummy will be an angel too. She will come to Heaven and look after me'

increasing awareness of themselves as individuals, and of their relationship with other people. Helping them to respond to different environments provides a framework for cultural and religious experiences with which they may be familiar, such as reflection or meditation.

In the middle years, children have a greater understanding of themselves and an awareness of the faiths and cultures in which they grow up. Some families may choose to talk about death and dying, and perhaps the concept of the soul moving on to another form of life (see Figure 15.2). Children's relationships with members of the local and wider community will have an important influence on their sense of personal identity and purpose. Many children will have an awareness of the contribution they make to the communities to which they belong, and there should be opportunities to help them to create memories for the people who will grieve for them after they have died.

Young adults are often fiercely independent and they may seem to have an urgent need to get on with living their lives. This may conflict with having a life-limiting illness. There is often an impressive determination on the part of young people to deny the reality of the situation, and carers need to respect this. Opportunities to explore the common ground between their own experiences, and spiritual and religious questions of meaning and purpose, may be helpful. Where young people are members of families with a religious belief, their questions are likely to include a spiritual and religious context.

Figure 15.2 'When I die my soul will go to Allah'

Bluebond-Langner (1995) and Brown (1999) describe how life-limited children with special educational needs may have a sophisticated understanding of death that includes religious dimensions. Luchterhand and Murphy (1998) also worked extensively with young people with learning disabilities. Their research has included thoughts about death. Recurring thoughts about the person who has died are common.

Religious themes often appear in children's thoughts about death and an afterlife. Heaven is nearly always regarded as a desirable place where life continues after earthly existence is over, although mostly this life is in an altered form, such as becoming an angel. For some children, hell appears as an alternative destination, although young people rarely talk about it as a possibility for themselves. For some children, thinking about religion may be unhelpful. The relationship between religion and death-anxiety has been studied by a number of researchers (Kaczorowski 1989; Peterson and Greil 1990; Templar 1993). Where young people are actively involved as members of worshipping communities, death-anxiety appears to be lower, although personality, temperament and life-experience all play their part.

Children's questions

Many children are curious about death and their questions about their illness may be accompanied by a fascination about what happens next. Religions seek to give responses to mysteries such as these. Some children may question their faith, wondering how a just God can allow them to die. Others may turn to religion to find an explanation for what is happening to them. This may involve thoughts about sins they have committed, laws they have broken, or faith they have lost. Thus, children's questions probe the world around them, as they reflect on their past and present life and strive to make sense of the future. Children's attempts to answer questions such as 'Why do I suffer?' or 'Why will I die?' may help them to make sense of what is happening in their own life story. Hitcham (1993) writes that 'inside every child there is a story waiting to be told but, when that story involves difficult issues such as death and dying, it is neither easy to tell nor to listen to', (p.2). (See Chapter 10, 'Children's Developmental Understanding and Emotional Response to Death and Dying'.)

Religious and cultural care in practice

When people are ill or vulnerable, they need care that is focused on their needs and what is important to them. Professionals require skills, information and confidence to find out what each family wants, and organisational structures that are sufficiently flexible to enable them to provide it. Practices, beliefs and attitudes are continually emerging. Professional awareness of the range of such patterns can be a vital starting point in addressing the needs of families from ethnic minorities. Families will seldom mind if carers ask about their customs and beliefs, as long as the subject is approached in a respectful and polite way. Indeed, interest may well be welcomed and enjoyed.

At a time when services are under great pressure and resources are stretched, the demand for holistic family-centred care that takes into account different cultural, religious and personal needs may seem unrealistic. Holistic care for dying children and their families requires special skills and sensitivities. Identifying and meeting individual cultural and religious needs are important parts of that care. The first requirement for staff caring for families is to know something of the religion and cultures concerned. Families usually find it helpful and supportive to meet staff who do not regard them as 'different' or 'strange'. Being cared for by somebody who has taken the trouble to learn something about customs and beliefs can make an enormous difference to the relationship.

In order to be effective, members of the caring professions must be aware of their own social mores, prejudices and world-view. People's attitudes and beliefs profoundly affect the way they respond to others, particularly those whose life-styles are different from their own. In 1995, Infield, Gordon and Harper concluded that, 'while many people are individually knowledgeable and culturally sensitive, few hospices had systematically planned services to meet the needs of culturally diverse groups', (p.xii) . Not surprisingly, children's hospices in general are finding it difficult to attract referrals from minority ethnic groups (ACT/RCPCH 2003).

Spiritual grief, across faith traditions

When parents have a life-limited child, they will often have to face challenges, questions and painful decisions. At Acorns, parents' spiritual experience is manifested across many faiths and traditions. How faith communities support parents throughout their grief journey is tremendously important and Acorns' experience of some religious groups is that parents do not always find the help they seek.

> I can't take my son to the temple because he might do something in his nappy while he is in the prayer hall and some people wouldn't think that was OK.

All faiths have ceremonies and rituals to mark the birth of a child and children are considered to be gifts from God. One mother, a member of the Hindu tradition, described how in India her own mother had ritually washed her hands after helping to deliver her grandchild. She had saved the water and taken it to the village well where she emptied it as a symbol of fertility and blessing to be shared with the local community. When the child died some years later, the child's parents were distraught. If they wrote to the grandmother about the child's death, or made a phone call, the news might be perceived by the local Hindu community in India as a bad omen.

Another grandmother belonging to a Roman Catholic congregation said that her daughter had found the parish priest unable to provide her with comfort, or to give a reason how a loving God could let her child die. In this instance, the family had sought the services of a psychic woman, who had been tremendously supportive in helping the grandmother to recognise the child's continuing presence in earthly life through cherished memories and times when she was 'just around'.

For centuries, religious icons and deities have portrayed women as symbols of fertility and motherhood, through large stomachs, hips and breasts. For bereaved mothers, their child has died and yet they are continually reminded that their bodily form is symbolic of a capacity to bear and nurture children. In some societies, parenting is also a symbol used to describe the relationship between humankind and God. Thus God is portrayed as the Creator, Sustainer and Provider in Judaism; God is depicted as Father, Son and Holy Spirit in Christianity; Mary as Mother by Roman Catholic Christians; Krishna as the child in Hinduism; and Kali the mother of guidance and discipline in Hinduism. For bereaved parents, their child has died and they are denied their care-giving role. Indeed, some parents describe life after their child has died as farcical, because they feel compelled to present a facade to the rest of the world, whilst inside they are consumed by overwhelming grief.

For South Asian parents, the pain of loss seems to take on a special kind of significance. God has blessed parents with a child and then let the child die. How can a loving and just God do this? Two Muslim mothers described the nature of their pain when their child died as:

- 'An empty hole.'
- 'Deep guilt for past deeds.'
- 'Desolation and estrangement from others, especially by members of their faith community that do not share their loss.'

A number of United Kingdom Government publications (DoH 1997, 1998; Scottish Office 1997; Welsh Office 1998) recommend that the views of patients and families are included in planning the care they receive. In 1999, the Department of Health launched the National Carers' Strategy, which emphasised the importance of ensuring that services enabled parents to sustain an acceptable life-style, maintain paid employment (if desired), maintain their physical and mental health and integrate into local communities. This commitment was further underlined in the Department of Health (2000b) NHS Plan. In March 2000, the Prime Minister identified to Parliament a need to address palliative care services. For families from ethnic minority groups, needs are diverse and, increasingly, involvement in choosing care has become a benchmark against which many palliative care services are measured (DoH 2002a).

The 2001 Census reported that South Asian Communities make up 4 per cent of the United Kingdom population, comprising 1.8 per cent Indian, 1.3 per cent Pakistani, 0.5 per cent Bangladeshi, and 0.4 per cent Asian others, totalling about 2.3 million people (Office for National Statistics 2001). Since these communities have proportionately younger people compared to White communities, the number of people from the South Asian communities is rising and will continue to do so (Hatton *et al.* 2004). Furthermore, according to Hatton *et al.*'s survey, the number of people with chronic health needs and disabilities is also rising substantially, with the incidence of persons with severe learning difficulties greater in some South Asian communities compared with White communities (Kerr 2001).

Some statistics have shown that South Asian families with a person with chronic health needs or disabilities are likely to be disadvantaged in terms of paid employment, housing and income (Chamba *et al.* 1999; Hatton *et al.* 2004). Furthermore, according to a study by Karim, Bailey and Tunna (2000), people from black and ethnic minority populations are under-represented in adult palliative care services. The experiences of South Asian families with a life-limited child using paediatric palliative care services is largely undocumented.

Good care can be provided which is appropriate for families from a wide range of cultural and ethnic backgrounds, whether the child is being cared for at home, a children's hospital or a hospice. Where service providers are committed to meeting the needs of different groups, take-up has often been dramatic. For example, Acorns provides a network of care for life-limited children and their families throughout the West Midlands, Shropshire, Staffordshire, Warwickshire, Herefordshire, Worcestershire and Gloucestershire. Among these families there are a large number from South Asian cultures.

Acorns has a commitment towards family-led and family-centred care. Central to successful models of care for ethnic minorities at the three hospices has been the appointment of a full-time Asian Liaison Officer and an African Caribbean Officer. The Trust was also fortunate to receive a three-year grant from The Princess of Wales Memorial Fund which helped to support an Asian Sibling Worker. Placing advertisements in mother tongue languages has attracted volunteers from ethnic minorities who work as befrienders in Acorns' three hospices and in families' own homes. Families who encounter language difficulties are supported by an interpreter service, funded by the Trust. An Asian Mothers' Support Group has proved very successful and, as the mothers gained confidence and learned to trust the staff, they have contributed to research which has provided an evidence base for their care.

In 2000, Acorns conducted a small-scale research project which set out to determine the experiences and expectations of ten Asian mothers with a life-limited child using the hospice services. Semi-structured interviews took place in mothers' homes. Acorns' Asian Liaison Officer accompanied the interviewer and interpreted questions and responses as needed. This part of the chapter summarises the research findings.

Mothers implied that they encountered prejudice in their own faith or cultural community. It was common for them to experience patronising and dismissive approaches by some professional groups when they raised concerns about their child. Sometimes conflicting situations arose with their partner or spouse, or with other family members, or with neighbours, as mothers struggled to care for their sick child. Having a life-limited child had changed the pattern of all the mothers' daily lives. Often this happened from the time of the child's diagnosis.

Diagnosis

The degree to which mothers understand their child's life-limiting illness at the time of diagnosis seems to have far-reaching consequences for how well they are able to communicate with their family and with members of their community.

> I don't remember much apart from the way he looked at me and how he said, Azra has Batten disease. I tell everyone the name of her illness, like the doctor told me.

Some mothers thought the consultant had told them that their child had a disability, rather than being life-limited. Interestingly, half of the mothers who felt that they had understood their child's diagnosis at the time it was given already had another child with the same condition. There was a significant degree of dissatisfaction concerning how parents viewed the communication style of the specialist consultant at the time of disclosure. Even though some families had not fully understood all the information they were given, when the news was given in an emotionally supportive manner this was helpful.

All of the parents were told the news of their child's diagnosis in English. On one occasion, a mother reported that a translator had been made available. Four of the families received some written information at the time of disclosure, although all of the mothers interviewed felt that it would have been helpful to have had their child's diagnosis written down.

The importance of providing accurate and accessible information for South Asian families, particularly when English is not a first language, has been emphasised in previous studies (Mir *et al.* 2001). Furthermore, the manner in which White families are told the diagnosis of their child's life-limiting illness has been shown to play a significant part in how well individual family members adapt to the situation (Brown 2001). Mothers talked at length about their experience of the diagnosis process. In all cases, the disclosure was given by a paediatric consultant. None of the mothers felt they had received sufficient professional support in the following days and weeks. Two mothers said that they found difficulty telling their husbands, and all of them had experienced anxiety relaying the information to extended family members. Significantly, several families had struggled telling the news to their own parents, and, in two families, siblings had not been told that their brother had a life-limiting illness.

Because families did not always have detailed information about their child's life-expectancy and the implications of this for their family, many were unsure where to access ongoing support at the time of diagnosis. Where support was offered, some of the mothers resented professionals asking intrusive questions, although they recognised that this was often borne out of a desire to be helpful. Others described feeling suffocated by the constant flurry of clinic and hospital appointments and the intensity of the emotion they felt.

Family support

Despite the stereotype in the United Kingdom that people from ethnic minority families receive support from their family members, Chamba *et al.* reported in 1999 that, in fact, South Asian families receive less support compared with White families. One of the mothers interviewed was a widow. Little contact from the child's father's family had been forthcoming after his death, and this mother had already had a child who had died of the same condition. She spoke of missing practical and emotional support, and feeling pressurised by her own parents to remarry as soon as possible.

Six of the mothers reported no help from members of their extended family. Where extended families did offer support, this included care for the life-limited child, help with domestic chores, accompanying the family to hospital and clinic appointments, and providing transport and help with interpreting. When help was forthcoming, the mothers were unanimous in saying how much they appreciated it.

> My sister-in-law comes and changes my daughter's nappies and washes her. That is important for me. Her father would not be the right person to do it.

Occasionally, mothers reported that members of their extended family were too busy to help, or that they had not asked for help because they felt that other people would be unable to cope with their child.

> They never gave me any practical help – they just stay in their own place.

There seemed to be a range of views expressed by extended family members that related to the cause of the child's illness. These include the illness being a punishment for past actions by the parents. Some relatives dismissed a diagnosis of congenital abnormality, and suggested that the child would recover health.

> We don't have anyone else like that in our family. It must have come from the other side.

> My mother-in-law didn't want to eat in our house. She seems to think that you can catch what Aziz has.

Support from friends and community

Being able to talk to other Asian women with a life-limited child is tremendously important for mothers. Sharing experiences and concerns in group work situations helps to relieve the sense of isolation they often feel within their families. Few of the mothers reported receiving help from friends outside Acorns' Asian Mothers' Group, although two were able to talk about occasions where they had been surprised by someone offering support.

> My friend, she came and did the ironing and washed up the pans. I asked her why she did it and she told me, 'I have been thinking about how hard it must be, never being able to go to a wedding or a festival time.'

> When we come to the Mothers' Group, we talk about our children and we share our thoughts. It makes me have hope in my heart.

Support services

Support services available to the mothers included education, health, Social Services and the children's hospice. A significant factor was the level of collaboration between the service providers, a factor described in previous research studies (Quinton 2004). Chamba *et al.*'s (1999) study revealed that South Asian families with a disabled child had high levels of awareness of general health and welfare services, but much lower awareness of support agencies providing respite care, counselling and psychological support. In Acorns' study all of the mothers were aware of what was available to them. However, this was largely to be expected, since each family had a dedicated Community Worker from the Hospice, part of whose role was to help parents access services, or to negotiate access on their behalf. Where mothers had used support services, some of these had been deemed by them as being culturally inappropriate, particularly in relation to language and gender issues, a finding supported by Hatton *et al.*'s (2004) study of South Asian families with a disabled child.

> The counsellor was Asian, and although she spoke the same language as I do, she talked in English all the time. I can't think in English when I'm telling her upsetting things.

Interpreter services

Interpreter services can make a valuable contribution to improving access to palliative care services (Chamba *et al.* 1999). Two of the mothers who had received support from Acorns' interpreters felt that this had helped to maintain their self-esteem and that it had been good to be able to discuss their child's illness and family coping strategies without another family member present. However, where interpreters had been supplied by other support agencies, three mothers felt that the person concerned did not have an insight into life-limiting illness and therefore the support offered had been rudimentary. Indeed, one mother felt that her spouse had a greater understanding of the jargon used by the specialist consultant than the interpreter did. Information about available services written in relevant languages was also important to the families. Although most of the mothers did not express a preference for support services to be staffed by Asians, it was important to all mothers that, when they contacted a service or attended an appointment, the main contact person was female.

Eight of the ten mothers expressed frustration about the time that had elapsed between requesting support from services and receiving help. Generally, it appeared that this was due to poor liaison between services, or having to fight for the support they needed. In several cases, support had either been promised and had not been forthcoming, or had been given and was then withdrawn. There were other instances where the support offered had been inappropriate for religious or cultural reasons.

> They offered me a lifeline and then they took it away. It is hard because when he was at school I had some respite, but now he is 17 he is with me all the time.

Evidence from the 2001 Census suggests that young disabled adults from South Asian families are more than 50 per cent more likely to be cared for in residential settings compared with their White counterparts. The numbers of life-limited young people from South Asian families, cared for permanently outside their home, is not known. However, experience from Acorns reveals huge anxiety encountered by families concerning transition from paediatric palliative care services to adult palliative care. The Government Select Committee Inquiry Report, recommendations into Palliative Care (United Kingdom Parliament, 21 July 2004), calls for an increase in palliative care services for young adults.

Other than respite provided by school, none of the parents were able to enjoy a break apart from Acorns. At the time of writing, an evaluation is under way to determine the effectiveness of support offered to parents at the hospice. The families who took part in the Asian Mothers Project will have an opportunity to respond to a written questionnaire, or to answer questions through the help of an interpreter. Responses will yield data concerning satisfaction about the Community Team Worker support, same-sex carers, diet, culturally appropriate environment, availability of interpreting services and the quality of the experience offered through the Asian Mothers' Group.

Practical support in the home

Mothers were unanimous in expressing a wish for help with household chores, so that they could spend quality time with their life-limited child. Several suffered poor physical health themselves and would like help lifting their child, or carrying out personal care tasks in their own home, such as bathing and feeding, or toileting and dressing.

> It would be really nice if just once in a while someone could do things for him, so I don't have to feel the strain on my back and shoulders.

> After school finishes, it seems like that really will be the end of everything. Then we just wait for the time for him to die.

Education

All of the mothers with children of school age (nine in total) were able to take advantage of education. Six of these children attended special schools, one was in mainstream middle school, and two in further education. Overall, parents were very pleased with the education services their child received, feeling that the curriculum offered was appropriate to their child's cognitive development. School provided parents with valuable opportunities for respite during term-time. The exception was a family where a daughter had been assessed and accepted for a place in a further education college, but had arrived to find that the college was not staffed, or equipped, to meet her physical and intellectual needs. Understandably, this had caused huge distress to the family and to the young lady concerned.

Generally, parents felt their child's cultural and religious needs were well met by schools and they were delighted to find that care assistants were often the same gender as their child.

In all families, the statementing of Special Educational Needs had been explained well and parents had been able to have an interpreter present to explain how the school would meet their child's needs. Interpreter services had also been provided at the young person's transition interviews at 14 and 16 years. In some instances, the child's assessment of Special Educational Needs had triggered support from other services, such as physiotherapy.

Of the nine mothers interviewed with a school-age child, all felt that their child enjoyed education, and there were comments such as: 'It helps to make life more normal' and, 'A beautiful school – such lovely teachers – such a good time for my son.'

Mothers' health problems

Having a child with a life-limiting illness disrupts everyday life. Often parents become overwhelmed with their grief, and exhausted through trying to care for their other well children. Understandably, caring for a life-limited child in such circumstances takes its physical and mental toll on carers, and there is a trend for higher-frequency visits to doctors and hospitals for mothers' own personal needs (Hatton *et al.* 2004).

Mothers reported that they suffered a high rate of health-related problems. Whilst most of the interviewees talked in depth about physical problems, such as tiredness, backache, headache (from lifting their child) and stomach problems, they also referred to 'being exhausted, worried, depressed and feeling constantly anxious'. One mother said that the only factor that had sustained her during her life-limited child's 13-year illness was 'keeping hope in my heart'.

Generally, the coping strategies employed by mothers changed at different stages of their child's illness. At the time around diagnosis they had hoped (and in some cases prayed) that the child's condition could be cured. This was particularly evident when the child had a congenital degenerative illness. During phases of very poor health, mothers had relied on their family and friends for emotional support, and all the mothers interviewed cited their children's hospice Community Team Worker as a source of practical and psychological support. Where a child was nearly always very poorly, mothers still gained hope through celebrating any achievements that their child had accomplished.

> When he is still laughing, or he sleeps without pain, then I feel it has been a good day.

The outcomes of previous research have highlighted the stress experienced in families caring for a life-limited child. Brown (1999, 2001) Chamba *et al.* (1999) and Hatton *et al.* (2004) suggest that families from ethnic minority communities caring for a disabled child may experience greater restrictions than White families.

Seven of the mothers interviewed said they were unable to leave their child unattended, unless the child was asleep. Providing such a high level of care impacted greatly on the relationship they had with their partner. Where the family was headed by a lone parent, they suffered extreme poor health.

Outings and social occasions were rarely enjoyed, and only one of the families had been able to take a holiday during the last three years. Two mothers reported that they would like to visit relatives abroad, but that they were unable to do this, because of the cost. Even if financial support was forth-coming, they didn't feel able to leave their child in respite care at the hospice for long enough to warrant making a journey overseas.

> I haven't seen my mother since my wedding 17 years ago. I can't go to see her even though she is getting old, because there is nobody to take care of my children.

In addition to having a restricted social life themselves, mothers said that they felt that their life-limited child had few opportunities to interact with well children. In families where there were well siblings, the life-limited child was almost totally reliant on them for opportunities to play outside school.

The outcomes of the research at Acorns have resulted in the Trust review-ing policy and practice when caring for Asian families. Staff have increased their knowledge, understanding and sensitivity concerning religious and cul-tural aspects of care. There has also been a heightened awareness of the impact of having a life-limited child on ethnic minority families. Many of the mothers have been helped to identify strengths that have been previously un-noticed by themselves or their families. Staff have encouraged them to develop a posi-tive sense of their own identity, and strategies for managing the stress that they feel. They have been helped by the Asian Liaison Officer to learn how to com-municate their own needs effectively, within and outside their family unit. Some mothers have encouraged other family members to be involved in caring for their sick child. In the end-of-life stages of their child's care, mothers know the options available to them, for example having a place set aside for worship or meditation, or appropriate facilities to wash their child after they have died.

Secular beliefs

For many people, a secular point of view (that is one that does not accept the existence of god(s) or the notion of an afterlife) makes the most sense. This stance can include views about ethical and moral issues and is driven by a view that human life is time-limited, with no 'other world' to go to, or any notion of re-birth. Earthly life is the only existence – it is not a prelude to another existence or the consequence of a previous one. The British Association of Humanists is a well-established organisation that holds this view. There are also other individuals who might describe themselves as 'humanists', without necessarily belonging to a formal group.

Atheists believe that there is no god. Conversely, 'agnostics' are open to the possibility that a god or gods may exist, and that there may be an afterlife, but that there is no proof of either. Within these broad definitions, individuals hold a variety of views. Beliefs, or ways of life that are outside the church, or other organised religious bodies, are described as secular, a word that means 'non-religious'. Most people who live a secular life do so by choice. Their lives are not defined by an absence of, or lack of, god or faith, but an affirmation of all that is to be valued in human existence and potential.

Parents who do not hold a religious faith may be left with several dilemmas when they have to face the death of their child. First, the child's body has to be disposed of in a way that is acceptable, according to the law and the regulations of the country in which the child's death has occurred. For parents with a religious faith, this usually happens with the ritual and ceremony of a funeral, appropriate to the religious and cultural stance of the family. For example, a Christian funeral service takes place at the crematorium, at a church, and parts of a Muslim funeral take place at the family home, the mosque or the burial place. Parents with no religious convictions may fall back on a religious funeral because they are not aware that there are alternatives. Second, families will need to find meaning and solace in the death of their child. Third, this is a time when the family will need support and comfort.

Non-religious funerals

A funeral plays an important part in helping families to cope with the death of their child. Most cultures and communities have ways of marking major life events with rituals and ceremonies. These major changes are sometimes referred to as 'rites of passage'. The society and culture in which these rites of passage take place will largely determine the content and format of the proceedings. There will be some variations based on the personal preferences of the people involved. Emotionally and psychologically, funerals also provide an opportunity to say 'goodbye' and to accept the reality of the death. The family will have to 'let go' of the physical presence of their child – a huge and significant step in accepting the reality of the death. For people with religious faith, this leave-taking may be associated with notions of their child 'being with God' in another spiritual existence. To some extent, sadness may be mitigated by the belief that eventually, after their own death, they will be reunited with their child or that the child moves to a new life through re-birth. Families who choose a secular lifestyle may hold a different perception around the physical facts of death, for example the child's physical body returning to the earth, becoming one with the natural phenomena. The ceremony itself *can* incorporate a family's beliefs, wishes and feelings, if those people who are supporting the family encourage them to make their own choices.

The experience of becoming a parent is life-changing, and the effect of having a child (even if he or she lives a very short time) is profound, and unlikely to ever be forgotten. When a child dies, parents will want to celebrate their child's life, acknowledging all they brought to the family and to the community beyond immediate family or friends. A secular approach to death provides an opportunity to look back on the child's life as they have lived it, rather than focusing on a continued existence in a different form, after earthly life is over. It is important to respect and value the impact of the child's life on those who have loved and cared for the child. One of the ways the events in each person's life are given dignity and meaning is by linking them to something greater or universal. Each child is a part of their family, the local community and the wider community.

Carefully chosen words, songs, readings and even hymns may add to the sense of occasion and dignity, honouring the child's life and marking its significance. They also provide a means of expression at a time when people find it difficult to articulate their feelings in a way that they feel is appropriate to the situation. Symbols play a part in all the major world religions, and they also have their counterparts in the secular world. Flowers are often part of the funeral and they are as appropriate in a secular context as well as a religious one. Candles can be used as a symbol for the flame of the child's life (and the extinguishing of it). They also provide a soft and gentle light, more conducive to quiet reflection and contemplation.

Placing treasured possessions or useful items such as tools or food in the coffin or grave with a dead person has been a custom associated with ancient civilisations dating back to pre-historic times. Perhaps the modern equivalent of putting something of special significance to the child in the coffin or grave, such as a favourite toy, is the last expression of kindness and love that parents can offer their child. (See Chapter 7, 'The Child's Funeral'.)

Spiritual aspects of parental grief

Throughout life people encounter times, or perhaps enjoy relationships, that have a powerful impact on them, and these experiences make their mark in the future. Some people might describe such experiences as 'sacred' – others that their lives were 'touched' by an inexplicable event or encounter. Because the death of a child affects parents so deeply, some parents describe the emotional experience as 'soul pain'. This spiritual pain is not a place of solace and comfort; rather it is a state of existence, as parents grapple with their grief and find new meaning in life.

After their child's death, many parents speak about feeling as if they exist in the world but they are detached from everyday life. Eventually, bereaved parents say that the numbness seems to fade and it is replaced by a deep psychological pain, which they feel throughout their body. Even if the pain retreats, it is likely to surge up again, especially if memories are triggered unexpectedly.

In spite of their anguish, most parents learn to hide the pain that they feel from people who do not seem able to stand alongside them in their loss. Some appear to have a need to find ways of coping that fills the void in their lives.

> The spiritual lives of bereaved parents reach the depths of human suffering and their resolution points to the furthest possibilities of human living. (Klass 1999, p.54)

When parents are asked whether they ever stop grieving, almost universally they say 'no, but the pain doesn't stay the same'. The pain they describe is psychological, physiological and spiritual. Their anguish is often likened to having a limb amputated. Furthermore, parents often say that each of their children has a unique meaning in their family, so that a child who has died can never be replaced.

Against all the odds, bereaved parents usually learn to re-order their lives and continue in a way that is meaningful to them.

> We lost Jennifer, but we have not lost the memory of her – she is still so much a part of our lives – it is as if she is woven into every thread of our family's existence.

One of the sustaining hopes for bereaved parents is that their child's life counted for something to people outside their family. Indeed, hope has been recognised as a valuable human response in relation to life-limiting illnesses. Hendricks-Furguson (2004) conceptualised hope as a belief that there is a positive existence in the future. Urquhart et al. (1999) describe hope as the inner power or strength that can enable individuals to look beyond their turmoil. For bereaved parents, having their pain and new status in life acknowledged is an important part of being able to grow through their grief. Benzein (2001), speaking of hope in the midst of grief, says that, after a child has died, some parents may experience reconciliation and comfort.

Sometimes parents find that setting themselves goals, and feeling enabled to take small steps to achieving these, is helpful. When they feel particularly frightened and isolated and they sense the present and the future as being devoid of hope, they may be vulnerable to depression and anxiety. Professionals who help parents to form positive relationships with them play a substantial role in nurturing hope, and it is often small acts of kindness and being prepared to travel the journey of grief alongside parents that is most helpful. Ongoing support from family and friends can help parents to feel they still have a purpose in life.

Key points

- Although there is an increasing amount of literature available on the psychosocial needs of families with a life-limited child, scant attention has been paid to cultural and religious care.

- The ethnicity and culture of families will affect their experience of death, dying and bereavement.

- Little is currently known about caring for families from different ethnic groups in paediatric palliative care.

- Culture is not static. Cultures change in response to new local, national and international situations.

- All cultures have their own ways of dealing with loss, and there may be differences concerning spiritual beliefs, rituals and etiquette.

- All cultures attribute unique significance to the death of a child. Funeral rites may be very different from those performed when an adult dies.

- All religions teach that their deity or deities have control over the destiny of a person's soul after earthly life is over.

- The influence of religion on people's lives varies greatly.

- Children are influenced by parental attitudes to religion very early during their life and this is likely to influence their thoughts and attitudes later on.

- How people worship varies between communities, denominations and individual worshippers.

- A child's age, cognitive ability, emotional wellbeing and home background will influence their understanding of what happens at the time of death and beyond.

- Children often include religious themes in their ideas about death and dying. They are often curious about death and their questions may reflect this curiosity.

- Parents suffer intense psychological, physiological and spiritual pain when their child dies.

- Spirituality is extremely difficult to define, and spiritual care is often surrounded by misconceptions concerning what it entails.

- Mementos and objects can provide parents with a symbolic link with their child.

- For bereaved parents, having their pain and new status in life acknowledged is an important part of being able to grow through their grief.

Implications for practice

- The need to provide appropriate and accessible care to minority ethnic groups has been recognised as a service development issue.

- Providing families with opportunities to carry out ceremonies and rituals may enable them to express their feelings.

- Professionals' should be aware of the rules, laws and procedures surrounding death and dying in the communities where they work.

- Space should be set aside for families to carry out private worship.

- Children need age and developmentally appropriate opportunities to explore their feelings and concerns.

- Professionals need to be aware of what children have been taught by their families and communities.

- Professionals require skills, information and confidence to find out how they can match care to individual family needs.

- Organisational structures need to be in place to provide families with religious, cultural and spiritual support.

- Professionals' own attitudes and beliefs will affect the way they respond to other people, particularly those whose life-style is different from their own.

- Parents should be helped to identify their own past and present strengths and coping strategies.

- Professionals should endeavour to be accepting and in touch with parents' pain, rather than be overwhelmed by it.

- When parents are helped to form positive relationships with professionals, this can play a part in nurturing hope for the future.

16

Post Mortem, Organ Donation and Tissue Retention

Erica Brown

If a child has been suffering from a life-limiting illness, it is unlikely that a post mortem will be required, although this may happen occasionally. Post mortem rates are falling. However, the paediatric autopsy plays a vital role in understanding more about life-limiting illnesses, especially where a child has died from a genetic illness.

Role of the paediatric pathologist

Paediatric pathologists who perform post mortems are medically qualified doctors, many of whom have had clinical experience of paediatrics or obstetrics. Before training as a paediatric pathologist, they have undertaken extensive training in general and adult pathology. Most paediatric pathologists in the United Kingdom work in large regional centres. As well as autopsies, most paediatric pathologists also investigate surgical specimens from infants and children taken at operations.

Post mortem (autopsy)

There are two types of post mortem: a Coroner's post mortem and a clinical or hospital post mortem. Most post mortems are carried out within 72 hours of death. At the time of death certification the doctor must ask two questions: 'Do I know why this child died?' and 'Am I sure that the death was due to natural causes?' If the answer to either of these questions is 'no', the case must be referred to the Coroner who will usually order a post mortem. Hospital post mortems are requested after the child's death certificate has been signed and the likely cause of death has been recorded. The value of hospital post mortems is repeatedly emphasised in the literature. Leadbetter (1989) suggests that 27.5 per cent of adult death certificates state an inaccurate cause of death. Statistics for the record of cause of paediatric deaths are not known and the Allitt Inquiry (DoH 1994) highlighted the need for more rigorous policy and practice.

Quality standards in post mortem

In 2002, the Royal College of Pathologists, Paediatrics and Child Health Obstetricians, Gynaecologists and Pathologists produced professional guidelines on autopsy practice to consolidate, update and expand previous guidance. The guidelines recommend that post mortem examinations should be done according to these guidelines.

Coroner's post mortem examination

A Coroner's post mortem examination is carried out according to the provisions of the Coroners Act 1988 and the Coroners Rules 1984 in order to determine the cause of a child's death. Although the family's consent is not required, the reasons for the post mortem and the procedures to be followed have to be explained sensitively to the family. They should be given information about when and where the examination is to be performed and told of their right to be represented at the post mortem by a medical practitioner. A Coroner's Officer, or Police Officer, will usually make contact with the family. The Allitt Inquiry (DoH 1994) recommended that professionals request a post mortem examination of any child who dies unexpectedly. It also raised concern as to whether the system was being used correctly. A paediatric Coroner's post mortem is rarely requested for children who die in a hospice, as the cause of death is usually known.

After the post mortem, a copy of a Coroner's post mortem report has to be made available to the family – a fee will be charged for this. Unless the Coroner has reason to do otherwise, a copy of the post mortem report should also be sent to the family's GP, and the family may wish to discuss the findings. In rare cases, an inquest may also be necessary following a Coroner's post mortem. The reason for an inquest, and its procedure, should be fully and sensitively explained to the family in these cases.

Types of post mortem and consent

Post mortem examinations may be full or limited. A full post mortem examination involves opening all body cavities and examining all the organs. A limited post mortem examination may be limited to a single organ, for example the heart only, if it is suspected that there may be congenital cardiac malformation. A limited autopsy may also be restricted to an external examination only, supplemented by skin biopsy and X-rays as required. Generally, a limited autopsy will never give as much information as a full autopsy, but it may still be useful. Full written parental consent is still required for external examination.

When obtaining consent, it is vital that the parents have sufficient information to enable them to come to a decision about the post mortem. The parents have the right to refuse a clinical or hospital post mortem examination. In this case, refusal of the consent should be clearly documented in the mother's and the child's medical record. However, the parents also have the right to ask for a post mortem examination of their child. They also have the right to modify or withdraw their consent to post mortem examination before the post mortem takes place, even after they have already given their signed consent.

A post mortem is an important investigation and the parents should be aware of the information it will provide about their child's life and death. They should be given appropriate information in a sensitive manner to enable them to make the choices that best suit them. This should include:

- explaining the post mortem procedure
- how the post mortem will be performed, for example the incisions to be made, tissue samples taken, etc.
- the benefits and limitations of post mortem examinations
- the expected time before the issue of the report and feedback to the parents.

Obtaining consent

Consent for post mortem examination must be obtained before any procedure can take place. The only exceptions to this are in cases where the autopsy has been ordered by Her Majesty's Coroner, for example deaths in the community. By obtaining consent, the parents will be fully aware of the investigations that will be carried out. Obtaining consent is a procedure that requires good communication skills, sensitivity and empathy. Parents will be given a copy of their signed consent.

The Code of Practice 2002

The Code sets out recommended practice for all those involved in communicating with families, whether the post mortem examination is a hospital post mortem, or ordered by the Coroner. The Code seeks to ensure that the child's next-of-kin are given the opportunity to understand the reasons for the post mortem, the processes involved and their rights in the decision-making. In the case of a competent young person or young adult, any wishes that they may have expressed before they died must be respected. Where a competent child or young adult has made an advance decision for his or her body to be used for anatomical examination, this must be in writing and witnessed.

Organs and tissues may not be retained following post mortem without parental consent or the Coroner's authorisation. Any retained tissue or organs must be disposed of in accordance with the express wishes of the parents, subject to meeting legal and health and safety requirements. If a child dies and there is no one with parental responsibility, someone in a 'qualifying relationship' (as defined by the Human Tissue Act 2004) may give consent.

Discussing the post mortem with the family

The family needs to be offered full and clear information about the purpose of the post mortem examination, the procedures and the range of choices available to them. They need time to consider this. If possible, the family should have the option of changing their minds within an agreed time limit and they should be given the name and telephone number of someone with whom they can talk. Some parents will wish to know considerable detail about what will be done with their child's body. In these cases, the procedures should be sensitively, but honestly, and fully, explained. Details of post mortem examination procedures are included later in the chapter.

Parents who ask for information about a post mortem should be told:

- What happens in the examination (including the removal, retention and use of tissue samples for diagnosis).

- The benefits of post mortem examination. Why the doctor thinks it would be valuable. The reasons for the Coroner's involvement (if applicable).

- Where, when and, if possible, by whom the post mortem will be performed. Parents need to know where their child will be, for how long, and when they can see their child's body again.

- Information about any tests to be included in the post mortem.

- When, to whom and how the results of the post mortem will be made available and explained.

- Options for what will happen to the child's body or remains, and any organs or tissues removed (including tissue blocks and slides), after the examination.

- Whether consent is to be sought for retention or use of tissues or organs after the post mortem, and for what purposes.

- The possibility of images to be made (including photographs, slides, X-rays and CT scans). In accordance with General Medical

Council Guidance, specific consent is not needed for the taking of photographs of organs or body parts, or of pathology slides. Nor is specific consent needed to use them for any purpose provided that, before use, the images are effectively anonymised by the removal of any identifying marks.

- Whether organs or tissues can be retained, without limit of time, for medical research, and whether there are particular uses which the family would wish to exclude from any general consent given.

- If any tissue or organs have been removed, when they can be reunited with the body, if the family so wish. (This will need to be done in consultation with the pathologist and, in the case of the Coroner's post mortem, with the Coroner.) N.B. This will have implications for funeral arrangements.

In some faiths and cultures, it is important that a funeral should take place as soon as possible after death. Attitudes to post mortem examination, burial, cremation and the use of organs and tissues after death differ greatly.

Parents can only consent to a post mortem examination if proper communication has taken place. Consent forms should be available in all the main local community languages and staff should establish whether or not families can read them. Use should be made, wherever possible, of a professional interpreter who is trained in interpreting for people who are bereaved. The interpreter must be able to understand and subscribe to issues of clinical confidentiality (NHS 2003b). N.B. Children should never be used as interpreters in relation to post mortems.

Post mortem protocol

When informed consent is obtained, the child's body is transferred to the mortuary with the appropriate paperwork. The pathologist must see the signed consent form before the post mortem can take place. Verbal consent is not sufficient. The post mortem is usually performed either on the day the child's body arrives in the department, or the day after. The pathologist and the mortuary technical officer confirm the identity of the child's body, check the paperwork and consent form and organise photography and X-rays. Before the post mortem, skin samples may be taken. The child's body is carefully weighed and measured and the condition of the skin is noted.

The incision used is large so that the pathologist is able to see the internal organs in position in the body before they are removed. The incision is normally a Y-shape from shoulder to shoulder, meeting in the centre of the chest at the mid-point of the sternum, then extending down to the pubic bone. Parents should always be aware of the extent of the incision. Describing it as a 'small scar' or 'small hole' is inaccurate and misleading, and may cause considerable distress if the child's body is seen after the post mortem.

The child's face is always untouched. The limbs generally remain untouched. The only exception to this case is if there are skeletal problems, in which case it may be that a limb dissection is required. In this case, reconstruction is always undertaken although, obviously, there will be a row of sutures on the limb. The brain is removed by means of an incision in the skull that extends from ear to ear around the back of the head.

Some pathologists prefer to dissect the organs *in situ*; others will remove all the organs and dissect them once removed from the body cavities. The organs are examined in a systematic way. After examination, sections of tissue from each organ are selected for examination. If necessary, and if appropriate consent is given, certain organs may be retained for more detailed examination. This usually means the brain and, occasionally, the heart.

The remainder of the tissue is returned to the child's body, although the organs cannot be returned to their normal positions within body cavities. All tissue is normally placed within a plastic bag (to prevent leakage) and returned to the body cavity.

After the post mortem examination has taken place, the mortuary technician will reconstruct the body and wash the child for redressing. The body can then be released to the funeral director, unless there is consent for the temporary retention of organs, in which case the body will stay in the mortuary until these more detailed examinations have taken place.

There is no reason why parents should not see their child's body after a post mortem. When the child's body is dressed, the marks of the post mortem should be almost completely hidden.

Post mortem imaging

Photographic imaging is an essential part of the post mortem examination. This should not be confused, however, with taking pictures of the child for parents to keep. The photographs taken by the pathologist are clinical images. They are part of the diagnostic process and are used if the pathologist needs to consult with various specialists, such as geneticists. The Department of Health Consent Form (2002) requires separate consent from parents for post mortem imaging. Parents should be told that the images are taken for clinical use and that they will be retained as part of the mother's permanent medical record. Sometimes an X-ray will also provide supporting evidence as to why a child died. It is likely that MRI scans and needle biopsies will also be used in the future.

If a baby dies in the community, a post mortem may not be carried out until X-rays have been taken and the report has been reviewed by a paediatric radiologist. All images are stored securely. They are not used for medical, educational or research purposes, unless there is specific consent. In some departments, X-rays may be destroyed after a certain time because of storage space issues. The written report must be retained.

Tissue samples

Small samples of tissue are taken from each organ. These are sent to the laboratory for microscopic examination. It is essential that parental consent be obtained for this. The standard Department of Health Consent Form emphasises that tissue sections embedded in paraffin wax are retained as part of the family's medical record. Where consent has been given, the tissue may be used in medical research.

The tissue samples usually measure around $10 \times 10 \times 4$ mm. They are often described to parents as being the size of a thumbnail. The samples are placed in small plastic cassettes, fixed in formalin and then dehydrated and processed into paraffin wax, known as tissue blocks. Very thin slices of wax containing a slice of the tissue are cut from the block. These slices are about one-tenth of the thickness of a human hair. The slice of tissue is placed onto a microscopic slide and then stained with special dye to help differentiate the cells. In the wake of recent organ retention problems, many parents have been asking for the return of tissue blocks for burial. This is an option that is increasingly being made available to parents.

The Department of Health Code of Practice (2003) makes it clear that consent for the retention and use of tissues and organs after a post mortem must be separate from consent for the post mortem. N.B. Where a Coroner's post mortem is carried out, different regulations apply.

The Human Tissue Act 2004 (implemented 1 September 2006)

The Human Tissue Act 1961 stated that the hospital doctor responsible for the child could authorise removal of any organ or tissue, or part of the body, for the purposes of education and research. In many cases, this happened without parents being informed. However, the Alder Hey and Bristol Hospital Inquiries (1999–2000) raised concerns about the retention of children's organs and tissues. In 2001, the Chief Medical Officer for England recommended that there should be a fundamental and broad revision of the law in regard to human organs and tissues taken from adults or children, either during surgery or after death.

The Human Tissue Act (2004) received Royal Assent on 15 November 2004 and the Amendment Bill was introduced in the House of Commons on

12 January 2005. The Human Tissue Act (2004), which became law on 1 September 2006, replaces the Human Tissue Act (1961), the Anatomy Act (1984) and the Human Organ Transplant Act (1989), as they relate to England and Wales. It also repeals and replaces the Human Tissue Act (Northern Ireland) (1962 Order), the Human Organ Transplant (Northern Ireland) (1989 Order), and The Anatomy Act (Northern Ireland) (1992 Order). The Act is likely to have far reaching consequences for policy and practice regarding tissue removal and retention.

The purpose of the Act is to provide a consistent legislative framework for issues relating to whole body donation and the taking, storage and use of human organs and tissue.

Organ retention

Organ retention must be discussed with parents. There are several options available should organ retention be considered.

- The parents may decide not to permit any organ retention.
- The organ can be retained as long as it is returned to the body prior to the funeral.
- The organ can be retained but must be returned to the parents at a later date.
- The organ can be retained and disposed of after examination in a respectful manner by the pathology laboratory.
- The organ may be donated to the Pathology Department for use in medical education and research.

Each of these options should be carefully discussed with parents. If the organ is to be returned to the body, the funeral may need to be delayed since, in some cases, organs need to be preserved with chemicals before samples can be taken.

Organ donation

Sometimes a child's organs can be donated after their death and some parents may derive comfort knowing that their child's body may help others. The Department of Health Code of Practice concerning the removal, retention and use of human organs and tissues was published in 2001. The Code is part of a wider series of documents about consent in the National Health Service as described in the Health Service Circular 'Good Practice in Consent' (NHS 2002/2003).

If families have given consent for the retention and use of tissues and organs, they should be asked if they wish to receive information about how they will be used. Any restrictions imposed on the use of tissue, and wishes for its eventual disposal, should already have been clearly documented as part of the process for obtaining consent.

Parents must sign a form in the presence of a witness, stating their wishes regarding any tissue or organ removal and retention.

Maintaining proper documentation

Whether or not parents wish to receive information about the use of donated tissue, proper documentation of all tissues and organs retained must be maintained. The pathologist who undertakes the post mortem examination is responsible for ensuring that this happens. The record should include:

- details of parental consent
- which tissue or organs may be used, whether tissue may be used for medical, educational or research purposes following diagnostic use, and how the tissue is to be disposed of
- details of all tissue removed, and what is done to the tissues
- if relevant, when, where and to whom the tissue was transferred
- if relevant, when, and how, disposal is undertaken. Where the tissue is used for research, a record must include the date when, the place where and by whom ethical approval was granted.

Disposal of tissue and organs

Tissue and organs should be handled respectfully at all times, in accordance with the wishes of the child's family. The method of disposal must be legal. Where the family have given their consent to the retention of tissues or organs, they should be offered the option of allowing the hospital to dispose of any parts not required. Families may wish the hospital to arrange for collection of tissue or an organ (usually by a funeral director of their choice), so that they can make their own funeral arrangements for cremation or burial. Alternatively, the hospital may offer to retain the child's body in storage until the organ can be returned to it. Second funerals have significant emotional and financial implications for families and so, whilst the choice is theirs, the implications must be discussed with them.

If the child's body has already been buried or cremated and the family request that remaining tissue or organs are to be returned later, these must be released:

- to the funeral director of the family's choice
- with authoritative confirmation of the identity of the tissue or organ

- with confirmation that the cremation or burial authorities have agreed in principle to accept the remains for disposal.

N.B. There is no legal bar to releasing tissue parts directly to a family, but the method of disposal must be lawful and safe, and it may be difficult to ascertain this. The pathologist should notify the family and obtain confirmation that they are able to handle the tissue appropriately. Releasing organs and tissues directly to families for their indefinite retention is not generally advisable because of health hazards.

The post mortem report

Before any post mortem is carried out, the family should be informed as to when the results are likely to be available. For a hospital post mortem, parents should be given an appointment time that will allow them to discuss the results with the doctor responsible for the care of their child. They should also be told who performed the post mortem. Families will usually be anxious to receive results of the post mortem as soon as possible. Others will not want to know the results, or will not wish to discuss them in detail. Their views must be respected. However, an opportunity to discuss things later should remain open to them, and they should be told this.

In the case of a Coroner's post mortem (with the permission of the Coroner), a copy of a full pathologist's report should be offered to parents. They should be prepared for what the report may include. A copy of the report should also be sent to the family's GP.

After the post mortem, the pathologist will produce a preliminary report based on naked eye findings. The pathologist may give a verbal report immediately, and a written provisional summary is usually available within one or two days. This provisional report may be useful in answering some of the parents' questions about their child. However, the cause of death may not be apparent at this stage, and parents should be made aware that a further report will be available in due course, which will be more detailed.

Collating the results of the post mortem investigation may take several weeks. When the pathologist has examined all relevant tissue, a final report can be produced. The pathologist will attempt to provide a cause of the child's death, or a diagnosis of the condition affecting the child. However, it is advisable to warn parents that, in some cases, a cause of death may not be found.

A post mortem report is a confidential medical document and, as such, cannot be released to a third party without the consent of the parents. It is, however, sent to the consultant who has responsibility for the care of the child's mother and the child's GP.

204 / Supporting the Child and the Family in Paediatric Palliative Care

In the event of sudden death in the community, the report is released to Her Majesty's Coroner. This will help to decide whether an inquest is necessary, or whether a death certificate can be issued. The Coroner will release copies of the report to certain persons, but only on written request. The post mortem report is a medical document and parents may find the terminology difficult to understand. However, families should always be given the opportunity to have a copy of the report, and a time should be made when they can go through it and have their questions answered. Some pathologists will provide a 'lay person's' interpretation of the report.

A post mortem should never be interpreted as an unnecessary or hurried event, carried out without a specific purpose. Professionals have a duty to explain that autopsy is available to all parents. When time is taken to explain the procedure, and all aspects of consent are rigorously sought and recorded, families may find that the information the post mortem provides answers some of their questions and enables them to know why their child died.

Key points

- If a child has been suffering from a life-limiting illness, it is unlikely that a post mortem will be required.

- Where a child has died suddenly, or from a genetic illness, the post mortem can play a vital role in understanding life-limiting illness.

- The Allite Inquiry (DoH 1994), recommended that professionals request a post mortem examination of any child that dies unexpectedly.

- All paediatric post mortems must be undertaken according to professional guidelines set by the Royal College of Pathologists, Paediatricians and Child Health Obstetricians (2002).

- The Human Tissue Act became law on 1 September 2006.

- There are two types of post mortem: a Coroner's post mortem and a clinical or hospital post mortem. In rare cases, an inquest may be required after a Coroner's post mortem.

- Post mortems may be full or limited. A full post mortem involves opening all body cavities and examining all organs. A limited post mortem may be confined to a single organ, e.g. the heart, or it may comprise an external examination of the body only, perhaps supplemented by skin biopsies, X-rays or photographic imaging as required. The child's face always remains untouched.

- Parents have the right to request a hospital post mortem.

- Organs and tissues may not be retained following post mortem without parental consent, or the Coroner's authorisation. This consent is additional to parental consent for a post mortem.

- Parents may specify any restrictions imposed on the use of tissue and their wishes for the eventual disposal of tissue should be documented.

- Attitudes to post mortem, burial, cremation and the use of organs/tissue after death vary greatly.

Implications for practice

- Consent must be obtained from parents *before* any procedures can take place.

- It is advisable to warn parents before a post mortem that, in some cases, the cause of death may not be found.

- Although a family's consent is not required for a Coroner's post mortem, the procedures to be followed should be sensitively explained to the child's family.

- Parents should always be given appropriate information about the post mortem, including explaining the post mortem procedure (e.g. incisions and any tissue samples that will be taken; the benefits and limitations of post mortem examination; details of the expected time between the procedure and issue of the report).

- Consent forms should be available in all main community languages and staff should check that parents understand the content. Professional interpreters should be used whenever possible. Children should never be used as interpreters in relation to post mortem.

- Any wishes expressed by a young person before their death concerning post mortem or organ/tissue retention or donation should be respected.

- Organ retention must be discussed with parents and separate consent must be obtained before any organs are removed and retained.

- There is no reason why parents should not see their child's body after the post mortem.

- For a hospital post mortem, parents should be given an appointment time to discuss the results with the doctor responsible for the care of their child. For a Coroner's post mortem, a copy of the pathologist's report should be made available to parents as long as the Coroner agrees. A copy must be sent to the child's GP.

- The results of the post mortem must not be released to a third party (other than the child's GP and the consultant responsible for the child's mother) without permission from the parents.

17

The Education
of the Life-limited Child

Erica Brown

It is estimated that more than 100,000 children lose 10 million hours of education annually because they have interrupted schooling through ill-health (NAESC 1998).

Most studies of children with life-limiting conditions are clinically, psychologically or sociologically focused. Few address educational dimensions, yet education is the largest common ground for the general child population. Baum (1998) said:

> To school-age children, the daily routine of attending school and receiving an education is a basic right. For children with life-threatening illnesses, schooling is a manifestation of normality in a life otherwise largely caught up with an agenda of illness; symbolically it offers a ray of optimism – where there is school, there is life, and hope, so to speak.

The Government's commitment of excellence to education for all children (DfEE 1998) applies equally to life-limited children. However, in spite of sterling efforts by many teachers, the quality of education for sick children remains patchy and inconsistent.

Eiser (1999) recognises that life is never the same for young people and their families after a diagnosis of life-limiting illness. She does, however, point out that 'normality' is an aspiration that should be encouraged. Education has an important part to play.

Education is a statutory duty and a right for all children and young people (DfEE 1997; DfES 2001; UNESCO 1991). Section 19 of the Education Act 1996 extended the right of education to include children's hospices.

A working party on behalf of the Royal College of Paediatrics and Child Health (1997) reported that parents with a child diagnosed with a life-limiting illness needed:

- early identification of their child's special educational needs
- opportunities to choose educational resources to support their child
- coordinated provision from all the educational services supporting their child.

In spite of this, research by Closs and Norris (1997) highlighted the fact that many life-limited children, and those with chronic medical conditions, were unable to access the kind of support that would benefit their education. Professionals and policy makers have a key role in supporting the welfare and continuity of education for children with life-limiting illnesses.

The past two decades have seen major developments and expectations in terms of the education of children with a range of disabilities. The term 'Special Educational Needs' was introduced in the 1981 Education Act, when it replaced the previous list of disabilities used since the 1944 Education Act. The 1981 Act said:

> A child has a special educational need if she or he has a learning difficulty which calls for special educational needs provision to be made. A child has a learning difficulty if he or she has a significantly greater difficulty in learning than the majority of children of the same age, or has a disability which prevents or hinders the child from making use of educational facilities of the kind provided for children of the same age in schools within the area of the Local Education Authority (LEA).

The concept of education is very wide. It may include all aspects of bringing up children, wherever this takes place; or, it may refer to specific processes that occur in certain contexts and for which criteria have to be met to justify the term 'education'. Terms such as 'the maximum development of abilities and skills of which the child is capable', or phrases such as 'complete social, physical and emotional development', abound. They are terms applicable to *all* children regardless of their abilities or limitations and might apply to all ages and stages of development, emphasising that education is appropriate and justifiable for all children.

The Code of Practice 2001

A revised Code of Practice on the Identification and Assessment of Pupils with Special Educational Needs (DfES) was introduced in September 2001. This replaced the Code of Practice which was introduced in 1994. The revised

Code gives practical guidance to LEAs and school governors on their duties as laid down in the Education Act 1996. The guidance is intended to enable children with special educational needs to be fully included in all aspects of school life and learning. Although not statutory, schools must have *regard* to the Code.

The Code and the National Association for the Education of Sick Children Report (1996) makes it clear that medical conditions can produce educational needs and it provides a broad framework for schools to record and to meet pupils' individual learning needs. Where pupils are not able to attend school, the Code of Practice provides guidance on liaison with 'out of school' education services.

When a child has a Statement of Special Educational Needs on grounds of disability and becomes sick in hospital, teachers and home tutors must have regard to the additional needs of the child as set down in their Statement of Special Educational Needs.

Statement of Special Educational Needs

A Statement is a record of the child's needs which sets out the targets to aim at in the immediate future. It also sets out the extra provisions which the Local Authority suggests as appropriate for the child. This may include specialist teaching, specific programmes to meet individual therapeutic needs, or specific teaching and learning strategies which teachers could employ with the child.

During the assessment, advice is gathered from various sources and copies of this are attached to the child's Statement. Advice will be sought from the parents, the school, the Educational Psychologist and the Health Service and maybe from other professionals such as the Community Paediatricians. The Statement is reviewed each year by the school, which will advise the Local Authority if any significant changes need to be made. Parents are always invited to attend an annual review meeting and their views are noted.

It is worth noting that not all children with a life-limited illness will have a Statement of Special Educational Needs, particularly if the onset of the illness has been quite rapid. Furthermore, some parents and young people may choose not to have a Statement as part of their desire to keep things as 'normal' as possible.

Consultation between the child's parents, the school, the school nurse, the school doctor or the family GP, the Community Paediatrician and any specialist services should ensure that the child is not excluded from any part of the school curriculum or school activity, unless this would be detrimental to the child's health. However, since the Code of Practice is not statutory, there appears to be wide variation of practice.

Children under the age of two with profound and complex needs are entitled to an early assessment by the Local Education Authority, which helps families to access specialist support and home-based services. Where a child attends a nursery school or is at first school, an assessment of the child's needs will be carried out by the Special Educational Needs Coordinator in the school.

The rationale for providing educational opportunities for life-limited children

Bolton's (1997) report provides compelling evidence that education for all sick children is a way of maintaining 'normality', boosting self-esteem and a valuable distraction from pain and the fear of isolation. Children should be enabled to attend school for as long as possible. If a child is too sick to go to school, education should continue through the hospital school, the hospice, or the home tuition service.

For many families and their life-limited children, opportunities for education provide a place for the celebration of personal achievements and social interaction.

> Being interested in other things did seem to help her and it gave her a sense of hope too.

However, including children with life-limiting illness into mainstream education challenges schools and often has significant financial implications in terms of staffing and other resources.

Because life-limited children may receive education in a variety of settings, there is a need for a holistic approach. An effective educational system will support a child of statutory school age throughout their life. This requires excellent management, matched to individual needs.

The impact of illness on children's development

The impact of chronic illness on children's emotional and social development has been described elsewhere in the book. There is little doubt that life-limiting illness may interfere with the attainment of normal educational tasks. Eiser (2000) believes that, for a child with chronic illness, restricted social experiences, hospitalisation and family emotions surrounding an uncertain prognosis may interfere with the attainment of normative goals. However, there are very few conclusive research findings concerning the impact of life-limiting illness on children's academic performance. This is particularly so in the case of the growing number of children with profound and complex learning difficulties, in addition to life-limiting illness.

Access to a broad and balanced curriculum

The principle of differentiation in the curriculum should allow children to work to their own potential. However, tests and exams may be problematical for those children who are sufficiently cognitively able to be assessed. Failing to meet the grade can be a disappointing experience and result in stress, which undermines school as an essential part of a child's growth and development.

Ensuring that all children, including those with life-limiting illnesses, have access to a broad and balanced curriculum relevant to their individual needs is an ongoing challenge. It requires regular review of curriculum content, teaching approaches, accommodation, management, resources and staffing. The introduction of the National Curriculum which resulted from the introduction of the Education Reform Act (1988) was the catalyst that helped schools to significantly broaden a curriculum that had become increasingly narrow in special schools. Arguably, there has been an over-emphasis on the development of children's communication and independence. In the document *Meeting Special Education Needs – A Programme for Action* (DfEE 1998) a framework for special education provision was set out. In addition, a review of the National Curriculum was instigated which was fully implemented in schools by 2002. Space prevents an in-depth discussion of all the subject areas of the school curriculum and how schools might meet individual pupil needs.

How illness disrupts education

When a school-age child has a life-limiting illness but they are still sufficiently well to attend school, there are potentially a number of ways that education may be disrupted:

- episodes of chronic illness which lead to a 'stop-go' pattern of school attendance
- degenerative conditions where a child may develop cognitive and physical difficulties, and become less academically and physically able, over a period of time
- regular short absences for treatment
- where a child attends school during periods of remission but is absent for important transitional stages of education, for example primary/secondary transfer.

Such disruption can impact on the acquisition of basic skills and the development of subject knowledge, organisational skills, self-motivated learning, group learning skills and developing and maintaining peer friendships.

A child who misses, on average, one day a week at school, misses 20 per cent of their education. However, it is often only in cases of complete absence that a child is offered educational support at home, in hospital or at a children's hospice. After a period of absence, a child may return to school having had little or no contact from teachers. Given the fact that there is evidence to support the idea that anxiety may exacerbate psychosomatic illnesses, and lower a child's resilience to infection, this can result not only in a child falling behind their peer group academically, but also feeling that they have lost their place in the school community.

Because they may have difficulty in integrating socially, there is some evidence to suggest that children may be more likely to be victims of bullying (Brown 2001). A child's successful return to school after a period of absence is likely to depend on factors such as:

- the length of time they were absent
- the impact of previous periods of absence
- the health of the child when they return to school
- the level of educational impact while the child was away from school.

Home tuition

Some children will receive home tuition for a few hours each week either instead of, or in conjunction with, some school attendance. Home teachers have a social, as well as an educational, function and can reduce the child's feelings of isolation when the teaching relationship works well. Families find that home teaching gives children opportunities that would probably not be available to them otherwise. Often children are too ill to go to school, and they have limited opportunities to meet adults outside their family and care network. However, home tuition is always fragmented and, generally, teachers are unable to provide the full range of curriculum subjects. One of the most frequent criticisms from parents is that there is not sufficient time available for their child to benefit fully.

Maintaining educational continuity is a complex task. It will include factors such as protecting and promoting children's learning skills, encouraging good peer relationships, minimising the effects of isolation, promoting equality of opportunity for all children, and facilitating a child's return to school (if appropriate).

Children with profound, multiple and complex learning difficulties

In the majority of children with profound complex learning difficulties, the cause and extent of the disability usually has its origins during the development of the foetus or the newborn baby. Pre-natal causes include genetic and chromosomal abnormalities; infections during pregnancy; and external factors like alcohol or drug abuse. Extreme prematurity may render children as life-limited through restricted lung capacity, lung damage or through ventricular haemorrhage. Perinatal causes include birth trauma, asphyxia, infection and jaundice, any of which may damage the newborn baby and result in cerebral palsy, with or without additional cognitive impairment. Later post-natal causes include infections, such as meningitis and encephalitis, non-accidental injuries and cardiac conditions associated with other medical problems, such as epilepsy. Often children are physically small and under-developed for their age, and some treatments are also associated with changes in body shape and size.

The health of children with life-limiting illnesses may be marked by spells of good health followed by periods of ill health. Others may experience slow progressive deterioration, for example those affected by neuro-degenerative conditions.

Children in hospital

For the majority of life-limited children, their developmental progress will be affected by limited social experience, periods of hospitalisation, the impact of treatment and emotional anguish for what the future holds.

Young hospitalised children will be adversely affected by periods of separation from their parents, at a time when they are also undergoing multiple physical assaults through injections and other powerful medical procedures. Parents may feel totally powerless when they are absent and their child may not have the capacity to understand what is happening. If they are present during treatment and unable to cope with their child's fear and pain, this may also affect the child adversely. Of course, many parents do remain with their child throughout their stays in hospital which, while supporting the sick child, may have detrimental effects on the rest of the family. (See Chapter 11, 'The Impact of Life-limiting Illness on the Family'.)

Community children's nurses can provide a vital link between children in hospital and their school, and direct contact between the child's teacher in school or the school Special Educational Needs Coordinator (SENCO). Indeed the Community Health Team has been identified as particularly useful. School nurses also provide a valuable link with other members of the multi-disciplinary team supporting the child and their family. Connexions Advisers for young people over 13 can also offer valuable assistance (Coles, Britton and Hicks 2004; Lightfoot 2003; Sloper 2001).

Schools keeping in touch with absent pupils

Schools have a central role to play in an integrated educational response to life-limited children. The NAESC Report (1997) spoke about many ill children suffering from 'out of sight, out of mind' reactions. At best, contact with schools was often intermittent and inconsistent.

Schools are required to think through their practice with regard to meeting the needs of children with medical conditions. In mainstream educational settings, having a life-limited child on roll may be rare. Therefore, a planned approach is essential, particularly in secondary schools, where many subject teachers would normally work with a child throughout a school week. All the child's teachers should have information about the child when they are away from school.

Maintaining social contact is important for parents, for example when a school sends cards or telephones. Children are generally described as gaining from contact with their school 'family'.

The role and responsibility of the Special Educational Needs Coordinator

The DfES Revised Code of Practice (2001) sets out the various responsibilities for pupils with special educational needs. The overall responsibility for these pupils lies with the Governors and the Head Teacher, but every teacher has a responsibility for pupils with special educational needs in their classes, and parents, pupils and non-teaching staff have roles to play. The SENCO coordinates the day-to-day policy and practice for special educational needs at school. Individual schools, in partnership with Health Authorities, should devise education plans for children's medical needs. From 2005, every child and young person with a Statement of Special Educational Needs will have a Health Action Plan.

The Code of Practice (2001) defines the role of a named SENCO as having responsibility for:

- the day-to-day operation of the school's special educational needs policy
- liaising with, and advising, teaching colleagues
- coordinating provision for children with special educational needs and medical needs
- maintaining the school's Special Educational Needs Register and overseeing the records on all pupils for special educational needs and medical needs.

- liaising with parents of children with special educational needs and medical needs
- contributing to the in-service training of staff
- liaising with external agencies, including the Educational Psychology Service, Social Services, and other support agencies, including medical services and voluntary bodies.

Research has shown, however, that schools vary considerably as to how long they support a child with life-limiting illness (Nash 1999). Some schools will support children until they die. Others provide little or no support, regarding the needs of those children with life-limiting illnesses as health requirements, and not educational needs, and therefore as the Health Authority's responsibility. Teachers may feel uncertain about their own capacity to support life-limited children, which may further compromise the child's successful integration into mainstream education. In mainstream schools the SENCO may have undergone limited additional training in relation to working with life-limited children, and they may receive very little support themselves in coming to terms with the life-limited child's prognosis.

Meeting a child's physical or mobility needs

One of the greatest barriers to successful integration of ill children into mainstream education is that of access for those who are wheelchair users or dependent on other mobility aids. All Local Authorities should have a rolling programme of adaptations to schools and, by law, all new schools must be wheelchair accessible with appropriate adapted toileting, changing and washing facilities. All schools should have at least one member of staff (usually the SENCO) who has knowledge about special equipment, to enable optimal inclusion of pupils with physical disabilities, and skills for planning the learning environment. This person should also have regularly updated training in basic physiotherapy programmes, including:

- positioning and passive movement to encourage good posture
- limb movement
- moving and handling to safeguard against children and adult injury, for example transfers and toileting.

Communication difficulties

Children may experience receptive, expressive, articulatory and interaction problems. The success of communication will depend on the expertise of staff in augmentative and assisted communication systems. Collaboration between home and school is essential. The environment also plays a crucial part in enabling children's communication.

Research by Hanslik (1990) shows that, long before a baby is able to communicate, adults treat the infant as though he or she is able to understand verbal language and actions, and it is because of this that communication skills develop. However, there is also evidence (Cunningham 1991) that parents find it more difficult to respond to children with disabilities than to non-disabled children.

Children are more likely to experience negative or unsatisfactory interactions in a non-responsive environment. Furthermore, Ware (1996) states that children with profound and complex learning disabilities may vocalise less frequently, having less conventional communication behaviours such as tongue thrusts, eye blinks and changes of position. Some children will demonstrate very little interaction. Therefore, it is essential that those who work with life-limited children who have delayed or very limited cognitive development should:

- respond to any actions the child makes, even if this is slow or in an unexpected way
- have an expectation that a child will respond, for example stimulating the child
- consider the child as a communicator, wherever this is intentional or pre-intentional.

Medication

All Local Authorities and individual schools should have policies for the administration of medicines. Parents should provide written requests for any prescribed medicines their child needs, and there should be a planned medication regime for each child, so that disruption of the child's education is minimised. Administration of medicines may be particularly problematical in mainstream schools and the school nurse will often play a key role in this.

The capacity for the sick child and life-limited children to show resilience should not be underestimated (Barnard, Morland and Nagy 1999) although the physical effects of drugs and treatments may be hard to accept.

> My face has got all puffy and someone laughed at me. It isn't because I eat too much – it is the drugs.

Sensory needs

Staff working with children with sensory disabilities should respond appropriately to how these can impact on children's learning and functioning skills.

Play and relaxation are an important aspect of children's experience, especially when it takes place in groups, keeping individual children in touch with their peers.

Education in children's hospices

Local Authorities have a responsibility to provide education for children of statutory school age while they are staying at a hospice. Because an increasing number of children who receive respite care in children's hospices have Statements of Severe Learning Difficulties or Profound, Multiple and Complex Learning Needs, this section focuses on such children and, in particular, suggests a framework for assessing needs which may already be included in the child's Individual Education Plan at school. The profile is divided into four sections: physical development; perceptual development; intellectual development; and personal and social development. The resulting profile may also form part of a physiotherapy assessment and inform the Nursing Care Plan, as well as providing staff with an overall picture of a child's current developmental level.

Educational aims

1. Physical development

- To enable the child to operate effectively within their immediate surroundings.
- To encourage the physical development of the child.
- To minimise dysfunctional movements, resulting from the child's disabilities.
- To encourage the child's confidence in movement and enjoyment of physical activity.
- To promote the child's perception of movement and postural awareness.
- To increase self-awareness, enabling the child to construct a realistic body image, and sense of personal space.
- To encourage the child's spontaneous movement, and ability to control and shape own movements.
- To encourage the child's mobility, locomotive and manipulative skills.

2. Perceptual development

- To develop the child's perceptual abilities to the fullest possible extent, enabling the child to derive and use the maximum amount of information from their surroundings.
- To encourage the child's awareness of self in relation to their environment.
- To encourage the child to notice and concentrate on sources of stimulation.
- To facilitate the development of the child's sensory awareness.
- To encourage the child to form concepts related to sound, vision, touch, taste, smell and movement.

3. Intellectual development

- To encourage the child to demonstrate intentional and purposeful behaviours.
- To encourage the child to develop and exert some degree of control over their personal experience.
- To develop the child's communication.
- To facilitate the child's understanding of familiar surroundings and situations.
- To encourage the child's ability to make informed choices.

4. Personal and social development

- To encourage the child's awareness of their own personal needs and preferences.
- To encourage the child to achieve the maximum possible personal independence through eating, drinking, washing, grooming, dressing and toileting needs.
- To enable the child to exert some degree of influence and control over their everyday environment.
- To encourage the child's awareness of others and interaction with them.
- To encourage the development of social skills which will enable the child to be an active member of a group, and take part in activities involving sharing, turn taking and cooperation with others.

Section 1 – Physical development

The following are some questions for staff to consider.

General

Voluntary movement

- Is there a medical condition which restricts the movement of the child?
- Is there any physical condition which restricts the child's movements (whether active or passive)?
- Is there any significant disturbance of muscle tone which affects the range of the child's movements?

Range

- Is the full range of movement possible for the child?
- If the range is restricted, to what extent, and for what reason?

Control

- Are the child's early reflexes present, for example startle reflex?
- Are the child's movements involuntary and random, or are they under voluntary control and intentional?
- Are the child's movements goal directed, for example reaching for a toy?
- If the child's movements are goal directed, are they accurate and well-controlled, or laborious and imprecise?
- Do other limbs move unnecessarily when the child makes a movement?
- Is the child able to use limbs in a complementary way, for example holding objects in place with one hand while operating with the other?

Development

- Are the patterns of motor development normal for the child's age, normal but delayed, or abnormal?

Sitting/standing posture

Sitting

- Can the child sit unsupported on a chair?
- Can the child sit unsupported on the floor?
- When sitting, does the child need the support of a special chair?
- When sitting, does the child need support, for example at hips, chest, head, legs, knees, feet?
- When sitting, does the child need safety straps, for example full harness, lap harness, groin harness, chest or foot straps?

Standing

- Can the child support own weight through their legs?
- Can the child stand independently?
- Can the child stand using furniture for support?
- Can the child stand when assisted by another person?
- If the child can stand with assistance, how much support is necessary?
- Does the child use a standing frame for support, for example at hips, chest, knees, or with foot straps?

Mobility and locomotion

Unassisted movement

- Can the child move around?
- Can the child walk normally?
- Can the child use supports in the surroundings, for example furniture, rails to move around?
- Does the child move around by crawling?
- Does the child move around by bottom shuffling?
- Does the child move around by rolling?

Assisted movement

- Does the child walk with a walking aid, for example a frame?

- Does the child walk with adult support?
- If adult support is needed, how is it given?

Range

- How far can the child move independently?
- How far can the child move with assistance?
- Does the child move around actively in the environment?
- Does the child need encouragement or prompting to move around?

Positioning

- Which positions are beneficial for the child's physical development?
- Is any equipment necessary to maintain a good position for the child?
- What type and angle of seating does the child need?
- Which side should the child lie on, and is any support necessary?
- If a wedge is used, what size is used? If using a wedge, how much support is necessary?
- What type of standing frame is needed?
- Which positions encourage or enable the child to explore their surroundings?

Hand use

Awareness

- Is there any position in which the child habitually holds their hands?
- Does the child watch one or both of their hands moving in front of their face?
- Does the child suck thumb or fingers of either hand?
- Does the child touch own body parts with their hands?
- Are any of the above actions self-stimulatory or self-injurious?
- Does the child bring both hands together in the mid-line?

Contact with the surroundings

- Does the child reach towards objects?
- Does the child touch or finger surfaces?
- Does the child hold objects?
- Does the child pass objects from one hand to the other?

Grasp

- Does the child show grasp reflex when an object is placed in their hand?
- Does the child use a flat palmar grasp (fingers flat to palm of hand)?
- Does the child use scissor grip (between side of thumb and index finger)?
- Does the child use pincer grip (tips of thumb and fingers)?
- Does the child open hands voluntarily to grasp objects?
- Does the child open hands voluntarily to release objects?
- Does the child show any preference for using either hand?

Barriers to learning

- Does the child have to rely upon others to carry out actions?
- Is the child unwilling, or reluctant, to carry out movements of which she or he is capable?
- Does the child resist, or withdraw, when being moved?

Section 2 – Perceptual development

The following are some questions for staff to consider.

Awareness and acuity

- Has the child any apparent (or known) hearing defect?
- Has the child any apparent (or known) visual defect?
- Has the child any other sensory problem?
- Does the child respond to touch stimuli?
- Does the child respond to visual stimuli?
- Does the child respond to sound stimuli?
- Does the child respond to smell or taste stimuli?

- Does the child show a startle response as a reaction to change (stimulus) in the immediate surroundings?
- Does the child show excitement in response to change (stimulus) in the immediate surroundings?
- How intense must a stimulus be to produce a response?

Selective attention / discrimination

- Does the child respond more frequently, or consistently, to some stimuli than to others? If so, are these touch, visual, sound, smell, taste?
- Does the child habitually ignore some stimuli, for example touch, visual, sound, smell, taste?
- Does the child habitually respond to new stimuli?
- Does the child habitually respond to familiar stimuli?
- Does the child show preference for or dislike of certain things?

Consistency of response

- Does the child respond consistently, and in the same way, to change, or is the response variable in frequency and type?
- Does the child respond in the same way to all stimuli, or does the response change according to the properties of the stimulus?

Concentration

- Is the child's attention easily distracted by events in the surroundings?
- Can the child concentrate on an activity long enough to achieve a goal?
- Does the child constantly have to be brought back to task?
- Is it difficult to attract the child's attention?

Barriers to learning

- What prevents the child from acquiring information from the surroundings?
- What prevents the child from responding in appropriate ways?

Section 3 – Intellectual development

The following are some questions for staff to consider.

Attention control

- Does the child attend to people, or objects, that are near by?
- Can the child transfer attention from one person or object to another, and back to the first again?

Environmental understanding

- Does the child show any recognition or anticipation of daily routines?
- Does the child show any recognition of specific people, objects, sounds or events?

Exploratory behaviour

- Does the child actively explore objects?
- Does the child actively explore the immediate surroundings?
- Does the child use a range of actions, for example shake, bang, push, pull, drop, finger, when exploring objects?
- Does the child do the same thing with every object, or use different actions with different objects?

Use of objects

- Does the child put things in and out of containers?
- Does the child deliberately use two objects together?
- Does the child use objects purposefully to achieve a result?
- Does the child use objects appropriately?

Early concepts

- Does the child look for objects which have disappeared?
- Does the child expect objects to reappear?
- Does the child expect to find objects in their usual place?
- Does the child associate actions with results (cause and effect)?
- Does the child use objects purposefully to achieve a result?
- Does the child match objects by attributes, for example size, colour, shape?
- Does the child sort collections of objects?

Understanding symbols

- Does the child identify miniature objects with their use?

- Does the child associate realistic pictures and photographs with objects?
- Does the child carry out 'pretend play'?
- Does the child identify line drawings of objects?
- Does the child understand any words?
- Does the child use any words?
- Does the child understand any gestures or signs?
- Does the child use any gestures or signs?
- Does the child use a communication system, for example Rebus, or Makaton symbols?

Barriers to learning

- What is likely to cause the child difficulties in learning skills and understanding experiences?

Section 4 – Personal and social development

The following are some questions for staff to consider.

Activity level

- Does the child engage in any spontaneous activity?
- Is the child passive most of the time?
- Is the child constantly active?
- Do the child's actions seem to be random or intentional?
- Does the child react to changes in his/her surroundings?
- Is the child's activity directed towards objects, people or events in the environment?
- Does the child withdraw from contact with people or objects?
- Is any of the child's activity self-directed? If so, what form does this take?

Motivation

- Does the child need very strong incentives or encouragement to engage in an activity?
- What incentives or rewards, for example food, drink, favourite object, praise, physical contact, are effective with the child?

Independent skills

- How dependent is the child for personal needs?
- Does the child tolerate, cooperate or actively participate in personal self-care?
- How much can the child do unaided in eating and drinking?
- How much can the child do unaided in toileting?
- How much can the child do unaided in dressing?
- How much can the child do unaided in washing?
- Does the child show awareness of own needs, for example hunger, thirst, discomfort, toileting, attention?
- Does the child show any preference for specific people, certain foods or drinks, particular toys or objects, or activities?
- Has the child any means of attracting attention?
- Has the child any means of indicating needs or preferences?
- Is the child able to take responsibility for their own personal needs?

Response

- Does the child cooperate in activities?
- Does the child take an active part in activities?
- Does the child withdraw from activities, or refuse to take part?

Interaction with others

- Does the child show awareness of the presence of other people?
- Does the child accept physical contact?
- Does the child withdraw or resist when approached by others?
- Does the child accept approaches by others passively?
- Does the child show pleasure when approached by others?
- Does the child respond to verbal language directed towards self?
- Does the child respond to verbal language in general?
- Does the child demand attention?
- Does the child show different responses with certain people?
- Does the child engage in turn taking activities or vocalisations?
- Does the child interact intentionally?

Communication

- Does the child respond when someone attempts to communicate?
- Does the child appear to want to communicate?
- Does the child respond appropriately to simple communication through speech?
- Does the child respond appropriately to simple communication with gesture, signs or body cues?
- Does the child express need or discomfort by crying, vocalising or bodily movements?
- Does the child communicate consistently through body language or gesture?
- Does the child communicate consistently through vocalisation?
- Does the child communicate consistently through speech?
- Does the child communicate consistently through communication systems, for example Makaton?
- Does the child communicate consistently through symbols, for example Rebus symbols?

The above questions are based on unpublished research by the author and colleagues, Westminster College, Oxford 1997/8.

Home/school partnership

For many parents, school hours provide valuable time and respite from the physical and psychological stress of caring for their child. It should be recognised that, although a child's right to educational continuity during sickness is established in law, life-limited children, and their parents, may not always welcome teaching. Understandably, education is not necessarily a priority for them and, in any event, the appropriateness of education will be dependent on how sick the child is. There will be times when a child is not able to undertake educational tasks. Incorporating children's wishes and feelings into educational opportunities is important. There will be occasions when children and young people do not want their parents to be involved, and this should be respected. However, parents are children's first teachers. They play a crucial part in helping their children to learn. Research findings suggest that parents can help their child more effectively if they know what a school or home tuition service is trying to achieve, and how they can help. Professionals should acknowledge parental need for:

- continued support in adjusting to the emotional and psychological reactions to their child's life-limiting illness
- multi-agency support
- help in setting realistic and meaningful targets for their child
- information at each stage of their child's development
- opportunities to recognise and celebrate their parenting skills.

Helping children to take pride and pleasure in their educational achievements is very important. What is often forgotten is that the needs of life-limited children and their families need to be reviewed and reassessed at regular intervals. Education should enhance the quality of experience for all those involved, and provide true equality of opportunity.

Key points

- Education is a statutory duty and a right for all children and young people.
- Many life-limited children and those with chronic medical conditions are unable to access the kind of support that would benefit their education.
- The Revised Code of Practice on the Identification and Assessment of Pupils with Special Educational Needs (2001) is intended to enable children with special educational needs to be fully included in all aspects of school life and learning.
- A child's Statement of Special Educational Needs may include specialist teaching, specific programmes to meet therapeutic needs, or specific teaching and learning strategies to employ with a child.
- There are very few conclusive research findings concerning the impact of life-limited illness on children's academic performance.
- Disrupted schooling can impact on the acquisition of basic skills and the development of subject knowledge, organisational skills, self-motivated learning, group learning skills and developing and maintaining peer friendships.
- Ensuring all children have access to a broad and balanced curriculum, relevant to their individual needs, is an ongoing challenge.
- One of the greatest barriers to successful integration of sick children into mainstream education is that of access for those who use wheelchairs or other mobility aids.

- The environment plays a crucial role in enabling children's communication.
- Play and relaxation are important aspects of children's experience.

Implications for practice

- Maintaining educational continuity is extremely important. This includes promoting a child's learning skills, encouraging good peer relationships, minimising the effects of isolation, and promoting equality of opportunity.
- All schools should have at least one member of staff (usually the SENCO) who has knowledge of specialist equipment, to enable the optimal inclusion of pupils with physical disabilities in a planned learning environment.
- Regular updated training for SENCOs should include physiotherapy programmes.
- Staff expertise concerning augmentative and assisted communication systems will impact on how successfully children with receptive, expressive and articulatory and interaction problems are able to communicate.
- Professionals should ensure that education enhances the quality of life experience for all children and young people and provides true equality of opportunity.
- Nurses and care staff should assess children's physical development, perceptual development, intellectual development and personal and social development. The resulting profile will inform the child's Nursing Care Plan and physiotherapy regime, as well as providing staff with a detailed picture of children's individual needs.

18

Transition from Paediatric Palliative Care to Adult Services

Erica Brown

Improvements in medical and nursing therapies means children with life-limiting conditions are surviving longer. Therefore, the management of transition from paediatric services to adult services has become a vital component in holistic care and highlights the need for improved and expanded services. Statistical evidence reveals an increasing number of clients who are in the 13-year to 19-year age range, making up between 26 per cent and 54 per cent of life-limited young people (ACT 2003). It is estimated that, in a population of 10,000 young people, about two aged between 13 years and 24 years will die. ACT estimates the numbers of children within the United Kingdom requiring symptom management and daily care are likely to be between 6,000 and 10,000, and this will increase as medical science advances. The physical, psychological and developmental needs of this age group are specific and different from those of children or adults. The timescale for palliative care also varies enormously from a few days to many years.

Young people have a wide spectrum of life-limiting conditions. Some illnesses are congenital or genetic, contracted in early life and throughout childhood. Others are contracted and diagnosed in adolescence and young adulthood. The ACT and RCPCH Palliative Care Service Guidelines (2003) describe four main categories of conditions. (See Chapter 1, 'The Historical Background of Paediatric Palliative Care'.)

In 2001, the ACT/RCPCH Working Party made a plea for flexible provision matched to the needs of young people aged 13–24 years. Children's hospices have evolved to meet these needs and to care for children from 0 years to 19 years and their families. Respite care is one of the hallmarks of paediatric palliative care and, although children's hospices such as Martin House, Douglas House and Acorns have expanded care to provide for the needs of adolescents and young adults, there is a huge gap in the provision of care outside the home for this age group. The focus for many life-limited young persons requiring care remains family-based with some support from Primary Health Care Teams, Community Services and multi-agency teams. However, this is generally less well coordinated than adult services, and where they do exist Primary Care Teams may have sparse knowledge of life-limiting conditions such as metabolic disorders and progressive degenerative illnesses. Often there is a paucity of respite care provision, with palliative care services focusing largely on elderly patients with cancer.

ACT (2001) identified seven reasons why the transition process from paediatric services to adult services is inadequate:

- Families may have developed a strong attachment to paediatric services over many years and resist transfer to a specialist consultant they do not know.

- Consultant paediatricians may develop a strong relationship with families and be reluctant to hand over care.

- Parents fear that adult services will be less comprehensive and impersonal.

- Parents fear that adult services will be less well coordinated.

- Equivalent adult services may not exist.

- Families may fear that they will be unsupported in the end of life phase of their child's care, especially if this coincides with transition.

- The assessment of young persons' holistic needs (including their emotional readiness for transition) may have been neglected.

Understanding the developmental tasks of adolescence

Recognition of the specific and often subtle changes associated with the period of adolescence is almost universal. Adolescence is a time of immense change; physically, mentally, psychologically, spiritually and socially. The adolescent discovers new and previously uncharted ground, such as independence, body image, sexuality and personal identity. Furthermore, the adolescent's transition towards adulthood is a pathway that all of society expects adolescents to tread. Understanding the rapid changes in relation to the physical, social, emotional and cognitive development of young people is pivotal in matching the care to the needs of young people with life-limiting illnesses (Russell-Johnson 2000; Stevens 1998). Several studies have attempted to define the developmental tasks of adolescence, dividing the transitional period from childhood into young adulthood into three phases, namely: early, middle and late. For many life-limited young people, they may be intent on completing the developmental tasks but be inhibited from doing so, because of the impact of their life-limiting illness. Some may be almost completely dependent on their parents for their care at a time when chronic and progressive illness reaches a crisis.

The societal perception of adolescence and adult status varies between cultures. In Western society there is no accepted age that defines adult status in all aspects of life. For example, there are differences between when a young person may marry (16 years), hold a driving licence (17 years) and vote (18 years).

Adolescence is a journey of discovery, turmoil, challenge, experimentation, ambivalence, egocentricity, confidence and self-doubt combined with unfolding changes physically, emotionally and intellectually (Cooper 1999). Coping with a life-limiting illness is a monumental undertaking. Unlike young children, adolescents generally perceive death as irreversible. Therefore, acceptance of personal death is particularly difficult because for many young people their lives are orientated towards a future. It should be remembered, however, that many of the anxieties that life-limited adolescents encounter have their roots firmly seated in systemic and youth culture, which accentuates differences between life-limited young people and their non life-limited peers. It is therefore important to be mindful of the following developmental tasks that adolescents assume.

Developmental objectives for adolescents

- Emancipation from the family.
- Achieving autonomy, financially and socially.
- Developing a set of personal values and morals.
- Developing personal and peer group identity.
- Achieving a personally acceptable body image.
- Developing career pathways.

Emotional challenges of young people with life-limiting illnesses

Young people with life-limiting illnesses are faced with tremendous emotional challenges. They are often very knowledgeable about their illness and their prognosis and aware of the effects on those that care for them. Some will need to explore reasons for their life-limiting illness (Hart and Schneider 1997) and, in particular, why they have to endure physical and cognitive deterioration. Having a life-limiting illness can be exceptionally isolating and many young people lose contact with their peer group outside a palliative care or special needs setting.

The paradox of support versus adult status

Many young people with life-limiting illnesses will require extensive support from a range of agencies up to, and including, the end of life stage of their care. Support is often viewed as incompatible with adult status and as being inconsistent with autonomy. Furthermore, young people may experience support services as intrusive and controlling. True support enables personal autonomy and self-sufficiency, encouraging young people to choose how and when they use the services available to them.

There has been little written concerning the participation of life-limited young people in decisions concerning their care. Collaborative partnership extends beyond the relationship between the parents and the health professional to one that encourages the young person to be involved in decisions that are made on their behalf. Riley (1996), Fulton (1996) and ACT/RCPCH (2003), believe that all people should be able to voice their opinions, a view underpinned by the Children Act (1989), which states that 'children must be kept informed about what happens to them and participate when decisions are made about their future'.

Despite this recommendation, young people are not always given opportunities that enable them to make their views known. Arguably, the potential exists for young persons' autonomy to be overlooked under the umbrella of family-centred care, because the focus is often on parents making decisions on behalf of their child. Indeed, parents need support and encouragement to enable their son or daughter to develop as much autonomy as possible. A very limited number of life-limited young people will achieve independent living, providing they are given adequate assistance in moving away from home. However, comprehensive, coordinated inter-agency planning is probably the exception rather than the rule.

Working in partnership with other agencies

For many young people with a life-limiting illness, their families provide the major part of their care, supported by Primary Care Teams, community paediatricians, occupational therapists and nursing teams such as Diana Teams, working collaboratively with social workers, overseen by a community paediatrician. In some regions, multi-agency children's palliative care groups also exist, providing care and support for young people up to the age of 19 years.

In the case of young people who utilise the services of children's hospice care, whether this is community-based or hospice-based, there are very few equitable services available once they have reached the age of 19 years. Many adult palliative care services are for elderly people with cancer. The exception is the service at Douglas House in Oxford opened in 2004 for young adults aged 18–40 years. However, as yet it is too early to evaluate how service-users view the support they receive, and whether it helps them to develop strategies for 'continuing to make their mark' in a way that encourages them to gain a sense of purpose and meaning in the time they have left.

Meeting the transitional needs of young people with life-limited illnesses requires flexible working on the part of statutory agencies. They need to communicate and to agree policies and protocols that work towards providing a 'seamless' service. The objective should be to provide integrated, high-quality holistic support, focused on the needs of the young person and their family. Such provision should be based on a shared perspective and should build, whenever possible, on mutual understanding and agreement. Services should adopt a client-centred approach to service delivery to ensure the changing needs and priorities of each young person.

The roles of some of the most important agencies involved in transition are described below.

The Connexions Service

The Connexions Service (DfEE 2000) has responsibility for working with young people between the age of 13 and 19, providing guidance and support through the teenage years and into adult life. The service is delivered primarily through a network of personal advisers linking in with specialist support services. Personal advisers are supported by a comprehensive service delivery structure with local organisations working together within Connexions Partnerships. (See also Chapter 17, 'The Education of the Life-limited Child'.)

Learning and Skills Council

The Learning and Skills Council is responsible for the development, planning, funding and management of all post-16 education and learning (except higher education) and work-based training for young people. The Council has a statutory duty to take account of assessments arranged by the Connexions Service.

Health Authority

The Health Authority should agree with Primary Care Groups and Trusts how the local health authority can meet the individual needs of young people.

Health Authorities and Trusts should also inform young people and their carers about voluntary organisations that might provide support.

In summary, joint planning arrangements should:

- take account of good practice
- ensure consultation with relevant services
- agree priorities
- communicate information to the client and their parents
- regularly review policies and objectives.

Legislation regarding decisions about medical care

Until 1986, the right of children under 16 years of age to make their own decisions about their medical care did not exist. Cooper (1999) refers to a 'protectionist philosophy' underpinning childcare that views young people as fragile, incompetent, powerless and unable to care for themselves. The same author believes that this may result in young people being denied a right to be involved in their own care. In England, Wales and Northern Ireland, once a young person reaches 18 years of age provided they have the capacity to think and make decisions independently, decisions around their health care fall solely with them. Young people between 16 and 18 years may also be deemed competent under the Family Law Act 1969. Young people under the age of 16 years have no statutory rights, but can be 'Fraser competent' if they are able to demonstrate an understanding of the issues involved. Therefore, medical professionals are required to judge the competence of the young person and then to involve them in decisions made on his or her behalf. (In Scotland, young people of 16 are presumed to be competent to make decisions.)

The relationship between a young person and their clinician is confidential unless permission is given by the young person to disclose their wishes to others. Legal and ethical considerations with regard to confidentiality, consent or refusal to treatment are major issues for this group of young people. With good support and guidance, however, some youngsters will be able to take control of their own lives.

Education

Education is an entitlement for young people under the age of 19 years and it plays a major part in preparing young people for the transition to adulthood. Current provision in Further Education has been shaped by attitudes and political policies in recent years. This section of the chapter focuses on some of the more recent legislation and its possible effects on the services and transition of young people with life-limiting illnesses. The NHS Optimum Health Services Trust (1999) document highlighted that the time of transition for young people with special needs was particularly difficult. Furthermore, the Beattie Report (1999) suggested that 'young people with learning disabilities are at risk of social exclusion and difficult transition on leaving school and subsequent transitions'.

According to the Disability Discrimination Act (1995), Section 1(1), a person has a disability if they 'have a physical or mental impairment which has a substantial and long-term adverse effect on their ability to carry out normal day-to-day activities'. Most young people with life-limiting conditions will have a Statement of Special Educational Needs that outlines their individual needs and measures that need to be taken to meet these needs. The Special Educational Needs Code of Practice (DfES 2001) outlines several principles that underpin transition and transition planning, taking into account the requirements of a young person and their family. The transition process should be:

- participative
- holistic
- supportive
- evolving
- inclusive
- collaborative.

Managing transition to Further Education

All young people with a Statement of Special Educational Needs should, in law, have the Statement reviewed annually. Some young people will remain in school until they are 19 years of age. In the final year of their schooling, the Connexions Service has a responsibility (under Section 140 of the Learning and Skills Act 2000) to coordinate transition from school to the continuing education sector, and for assessing Social Services support. Where a placement in a specialist college is appropriate for a young person, a copy of the student's transition plan should be sent to the local Learning and Skills Council.

For any young person, a course at college or university necessitates a period of transition. For many, this period enables them to move from a dependent role in the world of childhood to an autonomous and independent role in the adult world. For young people with life-limiting illnesses, transition marks a significant and important part in their lives as they move from a childhood role to adult status. The major role of Further Education is to enable young people to make best use of this transition, offering them the educational and vocational opportunities to which they have a right. Opportunities will vary from location to location, but an increasing number of colleges now make Further Education available to a wide range of students, sometimes in conjunction with social or health services or voluntary organisations.

Full-time courses are usually:

- for young people between the ages of 16 and 21 years
- up to three years in length
- based at a College of Further Education
- varied in content, according to the curriculum offered by individual colleges
- based on personal skills and transition to adult life.

Further Education should aim to meet individual student needs through offering a tailored educational programme, which is constructed within a curriculum framework, using age and ability appropriate activities, language, resources and teaching strategies. Technological support may be an important component in individual student learning.

Part-time courses may sometimes be delivered through outreach services.

Vocational guidance

Vocational guidance is an important part of the transition plan, and the Connexions Service should assist the young person and their parents to access the most appropriate provision, providing counselling and support as appropriate. Where the young person concerned requires services from the Local Authority after leaving school, this should be arranged with multi-agency support, including the provision of Further Education. Some young people may become independent of their families, moving into Higher Education and pursuing other personal goals. Assessment of needs should be a discreet process that incorporates the development of a plan of action.

Involvement of Health Services

Where health professionals have been involved in the care of the young person before transition, they should attend the young person's review at 14 years of age and advise on the services that are likely to be required. The young person's health records should be transferred to Adult Services (with the young person's consent and that of their parents). The plan for transition to Adult Services is an important one. Time is required to prepare the young person and their family to liaise with the Adult Services.

Transition as an ideology and a process

The shift in emphasis, with adolescents being seen as people in their own right, neither adult nor child, has flagged up many issues for healthcare professionals, parents and the young people themselves. Transfer to Adult Services as both an ideology and a process reflects the success of medical advancements in the treatment of life-limiting illnesses. The ACT/RCPCH (2003) document states that 'the need for wider scale planning regarding transition is particularly important in those illnesses once considered to be confined to childhood, where modern treatment advances have led to longer term survival into adult life'. Subsequently, the transition pathway to Adult Services requires healthcare professionals, parents and the young person to identify and recognise that this group need an initiative whereby they receive a holistic service. This should facilitate a coordinated and developmentally appropriate transition and eventual transfer to Adult Services. Transition as a process, however, involves more than transferring medical notes and the young person themselves to Adult Services. It should be 'based on the purposeful and planned movement of adolescents and young adults' (Viner and Keane 1999).

Research by Powncenby (1996) suggests that critical elements in the transition process are:

- comprehensive written information about the adult unit at an early stage
- combined paediatric and adult clinics with the opportunity for young people to discuss and sample new facilities, whilst being accompanied by a paediatric team member
- joint visits to the young person by paediatric and adult nurses
- consideration of the young person's emotional wellbeing post transfer.

Case studies

In order to identify and illuminate some of the issues that life-limited young people may have in accomplishing adolescent objectives, it may be useful to read the following case studies and examine the implications for the young persons concerned (N.B. all names have been changed to safeguard anonymity).

Lara is 15 years old and has an osteosarcoma of her left leg. She has had radical surgery resulting in the amputation of her leg, received courses of chemotherapy and is currently receiving palliative radiotherapy. Lara is aware of her diagnosis and has been kept fully informed and involved since her diagnosis seven months ago. She has lost contact with many of her peers and has decided not to sit her GCSEs. A couple of her close friends still visit her at home once a week but they are busy revising for their exams. Lara has alopecia and is very underweight for her age and height.

Implications: Treatment for cancer usually results in physical changes to the young person that may cause stress and poor body image, at a time when self-esteem and a positive body image are all important. The loss of Lara's hair may signify the loss of her femininity, as may her weight loss. Lara's surgery may also leave her with feelings of gross disfigurement and difficulties accepting her already altered physique. It may also be a factor in why Lara doesn't want to continue with her studies or see many of her friends. She is likely to be isolated and withdrawn. She will fully comprehend her prognosis (as may her peers), but actually talking about her wishes and needs may be incredibly difficult. She has previously experienced life without life-limited illness and now she has all of the added anxieties of having cancer. She is becoming increasingly dependent upon her parents physically, emotionally and even financially. Her independence, self-image and personal role in her community has altered dramatically. Lara's parents may wrap her in 'cotton wool' in an attempt to protect her and extend her life. Her sexual identity will undoubtedly change and her realisation of the loss of future hopes and goals may also contribute to a real sense of immobilisation.

Neil is 17 years old and suffers with the progressive neuro-degenerative disorder Duchenne muscular dystrophy. He is unable to walk and uses an electric wheelchair in order to mobilise. He has limited upper body movement and is completely dependent on his mother for all aspects of his personal care. He has some learning difficulties but attends mainstream college. His communication skills are very good.

Neil's best friend has invited him to attend his 18th birthday party, which is being held at a wheelchair friendly venue in the next town. Neil has asked his mum if he can attend the party, and if she will take him. Unfortunately, Neil's mum is working that night and will therefore require the use of the family's only mode of transport, the vehicle adapted for Neil.

Implications: Duchenne muscular dystrophy affects boys and is an inherited condition with mothers being the carrier. Boys are usually in an electric wheelchair by the age of ten. Young people affected by this condition will experience the gradual loss of their motor skills over a period of years. They will have observed their peers and siblings becoming independent and watched them being encouraged to do so. Many young people with Duchenne muscular dystrophy will have lived with the knowledge that their condition means they will die during their adolescence. As they grow older, the realisation that they will probably not have children, experience a sexual relationship or follow the career path of choice may result in them questioning the point of their actual existence. By the very nature of their condition, these young people will not have physically, emotionally or socially been able to attain a level of independence. In turn, the amount of privacy they receive or, indeed, have expectations about, will differ greatly to that of their non-life-limiting peers.

In this particular case, Neil may feel a real sense of anger towards his mum for using the vehicle that has been specifically adapted for his use. However, how can Neil display anger towards his mum when he is totally dependent on her for all of his care needs? He cannot 'storm out' of the house, bang doors or 'take himself off' for a few hours to calm down. He is left with pent-up anger and emotions.

Both of the case studies above illustrate the real and visible differences that life-limiting adolescents encounter when journeying through the period of transition towards adulthood. During this time, young people usually strive to achieve emancipation from their parents. Shopping trips and cinema visits, as well as a reluctance to participate in family gatherings, are amongst some of the methods of attaining a level of freedom from parents. Disagreements and debate around politics, religion and the pop culture of the day may become commonplace as young people push the boundaries and begin to develop their own morals and values.

For young people suffering with a life-limited condition, the tasks that most of us take for granted become incredibly difficult, if not near impossible, to achieve. Neil is never likely to leave home and become physically and financially independent, and Lara may experience resistance from her parents if she strives to be autonomous. She will inevitably be inhibited by the progression of the disease. Both have to face a future, no matter how short. It is, however, very different from the life that these two young people want and which society expects.

The next case study highlights the difficulties of those adolescents who have an unheard voice, those that are unable to communicate their needs.

Assaya is 19 years old and has childhood onset leukodystrophy. She is often agitated, suffering with involuntary movements and has difficulties with feeding that require a jejunostomy. She is at home most of the week as there are no suitable education or respite facilities available locally.

Implications: Assaya is able to communicate non-verbally by using gesture and eye contact. Occasionally she uses an electric speaking machine. She watches the television and sees how people of her own age are leading their lives and how this differs vastly from her own experience. The clothes that she wears, the music that she listens to and the bedtime and personal care she receives may also be aimed at a much younger person than herself. This may result in frustration, anger and withdrawal. Physiologically Assaya will have undergone the same hormonal and body changes of those of any female. However, her limited communication skills may impede her from informing carers or professionals of her fears, anxieties or, indeed, the pain that she may be suffering.

Before the progression of her disease, Assaya may have had career aspirations. These career goals will have been stunted by her physical disability, limited communication skills and a lack of accessible resources. Another consideration is Assaya's own expectations for her future, as well as those of parents and professionals, who may well be unable to comprehend that she has young adult aspirations and hopes.

Concerns about the transition of young people with life-limiting conditions from paediatric to adult care were first highlighted by ACT in the 2001 Report, 'Palliative Care for Young People aged 13 to 24 Years'. The document stated: 'for rare disorders, especially degenerative conditions…where young people have outlived their predicted life expectancy there is no equivalent service to transfer them to'.

More recently the RCN document *Adolescent Transition Care* (2004) highlighted four potential areas of difficulty when planning adult provision for young people:

1. Lack of specialist knowledge in adult teams and lack of confidence in knowledge.

2. Lack of specific service provision for young people.

3. Lack of understanding and appreciation of young people's needs and issues in both paediatric and adult healthcare sectors.

4. Professional attitudes.

Within the Health Service there are still no regulations for managing the transition of young life-limited people to adult care settings, although the Government's Select Committee Inquiry into Palliative Care recommendations of 21 July 2004 makes a call for the overview of service provision.

Service providers have a duty to help young people to understand what is available to them and how to access the support available. They should also have a commitment towards working collaboratively with other agencies, on a regular, rather than a crisis, basis, and they should be suitably experienced and qualified to work with young people and their families. Understanding generic adolescence issues such as relationships, independent living and leisure interests, in addition to the specific needs of young people with life-limiting illnesses, will contribute enormously in planning transition from paediatric services to adult care. It is also likely to result in positive outcomes regardless of the prognosis for the young people concerned.

Key points

- Managing the transition of young people from paediatric services to adult services has highlighted the need for improved and expanded services.

- The physical, psychological and developmental needs of adolescents and young people are different from those of children or adults.

- Understanding the rapid changes in the physical, social, emotional and cognitive development of young people is pivotal in matching care to the needs of young people with life-limited illnesses.

- Education is an entitlement for young people under the age of 19 and it plays an important role in preparing young people for the transition to adulthood.

- Legal and ethical considerations with regard to confidentiality, consent or refusal of treatment are major issues for life-limited young people.

- The societal perception of adolescence and adult status varies between cultures.

- True support enables personal autonomy and self-sufficiency, encouraging young people to choose how and when they use the services available to them.

Implications for practice

- Young people should be involved in choices and decision-making at every level.

- Confidentiality should be respected and upheld at all times.

- Anticipating young people's needs should be integral to care at times of transition from children's services to adult services and at end of life care.

- Continuity of support should be provided at times of transition.

- Families should be included in care plans (in consultation with the young person).

- Tension between the dependency and inter-dependency of young people should be acknowledged.

- Psychological and spiritual aspects of care should be integral to service provision.

- Care packages should be reviewed frequently.

- Equipment and mobility aids should be regularly updated and matched to the individual needs of the young person.

- Personal relationships (including sexual experiences) should be encouraged and incorporated into care plans.

- Young people who have partners should be enabled to include them in choices regarding care (if the young person wishes).

- Peer group activities should be encouraged and provision made to enable these to happen.

- The environment in which young people are cared for should be age-appropriate.

19

Acknowledging Staff Stress and Providing Support

Erica Brown

Much of the literature relating to paediatric palliative care acknowledges that staff are subjected to extreme distress (Harding 1996; Spinetta, Jankovie and Arush 2001). The emotional state of the parents and the nature of the child's illness will all play their part. Staff often find uncontrollable symptoms particularly challenging, especially if the child is in pain or distress. Additionally, degenerative conditions, where a child's health deteriorates slowly, are likely to cause high levels of stress (Barnes 2001). Where a child is expected to die and death does not occur, this may also cause extreme anxiety amongst staff (Woolley *et al.* 1989a).

It is interesting to note, however, that Vachon (1997) determined that stress in palliative care was less common than in other settings. She concludes that this is most likely because the potential for stress is generally acknowledged in caring for life-limited patients. Job satisfaction and high staff ratio to patients may also play their part.

Cooke (1992) suggests that there are three key factors that sustain nurses in hospice care:

- opportunities to form close personal relationships
- opportunities to make a difference
- opportunities to learn from families.

Entering into relationships with grief-stricken families does, however, carry risks for carers. Often the reactions may not seem sufficiently dramatic for the carer to seek medical support, but they are still likely to make their life miserable. Johnson (1993) calls this 'depletion of the spirit'.

Carers bring their own personal philosophy, beliefs and prejudices to caring. They also come with knowledge, skills and experience gained through professional development and practice.

The vulnerability of carers

All people who work in palliative care settings are bound to have times of pressure as they care for families who are suffering and distressed. Many people who work in children's hospices are by their very nature sensitive (Johnson 1991), a characteristic well-suited to palliative care, but they are also very vulnerable to the painful effects of grief, and their needs should not be neglected. Emery (1994) suggests that caring can be particularly stressful if the length of time that the child is likely to live cannot be predicted.

Harding (1994) and Saunders and Velente (1994) describe a multitude of emotions that staff are likely to experience. However, they stress that staff generally hope and expect to grow personally from the close relationships that they form with the dying child and the child's family.

Kavanagh (2001) reminds professionals that there is no 'proper' way for carers to respond to a dying child and that staff are likely to encounter greater stress if they rely on exact rules and routines.

Mediating factors

Staff will not be equally susceptible to stresses and a person's susceptibility may vary over time. There will, however, be factors which serve to increase or decrease a care-giver's vulnerability to a stress reaction. These factors are known as mediating factors (Fisher 1991; Spinetta *et al.* 2001).

Age

When staff are involved in caring for life-limited children, their response is likely to be determined by their normal age-appropriate emotional defence around the stresses aroused by the death process. Younger staff may feel outraged by a child's death. They may be particularly susceptible to burn-out because of their own unrealistic expectations, and they may have had no previous experience of death (Ramirez, Graham and Richards 1998). Middle-aged staff may experience intellectual acceptance, while emotionally denying the meaning of death. Sometimes they may attempt to reduce the situation to the level of an intellectual exercise. Naturally, if this happens, it will hinder communication and interaction with the child and their family. Being under the age of 55 has been associated with greater burn-out (Ramirez *et al.* 1998). Older staff may be more prone to stress in relation to their perceived 'ideal' work situation and their 'real' work situation. They are, however, likely to have an increased personal acceptance of death as a natural life process. It is likely that they will have had some experience of exposure to death and to have had opportunities for professional development and training.

Carers of any age may experience heightened stress if they look after a life-limited child who is the same age as their own child.

The social class/ethnic background

Little attention has been given to the social class of carers as a mediating factor, other than to recognise that there appears to be some difficulties in communication if carers and families are from very different socio-economic backgrounds. Families who seem to be well-educated and well-informed about the child's condition or treatment may be perceived by the care-giver as a greater challenge. People of different social class or ethnic background may have differing values, and this may be more likely to occur where parents' own home background is radically different from that of the carer. For example, single parents, parents in same-sex relationships, or in families where one of the child's parents has remarried or has a new partner.

People's motivation to work with life-limited children may lead to stress reactions, for example if a person is drawn to be a carer in order to resolve their own past losses or feelings of guilt. Sometimes the strategies a person has used to cope with past stressful situations may be threatened by individual situations. People are less likely to be able to cope at work when they are also facing their own personal or family problems. Societal expectations may also impact on people caring for life-limited and dying children. These may include:

- increased advances in medicine which are perceived as being capable of preventing death
- a belief that carers are always patient and understanding and immune to human emotions of depression and despair
- a belief that carers should be able to relate equally well to all families
- a belief that carers are capable of separating the stresses of their personal and professional lives.

In children's hospices, some relationships with children and their families develop over a relatively short period of time; others develop over many months or years. Inevitably, close relationships evolve as staff share special times with children and their families. Sometimes carers feel that they are torn between expressing their feelings of sadness and upholding expectations of professional behaviour. Generally, it appears that when it is acknowledged that staff need to express their emotions, they are better equipped to manage their distress.

Palliative carers may give of themselves person-to-person and, sometimes, soul-to-soul over many years (Hutchins 1997). Often staff struggle with their distress when they realise that the child's death is inevitable. Sometimes they may begin to withdraw emotionally, although they may be expected to support families for years after a child's death. Carers who feel able to 'follow through' the end of life stage of a child's illness until their death are generally more likely to be able to reflect on the situation afterwards in a more positive light, than those who do not have an opportunity for 'closure'.

> It seems ironic to speak about a child's death as a good death, but that is how I see it. Because I was involved for the last day of his life, I'm not left with unfinished business.

People working in palliative care encounter a wide range of challenges including the psycho-social challenges imposed on them by families anticipating their child's death. Caring demands utilising a repertoire of skills and matching them to individual situations. When staff are able to acknowledge their distress through sharing their experiences and to apply their acquired knowledge and skills, there is a greater likelihood that they will be able to apply the knowledge and skills in caring for other children.

Acknowledging staff stress and encouraging staff to show emotions

It is widely accepted that grief in response to loss must be experienced in order for emotional healing to take place and for new relationships to be formed. However, carers in children's hospices may feel it is unprofessional to cry and they may also feel ill-equipped to deal with their own emotions. Indeed, professional nursing education tends to put considerable emphasis on the maintenance of composure, especially in the presence of patients and their families.

Recognising the signs of stress

Many staff will be familiar with the signs and symptoms of excessive stress, but they are often unaware that these become damaging for themselves, unless they are able to recognise their own likely responses. It is tremendously important that people are able to recognise if they are moving into a negative stress cycle.

Negative effects of stress

The early effects of stress will vary between individuals. They often start with:

- disturbed sleep – often falling asleep quickly and then waking at a regular time during the night and finding difficulty in getting back to sleep again
- a sense of being rushed and unable to focus and generally taking longer to complete tasks
- reluctance to embark on a course of action
- dishevelled appearance or carelessness in dressing
- strained facial expression.

As time passes, more serious effects emerge. Often, individuals feel extremely physically tired but they are reluctant to relax or rest. Some people may even miss meals, or overeat, with the result that they lose or gain weight. Work performance may suffer and there is a tendency for individuals to blame other people for their shortcomings. Anger and resentment may affect other team members. Eventually, the person under stress may suffer lowering of their immunity to infection and illness. Family relationships suffer, and this may lead to marital stress and social isolation, together with loss of job prospects and impaired work performance.

Creative stress

When acknowledging the harmful effects of stress, it is also important to consider how the creative side may enhance staff performance and personal wellbeing, creating a 'buzz' and contributing to healthy self-esteem. Positive stress can energise people in their home life and at work, helping them to meet challenges. The Health Education Authority document (1995) *Health at Work in the NHS* refers to 'constructive and positive stress'.

Teams

People who give care need to receive care. Owen (2000) believes that valuing staff for what they do, and communicating this to them, is likely to act as a buffer against stress, especially where this is in the form of positive feedback and encouragement. Good team leaders, who are able to engage groups in goal setting and decision-making, also have a beneficial effect (Cooper and Mitchell 1990).

Conversely, if senior staff are stressed, they will be less likely to be able to give support to other people. If team conflicts occur, this may be more of a stressor than working with life-limited children and their families (Vachon 1997).

Although all members of a team (for example, receptionists and volunteers) may not be involved with a life-limited child and the child's family, the death of the child will be experienced with some level of sadness and sorrow. It is extremely important that 'institutional' grief is dealt with, and that individuals are not left to cope alone without support. Adams, Hershatter and Moritz (1991) list five characteristics associated with accumulated loss:

- lack of closure
- concern about constant exposure to death and dying
- ideal versus reality mismatch
- distancing
- diminishing boundaries.

The same authors recommend that individual team members explore their feelings with regard to their own losses, identify available support within their personal and professional life, are realistic, are aware of clients with whom they are most likely to identify, and employ techniques to reduce stress. Kavanaugh (2001) recommends that carers develop skills in what he calls 'the art of distancing', which he describes as:

> To be as warm, open and giving as you can, limited only by your professional duties, your responsibilities to other patients, and the realities of your own personal life (pp.24–5).

Peer group support often has the greatest influence on stress management, closely followed by feeling valued.

> I feel energised and my batteries are recharged by my colleagues.

Sharing experiences may help to alleviate feelings of isolation. Staff support groups may also provide opportunities for goal-setting and decision-making, and provide time to enable carers to become reflective practitioners (Harvey 1992). It is generally acknowledged that groups should be facilitated by an experienced person from outside the hospice setting (Woolley *et al.* 1989a). McKee (1995) also advocates using social activities, humour and peer grief support as informal strategies to relieve stress and consolidate good working relationships within teams. However, there will be many variations in how people cope and, at times, personal space and solitude have their place.

Environmental factors

The conditions in which staff work may directly affect stress levels (Barnes 2001). In Woolley's (1989) study of children's hospices, staff appreciated the pleasurable working conditions. In situations where staff knowledge and expertise are valued, and where they are able to work with families and carry out a care plan, they are more likely to view a child's terminal phase of life, and the child's death, as positive occasions in their career. When staff witness a young person's condition deteriorating, they may struggle to maintain a sense of control, especially if they have built up a close relationship with the child and their family (Kushnir, Rabin and Azulai 1997).

Often, there seems to be a conflict between identifying staff needs and acknowledging stresses that are inherent in the job. In a climate where holistic care may sometimes seem to conflict with demands from government agents and bureaucracy, individuals and organisations may be vulnerable. Unrealistic expectations may accentuate staff feelings of being undervalued, although people will respond differently according to personality, expectations and experiences.

Key points

- Much of the literature relating to paediatric palliative care acknowledges the extra stress to which staff are subjected.
- A person's susceptibility to stress may vary over time.
- The long effects of stress are cumulative.
- Not all stress is negative. Creative stress may enhance staff performance and personal wellbeing.
- Positive feedback and encouragement and feedback from managers are likely to act as a buffer against stress.
- Team conflict is likely to cause enhanced levels of stress.
- The conditions in which staff work may directly affect stress levels.
- Volunteers and administrative staff are likely to encounter stressful situations.

Implications for practice

- Professionals need to possess a repertoire of skills which they are able to match to individual situations.
- It is important that carers recognise if they are moving into a period of negative stress.
- When professionals are valued and supported by their peers, this can have a tremendously positive impact on stress management.
- It is important to recognise the creative aspects of stress as well as acknowledging harmful effects.

Staff support

Children and families can find themselves being cared for by a wide range of professionals and carers, who themselves need to be supported (Capewell and Beattie 1996). The role of care-giving is a complex one in which families may feel out of control and emotionally very vulnerable. Entering into a relationship with grief-stricken people carries risk. When carers are constantly engaging in stressful work, symptoms of cumulative stress may develop. Johnson (1993) describes this as 'depletion of the spirit'.

Carers enter palliative care with a wide range of motives, attitudes and ambitions. Most have a deep vocation to work with life-limited children and their families but they are human, and if the ideals and expectations of their vocation become jaded under the stress of caring, negative aspects may come into play.

There is ample evidence to show that the effects of stress can be very costly, both in human terms on the individual and to the employer in resource terms. We have seen that a certain amount of stress helps people to function normally and that it can be creative if channelled into fulfilling activities. However, the balance may be disturbed if negative stress is unchecked.

People need to be cared for, and their concept of support varies greatly. A common myth that appears to abound within the caring professions is that those who need support should not be in the job (Capewell and Beattie 1996). Furthermore, carers are often very reluctant to accept help, preferring to be givers. The quality of care that families receive is highly dependent on the quality of care that staff receive. Staff support enables people to be fully effective in their role.

The philosophy of staff support

Central to the philosophy of staff support is the premise that individuals need care, just as carers who are committed to the principle that life-limited children and their families need care. Staff support is about valuing staff as an integral part of the organisation, so that each individual has a sense of personal self-worth and respect. When people value themselves it is likely that they will be able to value their colleagues.

An organisation's Statement of Purpose is likely to contain words such as respect, valued, attitudes, dignity, and so on. Staff need to be able to see the aims of Policy Statements and Charters lived out in practice, and to be able to identify how their contribution makes a difference. The translation of Statement of Purpose into practice will require:

- clear communication channels with jargon-free documentation
- good management and decision-making

- evidence that policies are being carried out
- professional development and training opportunities
- accessible support networks for all staff.

The purpose of staff care is three-fold: primarily, to ensure that families receive good service and are protected from staff who are unfit emotionally, physically and professionally; second, to ensure that the stress of work does not have a detrimental effect on the health of staff; third, to safeguard against high staff absenteeism, turnover and low morale.

Minimising the impact of stress

As we have seen earlier in the chapter, the first step towards minimising the impact of stress is to accept that it is an integral feature of normal life (Stoter 1997). From an organisational point of view, managing stress will involve:

- acknowledging there are stressful situations that can have harmful effects on individuals and teams
- identifying the detrimental effects of stress for individuals, teams and the organisation
- implementing sources of support for individuals.

Some stress arises from a person's internal responses or from their home and family pressures, while others have roots in caring for life-limited children and their families. Factors outside the home and work situation will also play their part. It is important to analyse these stresses, and their contribution to the overall levels of stress, before planning support.

Organisational responsibilities

No organisation can be held responsible for meeting all the needs of the staff, although Health and Safety requirements expect that employees will be safe-guarded against harm (including stress) in their working environment. Good practice in framing job descriptions, selection processes, induction and oppor-tunities for training should contribute towards reducing uncertainty and stress.

Staff can expect to receive:

- acknowledgment that they are engaged in highly stressful situations as part of their normal work
- help in managing work-related stress, including access to support systems.

There will be several starting points for assessing stress. The first stage is to identify the origins within the workplace from:

- organisational perspectives
- personal perspectives
- team perspectives.

Organisational and management systems

The culture of an organisation influences the way in which staff support operates. This ethos includes values, expectations and assumptions, and it helps to sustain cohesiveness for the members.

Vital to a successful organisation is the human resource, but human resources are diverse and affected by many factors within the workplace and outside. These variables will affect staff performance and their own expectations of balance between work and out-of-work activities.

Human resources deserve care and respect. Indeed, there will be an expectation that the organisation nurtures the people who work for it. Indicators of how staff are valued should include good systems for pay and reward, fair disciplinary systems and recognition of the rights and responsibilities of all employees. A caring environment attracts and retains good quality staff, and creates conditions that encourage and enable people to be creative, improving overall morale and staff performance.

Manager perspectives

All managers need to make an objective assessment of stress within their teams, taking into account the demands and pressures of the jobs, levels of responsibility, the role of the department, and the personal capacity of individuals to fulfil their roles. Managers also have responsibility to establish and maintain a good working environment. This includes recognising the effects of stress and an ongoing commitment to staff support. Staff need to know where they can seek help.

Where individuals work in a number of settings, for example with families in the community, with agencies outside the organisation and with colleagues within their workplace, factors such as geographical location, travelling and isolation need to be taken into account.

Freedom to express views will go a long way towards eliminating stressful pressures. Communication needs to enable staff to receive information and to feed back their own ideas. Good communication is about openness and willingness to listen, and about having opportunities to clarify difficult concepts.

Policy statements need to be based on clearly thought-through vision and purpose, showing manageable and achievable short-term, medium-term and long-term objectives. Managers should take every opportunity to cultivate and communicate a sense of valuing the individual, through demonstrating attitudes of fairness and recognition of what individuals can offer.

Staff taking responsibility for themselves

Taking responsibility for one's own wellbeing means taking care in all aspects of life, including personal, social and working aspects. It is important to know when to seek support and help, and to know where to get it. Having the backup of friends and colleagues is vital. Taking personal responsibility will include:

- recognising personal strengths and weaknesses
- taking stock of own life-style
- being able to identify sources of pressure
- recognising the signs of stress early on
- seeking help if pressures become excessive.

Each person will have had experiences and environmental influences that have contributed to their personality, and shaped their values. Most people will be able to reflect on these experiences within the context of their home and family or social setting. This will enable them to apply this to their job, and aspects of job satisfaction within their team and their working environment.

In paediatric palliative care, a carer's sense of identity usually rests heavily on their ability to support others, but there will inevitably be times where looking after life-limited children and their families disturbs their sense of self, and the equilibrium of their life is upset. Indeed, working with dying children and their families may cause people to call into question the widely held belief that childhood is a carefree, idyllic time. Care-givers under stress may notice that their view of the world becomes pessimistic as they perceive loss and suffering everywhere. Therefore, they need personal and professional 'anchors' that give opportunities to counteract the pressures of their work. Professionally, each care-giver needs at least one caring, safe and confidential relationship in which to address personal responses to their work. Clinical supervision is costly, but organisations should never compromise the wellbeing of their workforce.

Staff who take responsibility for themselves will help others to feel respected and valued. They are also much more likely to create a good working environment. Everyone needs adequate rest and recreation. These are not luxuries. People also need opportunities to keep up to date professionally, and time to reflect on their personal responses to pain and suffering. Self-knowledge is a pre-requisite for understanding others.

Team perspectives

The detrimental effects of stress on individuals and organisations has been well documented. What is less well reported is the demoralising effects of stress on teamwork and the resulting decline in group performance. Of course, any situation can be both a source of care and support, and a source of stress. Where members of a team are compatible, the team should provide what Capewell and Beattie (1996) describe as 'a cradle of support which acts as a buffer to the most distressing work'.

Well-functioning and supportive teams know their purpose collectively and individually. Boundaries between roles are clear and mechanisms are in place to resolve conflicts. Lines of authority will also be clear, as will lines of two-way communication. Team development and review will occur regularly and encourage individual members to become reflective practitioners. Working in teams can also bring rewards in terms of individual members learning from each other, and adding strengths to the care available. Stoter (1997) says that 'the sum total of a team's contribution is always more than the sum of the individual's contributions' (p.19).

Each team operates within the context of the organisation and a working environment is affected by the quality of the relationships within the team. In effective teams, individuals generate ideas and their skills are enhanced by the interactions within the team. Good team relationships are vital. Negative relationships create fear and anxiety and have a downward spiral effect (Stoter 1997). In a team with good relationships, stress is minimised and there is cohesion. Good relationships increase motivation and team loyalties, creating a pleasant working environment which enhances job satisfaction and reduces sickness and absenteeism. In good teams, each member values and cares for others, recognising their needs and encouraging them to accept help from within the group, and to seek outside help where appropriate.

Groups of people do not become teams by randomly throwing individuals together. Members need to work together and to share common goals so that they trust one another and value each other's skills, ideas, hopes, fear and achievement. Within a team it is important to:

- reflect on and acknowledge stressful situations
- allow for reassessment of situations
- reflect on how care is being delivered
- allow for review of team strategies
- facilitate the most effective use of each team member, taking into account their personality, experience and life-stage. (Based on Stoter 1997.)

Group support is arguably the most widely-established and appreciated form of staff care. Sometimes informal or ad-hoc groups form spontaneously, for example in team meetings. Other groups may be formed in response to a specific crisis, or as a way of solving a particular problem. Learning groups or seminars give staff opportunities to acquire new knowledge and to share ideas. Some of these groups require expert facilitation, and leadership, and the choice of approach will be determined by group needs and resources. In addition, there should be opportunities for support such as monitoring, supervision and 'buddying'. Supervision can be tremendously beneficial. Support should include line management, clinical supervision and counselling or therapeutic support. Where it is carried out well, it encourages staff to discuss both work-related and personal matters. Supervision should be an integral part of a person's work, even if some care-givers also make their own arrangements for support outside their workplace, bearing the cost personally.

Professional development opportunities should provide scope to reflect on practice, and good education and training should be at the forefront of caring organisations. Furthermore, there should be ongoing opportunities for individuals and teams as a whole to try out new ideas within a supportive atmosphere.

Those who work with life-limited children and their families need to find support and meaning in their work, that helps them resolve the stress and grief they feel. When they are able to tell their stories to empathetic colleagues, it is likely that this will help them to reflect on their experiences and find ways of coping that do not compromise their own well being.

Key points

- The effects of stress can be very costly, both in human terms on the individual, and to the employer in resources terms.
- Carers are often reluctant to accept help, preferring to be givers.
- Staff support is about valuing staff as an integral part of the organisation.
- The culture of an organisation influences the way in which staff support operates.
- The quality of care that families receive is highly dependent on the quality of care that staff receive.
- Nurses and care staff need to review their ideas about professional codes of conduct and ask for, and accept, support when it is offered.

Implications for practice

- Organisations should provide an environment that attracts and retains good quality staff and nurtures an atmosphere that encourages and enables people to be creative, improving overall morale and staff performance.

- Good practice in framing job descriptions, selection processes, induction and opportunities for training should contribute towards reducing uncertainty and stress.

- Helping staff manage work-related stress includes providing access to support systems.

- Younger, less experienced staff may need more assistance in coping with stress and in developing their own coping mechanisms.

- An holistic approach to caring for life-limited children and their families must be incorporated into nursing education.

- Supervision should be an integral part of a person's work, even if some staff receive support outside their workplace.

- Organisations should provide ongoing opportunities for individuals and teams to try out new ideas, within a supportive atmosphere.

Part 4

The Way Forward

20

Maintaining the Quality of Care

Ann Smallman

Measuring quality

Quality is defined as a degree of excellence (Concise Oxford Dictionary). Many people are drawn towards services or goods that they perceive to be 'high-quality'. Historically, quality was viewed as a recommendation of a 'good' service that was frequently passed on by word of mouth and, in many ways, this remains true today. The reputation of quality goes hand in hand with an expectation of the service that will be provided. However, this may be based on a personal definition of quality or individual experiences. Without a framework or standard of the average expected service expectations may be based purely on personal preferences, leading to dissatisfaction and complaint, if the expectations are not met. Maintaining the quality of a service and, therefore, the reputation of that service requires knowledge of 'where the service is at' – that is, a measurement of what is the acceptable standard – in order to evaluate any improvements or deterioration. This measuring of services also allows for comparison with other services of a similar kind.

The measurement of quality in palliative care today is firmly rooted in total quality management (TQM). TQM was implemented from the late 1960s onwards and enabled manufacturers to ensure that their goods were delivered to the customer to the required standard, minimising resources and costs and maximising output through three key stages – inspection, quality control and quality assurance. The TQM model emphasises effectiveness and efficiency, along with appropriate measuring, to identify deviation from the agreed standards. Another key principle is the involvement and empowerment of the whole team, from shop floor to senior managers. Equally, the development of relationships with other providers, such as suppliers, needs to be based on trust, commitment and mutual obligation. Gradually this model of measuring goods and services against agreed standards was rolled out to services such as education, social services and healthcare. Alongside the quality agenda was the importance of accountability and public protection, through inspection by responsible bodies, also measured against agreed standards.

Plans to reorganise the National Health Service (NHS) put quality firmly on the health agenda.

> The new NHS will have quality at its heart. Without it there is unfairness. Every patient treated in the NHS wants to know that they can rely on receiving high quality care when they need it. Every part of the NHS and everyone who works in it should take responsibility for working to improve quality. This must be quality in its widest sense: doing the right things, at the right time for the right people and doing it right first time. And it must be the quality of the experience as well as the clinical result – quality measured in terms of prompt access, good relationships and efficient administration. (DoH 1997)

Clinical Governance is defined as 'a framework through which organisations are accountable for continuously improving the quality of their services and safeguarding high standards of care by creating an environment on which excellence flourishes'. (DoH 1998).

The framework for Clinical Governance is built around seven key areas:

1. Research and development

2. Evidence-based practice

3. Audit and effectiveness

4. Risk management

5. Patient (client) involvement

6. Leadership accountability, support and the lifelong learning of staff

7. Use of information.

The National Minimum Standards for Care, produced in 2002 and 2006, provided a baseline for which services such as rest homes and hospices could be evaluated (DoH 2002a; DoH 2006). Since 2004, the Healthcare Commission has taken over the role of monitoring organisations against these standards and frameworks (DoH 2004). Reports are published that are accessible to the consumer (patient/family), allowing them to judge and/or compare the quality of service given. Since April 2005, there has been a move towards an evidence-based self-assessment process, which is targeting inspections more effectively. However, alongside this there is the need for each organisation to demonstrate their compliance with standards, providing evidence to support their self-assessment and demonstrating ongoing development and improvement.

The challenge in paediatric palliative care

Within paediatric palliative care there has always been a reputation of high-quality services. From 1984 onwards, when children's hospices were developed, they became widely recognised for the quality of care offered (Worswick 2000). Services were developed with the needs of the child and their family, central to planning and provision, with the emphasis on a 'home from home' environment. Staffing levels were set to meet the needs of the child and family, with great importance placed on training and development. The development of services under voluntary control enabled organisations to invest in bespoke equipment and purpose-built premises, with facilities for play and family comfort – very different from the environments and priorities of the hospitals so many families were used to. Little wonder that services were viewed with great satisfaction.

The numbers of referrals to children's hospices were reflective of a high quality and individualised approach to care. Recruitment benefited greatly from word-of-mouth and personal recommendation. However, from the perspective of validity, these perceptions of quality may also have held a degree of bias. From a family perspective, there was gratitude that the services were available and a relief at the sharing of the burden of care with others who understood their trauma. There may also have been a reluctance to complain if the service was unsatisfactory. Understandably, families were focusing on their child at the end of their child's life. Inevitably, they feared that a complaint could have negative impact on the care their child received.

With the introduction of Care Standards, Clinical Governance and inspections, children's hospices and other palliative care services found themselves struggling to evidence the quality service they knew they were providing. They were left feeling that many aspects of Clinical Governance were at odds with their philosophy of a 'home from home' service. There was perhaps also a reluctance to spend time on creating an evidence-base, viewing it as a distraction from the focus on the child and family. However, in recent years, with a degree of organisation and structure, existing work projects and care have been considered and incorporated into evidence for the measurement of quality. Some children's hospices, such as Acorns, have posts of responsibility for quality assurance, benchmarking, research and development and education and training.

Demonstrating and maintaining the quality of service

Clinical/nursing care

Clinical Governance requires that clinical and nursing care is underpinned by evidence-based practice. This includes national guidelines such as those from the National Institute for Clinical Excellence (NICE), Professional Standards and the Nursing and Midwifery Council (NMC), or locally developed guidelines and policies that refer to relevant literature or research. Whilst these can be time consuming to develop, they provide a framework to measure the quality of care and a teaching tool for new staff, together with a clear structure to support individual staff practice and accountability. Involving staff groups in the research, writing and reviewing of policies and guidelines reduces the burden on senior staff and ensures acceptance and easing implementation of identified changes in practice. Whilst guidelines and policies should be easy to read and refer to, they should also reference additional evidence sources for those with more time and inclination to refer to them.

Care pathways provide clear consistent guidance for staff. They are a valuable aid for new or temporary staff in leading them through expectations of care standards. They also allow for multidisciplinary use and can be easily monitored or audited.

An efficient administration system will ensure all policies are easily identified for updating. Good information technology (IT) is crucial in providing access to journals, updating evidence, and also providing access to sites such as notice boards and on-line forums that allow the exchange and sharing of existing policies and guidelines. Special interest groups (SIGs) may help develop evidence-bases for more complex or newer areas of care and offer opportunities to share policy and practice.

Child and family involvement and feedback

One of the strengths of paediatric palliative care services is the involvement of the family and child or young person in the planning and delivery of care (Tebbitt 2000). Family members are recognised as the experts in the care of their child and staff willingly tap into their expertise without hesitation or embarrassment. In return, family members quickly learn to respect and trust the expertise of staff. This high level of information and involvement is usually recorded within the child's care plan, providing clear evidence of collaboration. Care plans that enable family members to add comments, or home diaries, are also very valuable.

It has already been stated that there is a strong link between quality and expectation. Effective use of information and good communication ensures that service-users receive reliable and current information about the availability of services. These safeguard against unrealistic expectations of what can or cannot be offered or achieved. Wherever possible, families, children and young people can be offered choices but this should only be where *real* choices exist and not just pay lip service – don't offer the choice of red jelly if there is only orange in the cupboard!

Evidence of welcome packs, leaflets and newsletters are all valuable in demonstrating quality and consistency of information. They are even better when it can be demonstrated that families and children have actively contributed to the development, presentation and content. Contributions to newsletters and publications may provide considerable insight into a personal viewpoint that could never be achieved through interview or questionnaire.

One of the biggest challenges within a palliative care environment is that, as a child nears the end of life, there is often only one remaining opportunity to do things. Clear, confident communication enables staff to ask the family (and child) their wishes and allows the family to feel confident in asking for what they really need.

Feedback

Feedback and information from families, children and young people can be received in many ways. This may be in the form of letters and cards, contributions to newsletters and leaflets, comments boxes and both informal and formal complaints. Diaries and feedback sheets are also helpful. Episodes of care can also be followed up by telephone and give an excellent opportunity to discuss any problems. These can all be collated and used both as statistical data and qualitative evidence. Informal feedback may also be gained via existing support groups.

Specific information may be extracted using focus groups, surveys and questionnaires. Individual projects such as those using drama, video, photographs or drawings may be particularly useful in working with children and young people since they allow them to express their views or preferences in a non-threatening and fun way. They will, however, require extra planning and careful preparation to ensure that the necessary information is obtained in a valid and usable format. Some will also require Local Ethics Committee approval. All require robust evidence that issues around confidentiality have been considered and addressed.

More structured research projects may also be set up using questionnaires or interviews. A level of expertise is required to ensure that the research is valid and reliable but this will ensure the credibility of the results.

Feedback to families is equally important, providing an insight into hidden areas of life at the hospice. Not only do paintings, photographs and activities logs provide reassurance to families about their child's safety and happiness, they also provide treasured memories for the future.

Staff involvement and communication

Communication and involvement of the multi-disciplinary team in quality assurance are essential components of any quality service. Effective communication should take place at all levels of the organisation and should be two-way; that is to say, top to bottom and also bottom to top. There should be ample opportunities for feedback. These will include regular appraisals, plus specific communications such as exit interviews. Staff involvement can take many forms from contributing to staff meetings to participating in staff surveys. Many staff value opportunities to be involved in specific projects, workgroups or opportunities for taking on additional responsibilities. All staff should have access to clear and accurate information about their role and the organisational policies and guidelines, together with access to current sources of evidence, to support their practice. All of these can be easily evidenced through provision of regular meeting notes and copies of information leaflets and memos. Evidence of regular staff consultation, whether formal through a structured survey, or informal from a 'post-it note' exercise, is also very valuable. Good staff involvement is supported by clear lines of accountability and clear line management structures.

Staff support

Staff support has many guises. Access to staff health services and counselling to deal with workplace stress and anxiety are particularly important in high-pressure areas such as palliative care. Ideally these should be via a self-referral process. Other opportunities to debrief or reflect will include clinical supervision sessions (both group and individual), end-of-shift debrief opportunities, reflective workshops and completion of portfolios and reflective diaries.

Many staff will welcome opportunities for flexible working, self-rostering, and access to facilities such as safe car parking, refreshments, showers and a pleasant working environment.

Staff also benefit from opportunities to share concerns through incident reporting, management supervision and opportunities for whistle blowing. Again, evidence can be sought through staff consultation and audit of services. (See Chapter 19, 'Acknowledging Staff Stress and Providing Support'.)

Staff development and training

Opportunities for training and staff development are crucial to ensure an effective workforce. While staff value frequent and generous opportunities for training, it is important that this can be demonstrated as being part of a wider plan. Such a plan encompasses both mandatory training and supplementary training to ensure that there is the right staff, with the right skills, in the right roles. Mandatory training is becoming increasingly burdensome and may challenge an independent service with limited staff and resources. Staff may need to be encouraged to explore all forms of learning. This will include areas such as e-learning and distance learning, work shadowing, journal groups and seminars, as well as university accredited courses and professional conferences. Training should link in with individual personal development plans and identified objectives. Evidence can include training schedules, outlines of teaching sessions and workshops, evaluations of training and personal development plans.

Risk management

Risk management covers a range of practices to include health and safety, risk assessment and prevention, incident reporting and analysis, and dealing with patient complaints and litigation. It will also include the development of risk registers and links closely with policy development and training.

For many palliative care services, the ethos of risk management has been a difficult concept to integrate with the philosophy of a child and family-centred service. The process of risk assessment can seem restrictive and complex but many staff find it reassuring to be working in an environment where assessment and minimising risk are part of everyday practice. Families want to be reassured that their child will be safe and that any accidents or problems will be thoroughly investigated and lessons learned.

The development of incident-reporting procedures and analysis of trends and themes is fairly new within palliative care specialities and has been viewed with suspicion by many staff. Following the publications of key documents such as *Organisation with a Memory* (DoH 2000a), many NHS organisations have moved towards positive learning from critical incidents and moved away from a blame culture. However, at some children's hospices, the concept of reporting colleagues may still create anxiety. Proactive support from management, with a focus on identifying near misses and prevention, can overcome this as can the opportunity for confidential reporting. Good incident reporting and investigation provides strong evidence of service evaluation and can identify areas for change or development. The same principles of risk assessment apply to Health and Safety practice, where standards are easily identifiable through the relevant legislation.

Audit

Clinical audit is a quality improvement process that seeks to improve the patient care and outcomes through systematic review of care against explicit criteria and the implementation of change. Aspects of the structures, processes and outcomes of care are selected and systematically evaluated against explicit criteria. Where indicated, changes at an individual, team or organisational level and further monitoring is used to confirm improvement in healthcare delivery. (NHS and Clinical Governance Support Team 2005)

Audit is crucial in recording and evaluating progress within the quality agenda of an organisation and for informing future development. Audit can be either retrospective or prospective. Retrospective audit, using past data, is beneficial in review, for example following an incident or complaint. Prospective audit is more accurate as it allows for data fields to be chosen and 100 per cent of the data to be made available for analysis. Audit is a cyclical process allowing for evaluation, change and re-evaluation (see Figure 20.1).

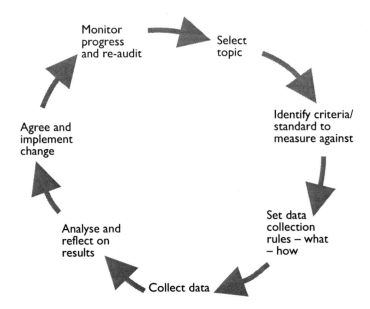

Figure 20.1 The audit cycle

Audit can be used for small or large-scale projects. These might range from the evaluation of a new record sheet through to the use of pain assessment tool, to a national study of symptom management. Ideally, each audit should have a lead person or facilitator. There are many sources of established guidelines, protocols and standards. These can be readily transformed into audit proformas, for example minimum care standards, professional guidelines, clinical guidelines. The sample chosen for audit should be small enough to allow for rapid data acquisition, but large enough to be representative. In some audits the sample will be time driven and in others it will be numerically driven. The type of data required will depend on what is being audited. Data may be computerised or recorded (numerical or written), or may require that specific questions are answered, space measured, or care observed.

The use of information

Other evidence that can be used to evaluate the quality of care will include recorded data. This includes bed occupancy, numbers of cancellations, frequency of bookings, numbers of new referrals, demography, staff turnover and recruitment success. Further measures of quality might include records such as infection rates or pressure sores. Clearly, computerised data are simpler to organise, retrieve and report on, so most children's hospices have invested in central computerised records, although these vary considerably in their complexity and the ways they are used. They range from simple 'Excel'-based programs storing client information, to complex purpose-built systems that also provide facilities for nurse rostering and computerised care planning. Given the principle that data is only as reliable as the person entering it, many hospices have had to invest in additional clerical and computer support roles to ensure that the data collected is robust and accurate.

Association of Children's Hospices Quality Assurance Project

Are We Getting it Right? was developed by ACH from 2001 with input from staff and families from many children's hospices. A comprehensive data-set was developed for each of six key aspects of hospice care, namely access; the child; the family; the staff; the environment; and communication. The purpose of the Quality Assurance Project is to enable hospice care teams to judge how well they are supporting life-limited children and their families and then to improve care following this assessment. Quality assurance link persons (QUALPs) were identified in each hospice to cascade and implement the project which was rolled out to all children's hospices from 2004 with the support of a facilitator and regional support groups. This work has now been recognised by the Healthcare Commission as an integral part of evidence to be provided for inspection. Many children's hospice services have implemented the process of self-evaluation and produced action plans to implement changes and innovations (ACH 2004).

Benchmarking

Benchmarking enables the quality of service delivery to be measured through the comparison of distinct areas of care with other services scoring against a core statement. This includes taking part in national benchmarking projects or taking part in special interest forums, such as the ACH benchmarking groups.

In conclusion, palliative care services are well-recognised for the attention to detail which ensures the best possible care at the end of life. There is ample evidence of high quality services but persistence, vision and training is required to ensure that the evidence collected reflects the breadth of holistic care being provided. A robust Clinical Governance framework that is supported and understood at all levels of the organisation will provide the tools to measure and demonstrate quality of the service and help to identify areas for future developments.

Key points

- The measurement of quality in palliative care today is firmly rooted in models of total quality management introduced in the United Kingdom in the 1960s.

- The National Minimum Standards for Care (2002, 2006) provided a baseline against which services could be evaluated in settings such as rest homes and hospices.

- From 2004, the Healthcare Commission has taken over monitoring against National Minimum Standards for Care. Many palliative care services have successfully introduced evidence-based self-assessment processes.

- For many palliative care services, the ethos of risk management has been a difficult concept to integrate with the philosophy of family-centred care.

- Audit is crucial in recording and evaluating progress within the quality agenda of an organisation and for informing future development.

- Benchmarking enables the quality of service delivery to be measured through distinct areas of care, scoring against a core statement.

Implications for practice

- Organisations need to be able to demonstrate their compliance with standards and to provide evidence to support self-assessment, demonstrating ongoing development and improvement.

- Involving staff in research, writing and the review of the organisation's policies and guidelines is likely to ease the implementation of identified changes in practice.

- Care pathways should be introduced that provide clear, consistent guidelines for staff leading them through expected standards of care.

- Efficient administration systems and good information technology is crucial to high standards of service-delivery.

- Clients and families can provide valuable evidence of user-involvement in service provision.

- Where families are involved in quality assurance, it is essential that there is evidence that their confidentiality is safeguarded and that ethical considerations have been addressed.

- Effective communication should be a two-way process at all levels within an organisation; that is to say, top to bottom and also bottom to top.

- Access to staff support is particularly important for people working in palliative care. Ideally this should be via a self-referral process.

- Palliative care services should provide regular opportunities for members of the workforce to participate in clinical supervision, debrief sessions, reflective workshops and the completion of portfolios and reflective diaries (as appropriate).

- Opportunities for training and development are crucial to ensuring an effective workforce. Training should link in with personal development plans.

- An organisation has a responsibility to nurture an environment where assessment and minimising risk is part of everyday practice.

- A robust Clinical Governance framework that is understood and supported at all levels of the organisation will provide the tools to measure and demonstrate service quality and help to identify areas for further developments.

- A person should be given designated responsibility as lead or facilitator for the process of audit.

21

The Role of Research and Development in Children's Hospices

Erica Brown

From the beginning of time humankind has sought after knowledge, because knowledge brings an element of control and power. Those who possess knowledge are often bestowed with authority and status. In many healthcare settings throughout the world there has been a move to set the standards of care with guidelines of 'best practice'. This is often associated with the development of clinical audit that systematically examines and evaluates clinical practice.

The need for research and critical evaluation alongside the delivery of compassionate holistic care was recognised at the time of the foundation of the modern hospice movement in the United Kingdom in the 1960s. In more recent times, research in palliative care has emerged as a practice speciality (Richards, Corner and Clark 1998). Since the 1990s the demand for an evidence-base in healthcare has been underpinned by several Health Service reforms, and a necessity for clear indicators of the outcomes and quality of the care given. The European Health Committee (1996) published a report on Clinical Research recommending that all qualified nurses should:

- be able to read and critically assess research literature relevant to their practice
- have a knowledge and understanding of data collection methods and analysis
- recognise the importance of research and evidence-based knowledge for the improvement of nursing practice and patient care.

Recent initiatives in the Health Service have included Clinical Governance, the National Institute for Clinical Excellence (NICE), and the Commission for Health Improvements. However, Goodman reported in 2000 that there was little evidence at the time of the effectiveness of the above legislation in improving standards of care. Field *et al.* (2001) noted that, although there were numerous texts addressing research in medical and social contexts, there was only one text addressing research in palliative care settings. Without a sound evidence-base it is impossible to audit whether families are receiving best practice.

Children's palliative care services have developed rapidly in response to the needs of life-limited children and their families. Therefore, meeting care needs has understandably been given priority over establishing a sound evidence-base. However, good quality research does have the potential for enhancing care. Several university-based research centres have contributed to adult palliative care development during the last two decades. The contribution of research and development to children's hospice services is, however, a relatively new concept, not least because of the ethical issues surrounding using children as subjects for research and the debate about whether patients and their families should be asked to engage in research when the patient is life-limited or dying. Posts to coordinate research in children's palliative care settings are still in the process of emerging. Acorns Children's Hospices took the lead with the appointment of a Head of Research and Development as an integral member of the Care Team in 2001.

Most other children's hospice organisations are small and are therefore unable to justify supporting the salary of a person responsible for research and development. Where this is the case, collaboration with similar organisations, including adult care services, is perhaps the way forward.

The contribution of research and development to paediatric palliative care

Theory may seem remote from everyday practice and, consequently, a certain amount of scepticism may prevail about the value of research. However, as we have seen above, recent policy decisions have highlighted the connection between research and practice.

In daily life, people gather information and draw conclusions. They have questions to which they seek answers and they talk to others and observe their behaviour in order to come to some conclusions. The difference between lay persons and researchers in finding answers to questions is that the latter are rigorous and systematic in their approach, taking steps to prevent their procedures influencing the decisions and actions they take. They describe in detail the steps taken throughout the investigation so that others are able to follow the process.

Although good research can provide insights into the practice being investigated, findings are not definitive: there is always scope to further knowledge and understanding, and to increase evidence-based policy and practice. Crow (1992) listed four areas that research could potentially contribute to practice:

- provide insights into current practice
- deepen understanding of concepts and philosophy of care
- contribute to the development of new and improved methods of care
- test the effectiveness of existing care.

According to the National Council for Hospice and Specialist Palliative Care Services, involvement in research is a vital element in palliative care, and the implementation of evidence-based practice is a key aspect of service quality. Research has been defined in many ways. One definition is 'an attempt to increase available knowledge, by discovery of new facts or relationships through systematic enquiry' (Macleod-Clark and Hockey 1998, p.4). Parahoo (1997) describes research as 'a private enterprise made public for the purpose of exposing it to the scrutiny of others, to allow for replication, verification, or falsification'. Payne (2000) says that 'research and the acquisition of new knowledge in palliative care are about numerous small footsteps towards the light, rather than giant leaps into the dark' (p.234).

Differentiating between research and quality improvement

It is necessary to make the distinction between research and quality improvement or clinical audit. The fundamental difference is that the aim of quality improvement is to evaluate and enhance the actual experience of the care families are receiving, whilst research strives to yield new evidence and information relevant to paediatric palliative care. Smith (1992) describes and differentiates between the two as:

> Research is concerned with discovering the right things to do, whereas quality improvement seeks to make sure that the right thing is done. (pp.105–6)

Research in palliative care services for children and their families has an enormous contribution to make to a public understanding of the effects of suffering, loss and grief, and to wider medicine and healthcare generally.

Paediatric palliative care services face the same demands for evidence of effectiveness and value for money as do adult general health services. Just over a decade ago, Frager (1996) described paediatric palliative care services as 'inadequate and inconsistent'. Indeed, many would argue that modern medicine focuses on investigation, diagnosis, treatment, and cure of illness, at the expense of caring for pain and suffering. Kane *et al.* (2000) believe that such an attitude has led to the belief that suffering is a scandal, and a problem to be conquered, rather than a challenge to be lived.

Evidence-based practice

Technology has increased the availability of research findings and the development of research methodology. Although evidence-based healthcare is not new, its popularity has grown with a need to record experience in an unbiased way. The term 'evidence-based' is an amalgam of scientific and professional practice. 'Evidence-based' implies scientific rationality, and 'practice' individual practitioner behaviour. Unfortunately, evidence-based research is not always what Brett (1997) refers to as 'practice ready', or clinically useful. Often it needs to be 'repackaged' and its significance and usefulness to practice determined.

In the children's hospice movement, evidence-based practice is generally understood as the process of finding, evaluating and applying evidence to the care of life-limited children and their families. Its ultimate goal is to bring about better care for families and to support practitioners in their decision-making.

It would be foolish to suggest that all members of an organisation should engage in research. Nevertheless everyone who contributes to family care should at least be sympathetic towards the contribution of research to practice, be aware of research findings, be willing to collaborate with colleagues in research activities, and safeguard the rights of families with regard to their involvement as research subjects. All research starts with an idea that needs to be fostered and nurtured into a research project. Discussing the idea within teams will safeguard against re-inventing the wheel, and ensure that the viability of the research focus has not already been discounted.

ACH and ACT have endorsed the important role research and development plays in the continuous improvement of care for life-limited children and their families. However, it is imperative that research methodology and data analysis is rigorous, and describes the holistic experience of families. It is important to ensure that any study is designed and carried out in a way that minimises bias and maximises the confidence that can be placed in its findings. The value of research as a source of information must be contextualised. Research results can be inconclusive if the research only attempts to answer questions the researcher wants answered. Indeed, Hunt (1997) believes that 'derided old wives' tales' and traditional beliefs sometimes have been found to have sound rationales, whilst research can be 'erroneous and even fraudulent'.

How a service provider uses research findings to enhance the quality of care provided is an integral part of the process. It will include the dissemination of the research so that the personnel involved in giving care can translate and demonstrate the findings into everyday practice and evaluate its impact.

> Research without practice is like building castles in the air. Practice without research is building castles on slippery ground. (Parahoo 1997)

Managers in paediatric palliative care can:

- encourage employees to disseminate research findings and to incorporate them into training
- seek out research reports themselves
- provide a forum to discuss research ideas at team and executive levels
- encourage service-users to be involved in research
- use learning from research as a springboard for practice.

Ethical considerations

Having a life-limiting illness is a multi-faceted experience. The situation threatens spiritual, physical and psychological dimensions of being, the relationships between parents and their child, and may raise questions to which there are no definitive answers. Therefore, the implications of the child's illness need to be considered holistically, with the child and their family at the centre of care. Research must *never* compromise the wellbeing of families.

Historically, discussion about ethical issues in medicine took place amongst clinicians. The Hippocratic Oath is still regarded as the basis for ethical issues in medicine. However, palliative care embraces many different disciplines which encompass a multi-professional approach to holistic care.

In recent years there has been a trend towards producing guidelines and regulations relating to research involving people in palliative care settings. In the United Kingdom these guidelines are known as 'Research Governance'. The guidelines are designed to minimise risk to participants and increase the quality of research undertaken.

The Research Governance framework for Health and Social Care in the United Kingdom embraces five areas:

1. *Ethics* – the rights, dignity, wellbeing, and safety of participants

2. *Science* – the appropriateness and quality of the research

3. *Information* – access to research findings

4. *Health and Safety* – of participants and staff

5. *Finance.*

(See the list of useful websites at the end of the references section for further information.)

Ethical issues change as children live longer and society responds to its involvement in healthcare. Indeed, Webb (2000) stresses that, although there are no finite and absolute answers to ethical dilemmas, ethical standards are essential to the practice of healthcare professionals. Children's palliative care has its own philosophy, code of conduct, and guidelines, deeply rooted in the International Declaration of Human Rights. Recent codes of conduct reflect earlier statements of practice in adult palliative care, such as the Geneva Convention of the 1940s, the Declaration of Helsinki, 1964, and British Paediatric Association, 1992. Paediatric palliative care is still a relatively new speciality.

In research relating to children's hospices, ethical considerations will include appropriate research methodology, inclusion of children and their families, and safeguarding confidentiality. There has been an established view that research involving adult patients who are dying and their families is intrusive (Webb 2000). However, given that the time-span for children's palliative care is markedly different in many cases from adult care, experience at Acorns Children's Hospices suggests that families are not only willing to participate in research that aims to evaluate the services provided, but they have an expectation of being partners in the process of the research and in the dissemination of findings.

Involving children in research is a relatively new concept. Prior to legislation such as the Children Act (1989), the Children (Northern Ireland) Order (1995) and the Children (Scotland) Act (1995), children were rarely asked to comment on the quality of care they received. In part, this may be the result of a number of assumptions: that adults believe that they are able to recall their own childhood experiences accurately, and that they are able to make balanced and relevant judgements on behalf of children; that children are unwilling to participate in discussions; or that the views of children are naïve. In recent years, studies have shown that children *are* able to offer their views and opinions (Doorbar 1995; Measelle, Ablow and Cowan 1998). This is endorsed by the Children Act (1989). Furthermore Article 12 of The United Nations Convention on the Rights of the Child (UNESCO 1991) states:

Children's views must be taken into account in all matters affecting them, subject to the child's age and maturity.

One of the most significant concerns about including children in research is about gaining consent (Coyne 1998). Often consent has been given via the child's parent or guardian, but, as Coyne states, for research to be valid it needs to be carried out 'with children rather than on children'.

Children with a high degree of cognitive disabilities have often been excluded from research because it has been thought that they are unable to articulate their views. This has been refuted by studies such as Farnfield and Kaszap (1998) and Erling (1999), who argue that, as long as appropriate communication methods are used, these young people's opinions can make a valuable contribution to practice.

Ethical practice requires that professionals are committed to the best interests of service users. Research should always be deeply rooted in professional values so that the evidence that it provides contributes to reflective practice.

The key stakeholders in research projects that involve an evaluation of care will include the organisation, families, other providers of care services, local community healthcare groups and sources of funding or organising and planning the services which families use. Vigilance is necessary to protect the interests of families first and foremost. Many of the principles relating to ethics in paediatric palliative care are relevant to the care of the child and the family from the time of diagnosis onwards. Day by day, staff in palliative care settings find themselves in situations where decisions have to be made that include clinical, ethical and practical issues which may relate to ethical principles. Practitioners will recognise these principles as underpinning and supporting their philosophy of care. Applying them holistically means being open to matching the principles to individual families. Where parents are involved in drawing up their child's care plan, there is greater likelihood that research does not compromise individual needs. At every stage of the research, ethical considerations should be employed, including the choice of topics for research, the design of the enquiry, and how publication of the results will take place.

It has become generally accepted that researchers should underpin their work with four principles:

1. *Autonomy* – the research should be sympathetic towards the rights, wishes and needs of the research participants and gain their informed consent. The aims and nature of the research should be explained.

2. *Beneficence* – the participant(s) should benefit from participating in the research.

3. *Non-maleficence* – the researcher has a duty to safeguard against the research participant(s) experiencing nuisance, harm or risk as a result of the involvement in the research. Any potential changes in care should be explained.

4. *Justice* – the outcomes of the research should benefit all participants equally.

Issues of confidentiality

Information collected during the research should never be disclosed in a way that identifies a person without their permission. It is also important to determine with the participants how the outcomes of the research may be shared, for example through journal articles and conference papers.

Ethics Committee approval

Approval to conduct research should be obtained from a local Research Ethics Committee *before* it starts. The Ethics Committee is an independent body whose role is to protect research participants from unacceptable risks or exploitation (Blunt, Savulescu and Watson 1998). Most Primary Care Trusts and Health Authorities have established local Ethics Committees and all children's palliative care providers should have links with their local committee.

Involving families in research

Involving service users as partners in research, design and implementation is becoming increasingly common (Acorns 2000, 2006). In children's palliative care settings, families often use the services for many years and they may show a willingness to be actively involved in research, both before and after their child's death. Involvement for altruistic reasons has been recognised amongst parents who have a child with special needs for many years (Hornby 1998) and Acorns' experience demonstrates that other family members such as siblings and grandparents also wish to be involved. However, the supportive nature of children's palliative care may make families particularly willing to engage in research in an attempt to show service providers gratitude for the care they are receiving. This does, however, make families particularly vulnerable and prone to feeling that they should adhere to requests. Therefore, it is absolutely vital that researchers should be on their guard so that they do not take advantage of families.

If questionnaires and surveys are used to collect information, families may find it extremely difficult to be honest about the care they have already received or are currently receiving. The viewpoints of different individuals will not always coincide. Indeed, there may be times when they conflict with one another.

Before inviting families to become involved they should be given the following information in ways that are accessible to them:

- what the research aims to achieve
- how long the project is likely to last
- what benefits families can expect to gain from their involvement
- that families are able to withdraw from their involvement in the project at any time
- how the confidentiality of individual family members will be protected.

Defining types of research

Research in palliative care is many faceted and can include clinical research, Health Services research, sociological and health psychology research, epidemiological research and economic evaluation.

Clinical research

The term 'clinical' includes care for the child or their family that involves medical interventions that may be nursing, psychosocial, spiritual or physiotherapy-based. Generally the focus of the research will be the impact and outcomes of the care provided.

Health Services research

Health Services research includes studying the health needs of a community and evaluating the efficiency and effectiveness of services to meet those needs. For example, where children's palliative care services are best matched to the needs of life-limited children and their families, rigorous enquiry will have taken place before service provision has been planned and implemented.

Sociological research

Sociological research addresses issues such as the values and beliefs that people hold and the significance of psychosocial interactions that take place during the process of care-giving.

Epidemiological research

This focuses on groups of people or larger populations rather than individuals. Generally epidemiological research concentrates on a statistical analysis of records, rather than collecting data as the result of interactions with individuals. A statistical analysis of the numbers of clients from South Asian communities using Acorns' services has contributed to a recently published text on palliative care (Brown, Gatrad and Sheikh 2005).

Size of research sample

Research studies do not have to use large numbers of people to be informative. Small research projects may yield rich data that can illuminate policy and practice. They can also serve as valuable pilot studies that demonstrate that the research is feasible within a defined time scale. It is, however, imperative that findings that are used to inform practice are valid. All research methods are flawed. The research question or hypothesis will determine the best suited method of data collection.

Qualitative research versus quantitative research

For many people, establishing evidence means identifying the impact of service delivery as scientifically as possible, carefully evaluating cause and effect. Others will challenge this approach, believing that a more accurate picture of service users' views is obtained through actively recording their perceptions and experiences. Field et al. (2001), in their seminal text on researching palliative care, say that, 'although some consideration needs to be given to the difference between research approaches, there are no best or worst methods' (p.7).

Distinguishing between qualitative and quantitative research can be problematic. The popular notion that quantitative research deals with quantity and numbers and that qualitative research deals with quality and anecdotal evidence is simplistic. Until fairly recently, quantitative research was perceived to be of greater value to patient care because it provides hard objective facts that can be statistically analysed and interpreted. Objectivity means that the researcher can stand 'outside' the phenomenon in order to study it, so that their personal preferences are unlikely to compromise the validity of the findings.

The philosophy of children's palliative care is congruent with research methods that are patient-centred and holistic. Data collection methods should therefore take into account how social, cultural and other factors influence the experiences and behaviour of the families concerned. The views of individual family members need to be taken into account so that their experiences, wishes and rights are respected. Qualitative research focuses on the way in which those who are the subjects of the research make sense of their experiences. Thus, the process involves personal involvement between the researcher and the patients and their families.

Payne (2000) has provided an insight into how qualitative research methods may contribute to research in palliative care settings. Critics of qualitative research argue that over-involvement of researchers in the research process means that they are unable to remain objective. Mays and Pope (1995) refer to qualitative research as 'an assembly of anecdote and personal impressions, strongly subject to researcher biases' (p.110).

There have been numerous texts which advocate the use of either qualitative or quantitative research methodology to inform policy and practice. Rather than providing an in-depth discussion as to the merits or otherwise of either of these approaches here, the following text outlines some of the factors that staff are encouraged to take into account before deciding on data collection methodology at Acorns Children's Hospices.

Whichever research methodology is chosen, the outcomes are only likely to be as good as the questions that underpin the enquiries. Using the method of data collection, questions should always be clear and unambiguous and must never be biased towards a particular response. Therefore, the data collection process should:

- be geared in length to the likely tolerance of the respondents
- be unbiased
- be unambiguous
- generate ease
- use language familiar to respondents
- indicate the level of detail required
- have a coherent structure, with clearly defined introduction and conclusion.

The range of data collection methods that may be used include:

- observation – the researcher is at the heart of the research, setting questions, reporting events and circumstances first-hand, often recording these in a field work diary
- interviews (individual or group) – using a check list of topics or themes for discussion
- focus groups – where the researcher acts as a facilitator of discussion about topics determined in advance

- documentary analysis, including care plans
- case studies – including observation and interviews with individual family members, staff etc.

Questionnaires are appropriate when:

- large numbers of respondents are involved across a wide geographical area
- 'facts' rather than opinions are sought
- data are analysed in a standard format
- respondents prefer time to reflect before responding to the questions asked
- researcher time is at a premium.

Interviews are appropriate when:

- small numbers are involved
- the enquiry is exploratory in nature
- attitudes of respondents are sought
- sensitive areas are explored
- complex situations exist
- non-verbal responses may have significance
- flexibility is required.

Interest is growing in children's services responsible for paediatric palliative care. This is evident by the number of invitations to give conference papers and write journal articles, or to attend meetings, by staff from Acorns Children's Hospices. Evidence-based practice has already had a major impact on the development of care in adult palliative care settings. In the future, it is likely that resource allocation will be based on efficacy and also on cost-effectiveness, with the result that, where efficacy is lacking, funds will not be provided. This has enormous implications for paediatric palliative care because research-based evidence is sparse, and most paediatric palliative care services are voluntary organisations.

The planning and evolvement of paediatric palliative care depends on accurate knowledge of the families it serves. What appears to be a greater number of service providers in geographical regions such as the South East of the United Kingdom compared with the remainder of the country, and the planned amalgamation of some established services, may beg the question whether there has been a sufficiently rigorous assessment of need, prior to the planning, building and operation of children's hospice care units.

Paediatric palliative care is at a critical stage in its evolution. Evidence-based practice is not a new idea. It has always been implicit that practice should be based on the best possible evidence. The challenge in children's palliative care is not only to consider the quality of everyday practice but to assess the needs of all families. This ensures that the evidence-base continues to grow so that care is truly matched to the unique needs of individual family members.

Key points

- Demand for an evidence-base in healthcare has been underpinned by several Health Service reforms and the necessity for clear indicators of the outcomes and quality of the care given.

- The contribution of research and development to children's hospice services is a relatively new concept, not least because of ethical issues surrounding involving patients and their families.

- Although good research can provide insights into practice, findings are not definitive: there is always scope to further knowledge and understanding, and to increase evidence-based policy and practice.

- The distinction should be made between research, and quality improvement, or clinical audit. The aim of quality improvement is to evaluate and enhance the actual experience of care families are receiving. Research strives to yield new evidence and information.

- In the children's hospice movement, evidence-based practice is generally understood as the process of finding, evaluating and applying evidence to the care of life-limited children and their families. The ultimate goal is to bring about better care for families and to support practitioners in their decision-making.

- Experience at Acorns suggests that families are not only willing to participate in research that aims to evaluate the services provided, but they have an expectation of being partners in the research process, and in the dissemination of findings.

- Children with a high degree of cognitive impairment *are* able to express their opinions and make a valuable contribution to an evidence-base, as long as appropriate communication methods are employed.

- Distinguishing between qualitative and quantitative research can be problematic. The popular notion that quantitative research deals with quantity and numbers and that qualitative research deals with quality and anecdotal evidence is simplistic.

Implications for practice

- Organisations should recognise that, without a sound evidence-base, it is impossible to audit whether families are receiving best practice.

- Research must *never* compromise the wellbeing of families.

- All persons involved in family care should at least be sympathetic towards the contribution of research to practice; be aware of the outcomes of research; and be willing to collaborate with colleagues in research activities, and safeguard the rights of families with regard to their involvement as research subjects.

- Small research projects may yield rich data and they may also serve as valuable pilot studies.

- At every stage of research, ethical considerations should be employed, including the choice of topic for research, the design of the enquiry, and how the publication of the results will take place.

References

ACH (Association of Children's Hospices) (2004) *Are We Getting it Right? A Tool to Measure the Quality of Children's Hospice Services.* Bristol: ACH.

ACH (Association of Children's Hospices) (2006) *Factsheet.* Bristol: ACH. [See Useful websites]

Acorns (2000) *The Experiences and Expectations of Asian Mothers with a Life-Limited Child.* (Unpublished research) Birmingham: Acorns Children's Hospice Trust.

Acorns (2003) 'The experiences and expectations of Asian mothers.' *Asian Mothers' Newsletter 1,* 2, 1–2.

Acorns (2006) *An Evaluation of Routine Respite Care at Acorns 3 Hospices.* (Unpublished research) Birmingham: Acorns Children's Hospice Trust.

ACT (Association for Children with Life-threatening or Terminal Conditions and Their Families) (2001) *Palliative Care for Young People Aged 13–24: A Joint Report by ACT, National Council for Hospice and Specialist Palliative Care and Scottish Partnership Agency for Palliative and Cancer Care.* Bristol: ACT.

ACT (Association for Children with Life-threatening or Terminal Conditions and Their Families) and RCPCH (Royal College of Paediatrics and Child Health) (2003) *A Guide to the Development of Children's Palliative Care Services,* 2nd edn. Bristol: ACT/RCPCH.

Adams, J., Hershatter, M. and Moritz, D. (1991) 'Accumulation loss phenomenon among hospice caregivers.' *American Journal of Hospice and Palliative Care 21,* 6, 452–8.

Adler, S. (1990) 'Taking children at their word: pain control in paediatrics.' *Professional Nurse,* May, 398–401.

Affleck, G., Tennen, H. and Rowe, J. (1991) *Infants in Crisis. How Parents Cope with Newborn Intensive Care and its Aftermath.* New York: Springer.

Ahmad, W. (1996) 'Family obligations and social change among South Asian communities.' In W. Ahmad and K. Atkin (eds) *'Race' and Community Care.* Buckingham: Open University Press.

Aldred, H. (2001) *Research Proposal to Explore the Impact of the Word 'Hospice' on Parents Caring for a Life-Limited/Life-Threatened Child.* (Unpublished dissertation.)

Almond, B., Buckman, W. and Gofman, H. (1979) *The Family is the Patient – An Approach to Behavioural Paediatrics.* London: Mosby.

Altschuler, J. (1997) *Working with Chronic Illness.* London: Macmillan.

Amene, M. and Treves, S. (2000) 'Last Offices.' In J. Mallet and L. Dougherty (eds) *Royal Marsden Hospital Manual of Clinical Nursing Procedures.* Oxford: Blackwell Science.

Anand, K.J. and Craig, K.D. (1997) 'New perspectives in the definition of pain.' *Pain 67,* 1, 3–6.

Armstrong Dailey, A. and Zarbock, S. (2001) *Hospice Care for Children,* 2nd edn. Oxford: Oxford University Press.

Atkins, K. and Rollings, J. (1998) 'Looking after their Own? Family Care Giving among Asian and Afro-Caribbean Communities.' In W. Ahmad and K. Atkins (eds) *Race and Community Care.* Buckingham: Open University Press.

Attig, T. (1996) *How we Grieve: Relearning the World.* New York: Oxford University Press.

Aynsley Green, A. (2005) Interview, 29 June, *Children Now.*

Barnard, P., Morland, I. and Nagy, J. (1999) *Children, Bereavement and Trauma – Nurturing Resilience.* London: Jessica Kingsley Publishers.

Barnes, K. (2001) 'Staff stress in the children's hospice: causes, effects and coping strategies.' *International Journal of Palliative Nursing 7,* 5, 254–6.

Barnett, W.S. and Boyce, G. (1995) 'Effects of children with Down's syndrome on parents' activities.' *American Journal of Mental Retardation 11,* 2, 115–17.

Baum, D. (1998) 'Life-limited Children.' In T. Nash, 'Medical Support at School: Children with Life-threatening Illness.' *Childright,* October.

Beattie, R. (1999) *Implementing Inclusiveness: Realising Potential.* Edinburgh: Scottish Executive.

Bennet, F. and Abrahams, C. (1994) *Unequal Opportunities: Children with Disabilities and their Families Speak Out.* London: NCH Action for Children.

Benzein, E. (2001) 'The meaning of the lived experience of hope in patients with cancer in palliative home care.' *Palliative Medicine 15*, 2, 117–26.

Beresford, B. (1995) *Expert Opinions: A National Survey of Parents Caring for a Severely Disabled Child.* Bristol: Policy Press.

Bjornberg, U. and Buck-Wiklund, M. (1990) *The Organisation of Everyday Family Life in the Family and the Neighbourhood.* Goteborg: Daidalos.

Black, D. (1989) 'Life threatening illness, children and family therapy.' *Journal of Family Therapy 22*, 18–24.

Black, D. (2002) 'Bereavement.' In A. Goldman (ed.) *Care of the Dying Child.* Oxford: Oxford University Press.

Black, D. and Wood, D. (1989) 'Family therapy and life-threatening illness in children and parents.' *Palliative Medicine 3*, 113–18.

Bluebond-Langner, M. (1995) 'Worlds of dying children and their well siblings.' *Death Studies 13*, 1–16.

Blunt, J., Savulescu, J. and Watson, A.J. (1998) 'Meeting the challenges facing research ethics committees: some practical suggestions.' *British Medical Journal 316*, 58–61.

Bolton, A. (1997) *Losing the Thread: Pupils' and Parents' Voices about Education for Sick Children.* London: NAEC.

Bottemly, V. House of Commons Hansard Debates. 15 Dec 1989. www.publications.parliament.uk

Bradford, R. (1997) *Children, Families and Chronic Disease.* London: Routledge.

Bray, A. (1997) *Fathers and Children with Disabilities.* Seminar at Westminster College, Oxford, 15 May 1997.

Brett, J. (1997) 'Use of nursing practice research findings.' *Nursing Research 36*, 6, 344–9.

British Paediatric Association (1992) *Guidelines for the Ethical Conduct of Medical Research Involving Children.* London: British Paediatric Association.

Brown, E. (1999) *Loss, Change and Grief – An Educational Perspective.* London: David Fulton.

Brown, E. (2001) 'The Trauma of Life-limiting Illness.' In E. Brown and D. Kinchin (eds) *Supporting Children with Post Traumatic Stress Disorder – A Handbook for Teachers and Professionals.* London: David Fulton.

Brown, E. (2002) *The Death of a Child – Care for the Child, Support for the Family.* Birmingham: Acorns Children's Hospice.

Brown, E. (2004) *The Experiences and Expectations of Asian Mothers with a Life-limited Child.* Birmingham: Acorns Children's Hospice.

Brown, E. (2005a) *Enhancing the Quality of Experience for Christian Families.* Birmingham: Acorns Children's Hospice.

Brown, E. (2005b) *Enhancing the Quality of Experience for Muslim Families.* Birmingham: Acorns Children's Hospice.

Brown, E. (2005c) *Enhancing the Quality of Experience for Hindu Families.* Birmingham: Acorns Children's Hospice.

Brown, E. (2005d) *Enhancing the Quality of Experience for Sikh Families.* Birmingham: Acorns Children's Hospice.

Brown, E. and Arens, G. (2005) *Siblings Project – Listening to Brothers and Sisters.* Birmingham: Acorns Children's Hospice Trust.

Brown, E. and Mercer, A. (2005) 'The Mercer model of paediatric palliative care.' *European Journal of Palliative Care 12*, 1, 22–5.

Brown, E., Gatrad, R. and Sheikh, A. (2005) *Palliative Care Amongst South Asians.* London: Quay Books.

Bruce, E. and Schultz, C. (2001) *Non-finite Loss and Grief – A Psycho-educational Approach.* London: Jessica Kingsley Publishers.

Bullard, I.D. and Dohnal, J.T. (1994) 'The community deals with a child who has a handicap.' *Nursing Clinics of North America 19*, 309–18.

Burnard, P. (1994) *Counselling Skills for Health Professionals*, 2nd edn. London: Chapman and Hall.

Callery, P. (1997) 'Maternal knowledge and professional knowledge: co-operation and conflict in the care of sick children.' *International Journal of Nursing Studies 34*, 1, 27–34.

Callery, P. and Smith, L. (1991) 'A study of role negotiation between nurses and the parents of hospitalised children.' *Journal of Advanced Nursing 16*, 772–81.

Capewell, B. and Beattie, L. (1996) 'Staff Care and Support.' In B. Lindsay and J. Elsgood (eds) *Working with Children in Grief and Loss.* London: Balliere Tindall.

Carers and Disabled Children Act. (2000) London: HMSO.

Carlisle, D. (1988) 'From hospice to respice.' *Nursing Standard*, 13 August, p.20.

Carpenter, B. (ed.) (1997) *Families in Context: Emerging Trends in Family Support and Early Intervention.* London: David Fulton.

Carter, B., McArthur, E. and Cunliffe, M. (2001) 'Dealing with uncertainty: parental assessment of pain in their children with profound special needs.' *Journal of Advanced Nursing 38*, 5, 449–57.

Casey, A. (1988) 'A partnership with child and family.' *Senior Nurse 8*, 4, 8–9.

Centre for Bereavement Research and Intervention (University of Utrecht, Netherlands) (1997) 'Couples at risk following death of their child.' Paper given at University of Utrecht, July.

Chadwick, H. (1999) 'A Comparison of General Practitioners and Parents' Perceptions of a Children's Hospice.' In C. Robinson and P. Jackson (eds) *Children's Hospices – A Lifeline for Families?* London: National Children's Bureau/Joseph Rowntree Foundation.

Chamba, R., Ahmad, W., Hirst, M., Lawton, D. and Beresford, B. (1999) *On the Edge: Minority Ethnic Families Caring for a Severely Disabled Child.* Bristol: The Policy Press.

Chapman, J.A. and Goodall, J. (1980) 'Helping a child to live whilst dying.' *Lancet 1*, 8171, 753–6.

Children Act. (1989) London: HMSO.

Children (Northern Ireland) Order. (1995) London: HMSO.

Children (Scotland) Act. (1995) Edinburgh: Stationery Office.

Clark, J. and Jacinta, S. (1995) *Caring for the Dying Patient and the Family.* Cheltenham: Nelson Thornes.

Closs, A. and Norris, C. (1997) *Outlook Uncertain: Enabling the Education of Children with Chronic and/or Deteriorating Conditions.* Edinburgh: Moray House Institute of Education.

Coleman, J.C. and Hendry, L. (1993) *The Nature of Adolescence and Illness.* London: Routledge.

Coles, B., Britton, L. and Hicks, L. (2004) *Building Better Connexions – Interagency Work with the Connexions Service.* York: Joseph Rowntree Foundation.

Collier, J. (1997) 'Attitudes to children's pain: exploring the pain "myth".' *Paediatric Nursing 9*, 10, 15–18.

Cook, P. (1999) *Supporting Sick Children and their Families.* London: Balliere Tindall.

Cooke, M. (1992) 'The challenge of hospice nursing.' *American Journal of Hospice and Palliative Care 9*, 1, 34–7.

Cooper, C. (1999) *Continuing Care of Sick Children – Examining the Impact of Chronic Illness.* Salisbury: Quay Books.

Cooper, C. and Mitchell, S. (1990) 'Nursing the critically ill and dying.' *Human Relations 43*, 297–311.

Corden, A., Sainsbury, R. and Sloper, P. (2001) *Financial Implications of the Death of a Child.* York: Joseph Rowntree Foundation.

Corlett, J. and Twycross, A. (2006) 'Negotiation of care by children's nurses – lessons from research.' *Journal of Palliative Nursing 18*, 8, 34–7.

Coroners Act (c.13). (1988) London: HMSO.

Coroners Rules. (1984) London: HMSO.

Cowles, K.V. (1996) 'Cultural perspectives of grief – an expanded concept analysis.' *Journal of Advanced Nursing 23*, 287–94.

Coyne, I.T. (1998) 'Researching children: some methodological and ethical considerations.' *Journal of Clinical Nursing 7*, 409–16.

Craig, K., Lilley, C.M. and Gilbert, C. (1996) 'Social barriers to optimal pain management in infants and children.' *Clinical Journal of Pain 12*, 232–42.

Cremation (Amendment) Regulations. (2006) London: HMSO.

Crow, R. (1992) 'How nursing and the community can benefit from nursing research.' *International Journal of Nursing Studies 19*, 1, 37–45.

Cummings, E.A., Reid, G.J. and Finley, A. (1996) 'Prevalence and sources of pain in paediatric infants.' *Journal of Pain 68*, 25–31.

Cunningham, C. (1991) 'Behavioural and linguistic development in the interactions of normal and retarded children with their mothers.' *Child Development 52*, 62–70.

Davies, B. (1999) *Shadows in the Sun – The Experiences of Sibling Bereavement in Childhood.* Philadelphia: Bruner Mazel.

Davies, B. and de Vlaming, D. (2006) 'Symptom Control at the End of Life.' In A. Goldman, R. Hain and S. Liben (eds) *Oxford Textbook Palliative Care for Children.* Oxford: Oxford University Press.

Davis, H. (1993a) *Counselling Parents of Children with Chronic Illness or Disability.* Leicester: BPS Books.

Davis, P. (1993a) 'Opening up the gate control theory.' *Nursing Standard 7*, 45, 25–7.

DfEE (Department for Education and Employment) (1997) *Making Connections: A Guide for Agencies Helping Young People with Disabilities Make Transition from School to Adulthood.* London: The Stationery Office.

DfEE (Department for Education and Employment) (1998) *Excellence for All Children: Meeting Special Educational Needs – A Programme for Action.* London: DfEE.

DfEE (Department for Education and Employment) (2000) *Connexions: The Best Start in Life for Every Young Person*. London: The Stationery Office.

DfEE/DoH (Department for Education and Employment and Department of Health) (1996) (Circular 14/96) *Supporting Pupils with Medical Needs in School*. London: DfEE.

DfES (Department for Education and Science) (1988) *Education Reform Act*. London: HMSO.

DfES (Department for Education and Science) (2001) *The Special Educational Needs Code of Practice*. Nottingham: Department for Education and Skills.

DfES (Department for Education and Skills) (2004a) *Every Child Matters: Change for Children*. DfES, www.everychildmatters.gov.uk

DfES (Department for Education and Skills) (2004b) *Children Act 2004*. www.dfes.gov.uk/publications/childrenactreport

DfES (Department for Education and Skills) (2005) *Professional Guidance for Children with Additional Needs*. London: DfES.

Disability Discrimination Act (1995) London: HMSO.

Dobson, B. and Middleton, S. (1998) *Paying to Care: The Cost of Childhood Disability*. York: Joseph Rowntree Foundation.

DoH (Department of Health) (1984) *Public Health (Control of Diseases) Act*. London: HMSO.

DoH (Department of Health) (1989) *Official Report, 15 December 1989;* Vol 163, c. 847. London: DoH.

DoH (Department of Health) (1991) *The Children Act and Regulations. (Volume 6) Children with Disabilities*. London: HMSO.

DoH (Department of Health) (1994) *The Allitt Inquiry*. London: HMSO.

DoH (Department of Health) (1997) *The New NHS: Modern and Dependable*. London: The Stationery Office.

DoH (Department of Health) (1998) *A First Class Service. Quality in the New NHS*. London: DoH.

DoH (Department of Health) (1999) *National Carers' Strategy. London: DoH*.

DoH (Department of Health) (2000a) *An Organisation with a Memory – Report of an Expert Group on Learning from Adverse Events in the NHS*. London: DoH.

DoH (Department of Health) (2000b) *The NHS Plan*. London: DoH.

DoH (Department of Health) (2002a) *Independent Health Care: National Minimum Standards Regulations*. London: The Stationery Office.

DoH (Department of Health) (2002) *Form 2HSC 2001/023: Parental Consent to Investigation or Treatment for a Child or Young Person*. London: DoH.

DoH (Department of Health) (2003) *Families and Post Mortems: A Code of Practice*. London: The Stationery Office.

DoH (Department of Health) (2004) *National Service Framework for Children, Young People and Maternity Services* (NSF). London: DoH.

DoH (Department of Health) (2005) *Common Core Skills and Knowledge for Children's Workforce*. London: HMSO.

DoH (Department of Health) (2006) *Standards for Better Health*. London: DoH.

Doka, K. (ed.) (1993) *Children Mourning, Mourning Children*. Washington: Hospice Association of America.

Dominica, Sr. F. (1997) *Just My Reflection – Helping Parents do Things their Way when a Child Dies*. London: Darton, Longman and Todd.

Doorbar, P. (1995) *Children's Views of Healthcare in Portsmouth and South East Hampshire*. Portsmouth: PDA and Portsmouth and South East Hampshire Health Authority.

Down, G. and Simons, J. (2006) 'Communication.' In R. Hain, A. Goldman and S. Liben (eds) *The Oxford Textbook of Palliative Care for Children*. Oxford: Oxford University Press.

Dyregrov, A. (1994) *Grief in Children – A Handbook for Adults*. London: Jessica Kingsley Publishers.

Education Act. (1944) London: HMSO.

Education Act. (1981) London: HMSO.

Education Act. (1996) London: HMSO.

Education Reform Act. (1988) London: HMSO.

Eiser, C. (1993) *Growing Up with a Chronic Disease: The Impact on Children and their Families*. London: Jessica Kingsley Publishers.

Eiser, C. (1999) 'Making sense of chronic disease.' The Eleventh Jack Tizzard Memorial Lecture. *Journal of Child Psychology and Child Psychiatry 35*, 8, 1373–89.

Eiser, C. (2000) 'The Psychological Impact of Chronic Illness on Children's Development.' In A. Closs (ed.) *The Education of Children with Medical Conditions*. London: David Fulton.

Emery, J. (1994) 'Perceived sources of stress among paediatric oncology nurses.' *Journal of Paediatric Oncology Nursing 10*, 3, 87–92.

Environmental Protection Act. (1999) London: HMSO.

Erling, A. (1999) 'Methodological considerations in the assessment of health related quality of life in children.' *Paediatric 88*, 428, 106–7.

European Health Committee (1996) *Nursing Research: Report and Recommendations.* European Health Committee: Brussels.

Family Law Reform Act. (1969) London: HMSO.

Fanurik, D., Koh, J.L., Schmitz, M., Harrison, R., Conrad, T. and Tomerlin, C. (1999) 'Children with cognitive impairment. An exploration of self-report skills.' *Clinical Nursing Research 7*, 103–19.

Farrell, M. (1996) 'The role of children's hospices.' *Paediatric Nursing 8*, 4, 6–8.

Farnfield, S. and Kaszap, M. (1998) 'What makes a helpful grownup? Children's views of professionals in the mental health services.' *Health Informatics 4*, 3–14.

Fessi vs. Whitmore (1999) FCR 767, Chancery Division, Judge Boggis, Q.C. sitting as a Judge in the High Court, 2 June 1997.

Field, D., Clark, D., Corner, J. and Davis, C. (2001) *Researching Palliative Care.* Buckingham: Open University Press.

Firth, S. (1996) 'The Good Death: Attitudes of British Hindus.' In G. Howarth and P.C. Jupp (eds) *Contemporary Issues in the Sociology of Death, Dying and Disposal.* Basingstoke: Macmillan.

Firth, S. (2000) 'Cross Cultural Perspectives on Bereavement.' In D. Dickenson, M. Johnson and J. Samson (eds) *Death, Dying and Bereavement.* London: SAGE and Open University Press.

Firth, S. (2001) *Wider Horizons – Care of the Dying in a Multicultural Society.* London: National Council for Hospice and Specialist Palliative Care Services.

Fisher, M. (1991) 'Can grief be turned into growth? Staff grief in palliative care.' *Professional Nurse 7*, 3, 178–82.

Frager, G. (1996) 'Paediatric palliative care: building the model, bridging the gaps.' *Journal of Palliative Care 12*, 9–12.

Fulton, Y. (1996) 'Children's rights and the role of the nurse.' *Paediatric Nurse 8*, 10, 29–31.

Galinsky, N. (1999) *When a Grandchild Dies: What to Do, What to Say, How to Cope.* Houston: In Sky Publishing.

Gascoigne, E. (1995) *Working with Parents as Partners in SEN – Home and School. A Working Alliance.* London: David Fulton.

Geertz, C. (1993) *The Interpretation of Cultures.* London: Fontana.

Glaser, B.G. and Strauss, A.L. (1996) *Awareness of Dying.* Chicago: Aldine Publishing.

Goldman, A. (ed.) (2002) *Care of the Dying Child,* 2nd edn. Oxford: Oxford University Press.

Goldman, A. and Schuller, I. (2006) 'Models of Curative and Palliative Care Relationships.' In J. Cooper (ed.) *Occupational Therapy in Oncology and Palliative Care.* London: John Wiley.

Goldman, A., Hain, R. and Liben, S. (eds) (2006) *Oxford Textbook of Palliative Care for Children.* Oxford: Oxford University Press.

Greenburg, H.S. and Meadows, A.T. (1991) 'Psychological impact of cancer survival on school age children and their parents.' *Journal of Psychosocial Oncology 9*, 4, 43–56.

Hain, R. (2002) 'The view from a bridge.' *European Journal of Palliative Care 9*, 2, 75–7.

Hamers, J. (1996) 'The influence of children's vocal expressions, age, medical diagnosis and information obtained from parents' and nurses' pain assessments and decisions regarding interventions.' *Pain 65*, 53–61.

Hanslick, J. (1990) 'Non-verbal interaction patterns of mothers and their infants with cerebral palsy.' *Mental Retardation 25*, 4, 333–4.

Harding, R. (1994) *Causes and Management of Stress for Trained Nurses Caring for Children with Cancer and Leukaemia.* Bristol: Avon and Gloucester College of Health.

Harding, R. (1996) 'Children with cancers: managing stress in staff.' *Paediatric Nursing 8*, 3, 28–31.

Hart, D. and Schneider, D. (1997) 'Spiritual care for children with cancer.' *Seminars in Oncology 13*, 4, 263–70.

Harvey, P. (1992) 'Staff support groups: are they necessary?' *British Journal of Nursing 1*, 5, 256–8.

Hatton, C., Akram, Y., Shah, R., Robertson, J. and Emerson, E. (2004) *Supporting South Asian Families with a Child with Severe Disabilities.* London: Jessica Kingsley Publishers.

Health Education Authority (1995) *Health at Work in the NHS: Organisational Stress in the NHS.* London: Health Education Authority.

Heath, I. (2000) *The Mystery of General Practice. The John Fry Trust Fellowship Lecture.* Royal College of General Practitioners. www.rcgp.org.uk

Hendricks-Furguson, V. (2004) 'Relationships of age and gender to hope and spiritual well-being amongst adolescents with cancer.' *Journal of Palliative Oncology 23*, 4, 189–99.

Herbert, M. (1996) *Supporting Bereaved and Dying Children and their Parents.* Leicester: British Psychological Society.

Hetherington, E. and Parke, R. (1991) *Child Psychology: A Temporary View.* 3rd ed. New York: McGraw Hill.

Hicks, M. and Lavender, R. (2001) 'Psychosocial practice trends in paediatric oncology.' *Journal of Oncology Nursing 18*, 4, 143–53.

Hill, D. and Penso, D. (1995) *Opening Doors: Improving Access to Hospice and Specialist Care Services by Members of Black and Ethnic Minority Communities.* London: National Council for Specialist and Palliative Care Services.

Hill, L. (ed.) (1994) *Caring for Dying Children and their Families.* London: Chapman and Hall.

Hillier, S. (1991) 'The health and healthcare of ethnic minority groups.' In G. Scambler (ed.) *Sociology as Applied to Medicine.* London: Jessica Kingsley Publishers.

Hindmarch, C. (2000) *On the Death of a Child*, 2nd edn. Oxford: Radcliffe Medical Press.

Hitcham, M. (1993) *All About the Rainbow.* Newcastle: Royal Victoria Infirmary.

Hofstede, G. (1991) *Cultures and Organisations – Software of the Mind.* London: McGraw Hill.

Hornby, G. (1998) *Counselling in Child Disability.* London: Chapman and Hall.

Hornby, G. (1999) *Working with Parents of Children with Special Needs.* London: Cassell.

Hornby, G. and Ashworth, T. (1995) 'Grandparent support for families who have a child with disabilities: a survey of parents.' *Journal of Child and Family Studies 3*, 403–12.

Horrocks, S., Somerset, M. and Salisbury, C. (2002) 'Do children with non-malignant life-threatening conditions receive effective palliative care? A pragmatic evaluation of a local service.' *Palliative Medicine 16*, 5, 410–16.

Human Tissue Act. (1961) London: HMSO.

Hunt, A. (2001) 'Towards an understanding of pain in the child with severe neurological impairment: development of a behaviour relating scale for assessing pain.' PhD thesis, University of Manchester.

Hunt, A. (2003a) *Paediatric Pain Profile.* www.ppprofile.org.uk

Hunt, A. (2003b) *Pain Assessment Tool.* www.ppprofile.org.uk

Hunt, A., Mastroyannopoulou, K., Goldman, A. and Seers, K. (2003) 'Not knowing – the problem of pain in children with severe neurological impairment.' *International Journal of Nursing Studies 40*, 171–83.

Hunt, M. (1997) 'The process of translating research findings into practice.' *Journal of Advanced Nursing 12*, 101–10.

Huntly, C. (1988) *Understanding Voluntary Organisations.* London: Penguin.

Hurley, A. and Whelan, A. (1988) 'Cognitive development and children's perceptions of pain.' *Paediatric Nursing 14*, 1, 21–4.

Hutchins, D. (1997) 'The hardiness of hospice nurses.' *American Journal of Hospice Palliative Care*, May/June, 110–13.

Hynson, J. (2006) 'The Child's Journey.' In A. Goldman, R. Hain and S. Liben (eds) *The Oxford Textbook of Palliative Care for Children.* Oxford: Oxford University Press.

Infield, D.L., Gordon, A.K. and Harper, B.C. (eds) (1995) *Hospice Care and Cultural Diversity.* New York: Haworth Press.

Irish, D.P., Lundquist, K.S. and Nelson, V.J. (1999) *Ethnic Variations in Dying, Death and Grief: Diversity in Universality.* London: Taylor and Francis.

Jenkins, K. (1995) *On 'What is History?'* London: Routledge.

Johnson, K. (1993) *Crisis Management.* California: Hunter House.

Johnson, W. (1991) 'Predisposition to emotional stress and psychiatric illness: the role of unconscious and environmental factors.' *British Journal of Medical Psychology 64*, 317–29.

Jonker, G. (1996) 'The knife's edge: Muslim burial in the disporia.' *Mortality 1*, 1, 27–43.

Judd, D. (1993) *Give Sorrow Words – Working with a Dying Child.* London: Free Association Books.

Kaczorowski, J.M. (1989) 'Spiritual well-being and anxiety.' *The Hospice Journal 5*, 4, 105–15.

Kagan, C., Lewis, S. and Heaton, P. (1998) *Caring to Work: Accounts of Working Parents of Disabled Children.* London: Family Policy Studies Centre.

Kane, J., Barber, R.G., Jordan, M., Tichenor, R. and Camp, K. (2000) 'Supportive/palliative care of children suffering from life-threatening and terminal illness.' *American Journal of Hospice and Palliative Care 17*, 3, May/June, 165–72.

Karim, K., Bailey, M. and Tunna, K. (2000) 'Non-white ethnicity and the provision of specialist palliative care services: factors affecting doctors' referral patterns.' *Palliative Medicine 14*, 471–78.

Katz, K.S., Baker, C. and Osborn, C. (1991) 'Home-based care for children with chronic illness.' *Journal of Perinatal and Neonatal Nursing 5*, 1, 71–9.

Kavanagh, R. (2001) 'Dealing naturally with dying.' *Nursing 76*, October, 23–9.

Kazak, A. and Nachman, G.S. (1991) 'Family research on childhood chronic illness: paediatric oncology as an example.' *Journal of Family Psychology 4*, 4, 462–83.

Kenny, G. (1998) 'An ethical investigation into the provision of pain relief in infants.' *British Journal of Nursing 7*, 17, 1022–5.

Kerr, G. (2001) 'Assessing the needs of learning disabled young people with additional disabilities.' *Journal of Learning Disabilities 5*, 154–7.

Kirk, S. (1999) 'Caring for children with specialised health needs in the community: the challenges for primary care.' *Health and Social Care in the Community 7*, 350–7.

Klass, D. (1999) *The Spiritual Lives of Bereaved Parents.* London: Taylor and Francis.

Klass, D., Silverman, P. and Nickman, S. (eds) (1996) *Continuing Bonds: New Understandings of Grief.* London: Taylor & Francis.

Knudson, A. and Natterson, J. (1960) 'An investigation of grief and adaptation in parents of dying children.' *Journal of Pediatric Psychology 8*, 3–20.

Kolf, J. (1995) *Grandma's Tears.* Omaha: Baker Books.

Kruijver, I., Kerkstra, A., Bensing, J. and van de Weill, H. (2000) 'Nurse–patient communication in care. A review of the literature.' *Cancer Nurse 23*, 1, 20–31.

Kubler-Ross, E. (1983) *On Children and Death.* New York: Macmillan.

Kushnir, T., Rabin, S. and Azulai, S. (1997) 'A descriptive study of stress management in a group of palliative oncology nurses.' *Cancer Nursing 20*, 6, 14–21.

Laakso, H. and Paunonen Ilmonen, M. (2001) 'Mothers' grief following the death of a child.' *Journal of Advanced Nursing 36*, 1, 69–77.

Lammy, D. House of Commons Hansard Debates. 1 May 2003. www.publications.parliament.uk

Lauer, M.E., Mulhern, R.K., Wallskoy, J.M. and Camitta, B.M. (1993) 'A comparison study of parental adaptation following a child's death at home or in hospital.' *Pediatrics 71*, 1, 107–11.

Leadbetter, S. (1989) 'Semantics of death certification.' *Journal of the Royal College of Physicians 20*, 129–32.

Learning and Skills Act. (2000) London: Stationery Office.

Lewis, M. and Prescott, H. (2006) 'Impact of Life-limiting Illness on the Family.' In A. Goldman, R. Hain and S. Liben (eds) *Oxford Textbook of Palliative Care for Children.* Oxford: Oxford University Press.

Lightfoot, J. (2003) *Service Support for Children with a Chronic Illness or Physical Disability Attending Mainstream School.* York: University of York.

Lloyd Williams, M. (2002) 'Breaking bad news to patients and relatives.' *British Medical Journal Care Focus 325*, 11.

Luchterhand, C. and Murphy, N. (1998) *Helping Adults with Mental Retardation Grieve a Loss.* London: Taylor and Francis.

McCaffery, M. (1992) 'Perceptions about paediatric pain.' In A. Twycross, A. Moriarty and T. Betts (eds) *Paediatric Pain Management: A Multidisciplinary Approach.* Oxford: Radcliffe Publishing.

McCaffery, M. and Wong, D. (1993) 'Nursing Interventions for Pain Control in Children.' In N. Schechter, C. Berde and M. Yaster (eds) *Pain in Infants, Children and Adolescents.* Baltimore: Williams and Wilkins.

McGrath, P.J., Rosmus, C., Camfield, C., Campbell, M. and Hennigar, A. (1998) 'Behaviours caregivers use to determine pain in non-verbal, cognitively impaired individuals.' *Developmental Medicine and Child Neurology 40*, 340–3.

McHaffie, H.E. (2001) *Crucial Decisions at the Beginning of Life – Parents' Experiences of Treatment Withdrawal from Infants.* Oxford: Radcliffe Medical Press.

McKee, A. (1995) 'Staff support in hospices.' *International Journal of Palliative Nursing 1*, 4, 200–5.

McLoughlin, I. (1986) 'Bereavement in the Mentally Handicapped.' *British Journal of Hospital Medicine 36*, 4, 256–60.

Macleod-Clark, J. and Hockey, L. (1998) *Further Research for Nursing.* London: Scutari Press.

Martin, T. and Doka, J. (2000) *Men Don't Cry – Women Do.* Philadelphia: Bruner Mazel.

Martinson, I.M. (1980) 'Dying children at home.' *Nursing Times 76*, 29, 129–32.

Mays, N. and Pope, C. (1995) 'Rigour and qualitative research.' *British Medical Journal 31*, 109–12.

Measelle, J.R., Ablow, J.C. and Cowan, C.P. (1998) 'Assessing young children's views of their academic, social and emotional lives: an evaluation of self-perception scales of the Berkeley Interview.' *Child Development 69*, 6, 156–76.

Melander-Mattala, U. (1995) *Content and Perspective in Doctor–Patient Conversation.* Uppsala: Department of Nordic Languages, University of Uppsala.

Meyer, D. (1997) *Grandparent Workshops.* Seattle: University of Washington Press.

Mir, G., Nocon, A., Ahmad, W. and Jones, L. (2001) *Learning Difficulties and Ethnicity.* London: Department of Health.

Mirfin-Veitch, B. and Bray, A. (1997) 'Grandparents: Part of the Family.' In B. Carpenter (ed.) *Families in Context: Emerging Trends in Family Support and Early Intervention.* London: David Fulton.

Moody, R. and Moody, C. (1991) 'A family perspective – helping children acknowledge and express grief following death.' *Death Studies 15,* 587–602.

Mulhern, R.K., Fairclough, D.L., Smith, B. and Douglas, S.M. (1992) 'Maternal depression.' *Journal of Paediatric Psychology 17,* 313–26.

Murgatroyd, S. and Woolfe, R. (1993) *Coping with Crisis: Understanding and Helping People in Need.* Birmingham: Open University.

Murphy, K.M. (1990) 'Interactional styles of parents following the birth of a high-risk infant.' *Journal of Pediatric Nursing 1,* 33–41.

NAESC (National Association for the Education of Sick Children) (1996) *Report into the Provision of Education by Local Education Authorities to Children who are Out of School for Reasons of Sickness.* London: NAESC.

NAESC (National Association for the Education of Sick Children) (1997) *Losing the Thread – Pupils' and Parents' Voices about Education for Sick Children.* London: NAESC.

NAESC (National Association for the Education of Sick Children) (1998) *Education for Sick Children: Directory of Current Provision in England, Scotland, Wales and Northern Ireland.* London: NAESC.

Nash, T. (1999) 'Medical support at school: children with life-threatening illness.' *Childright,* October, 17.

NHS (National Health Service) (1999) *Young Adults' Transition Project – Optimum Health Services.* London: NHS.

NHS (National Health Service) (2003a) *Scottish Executive Health Department Circular 2001/2003.* Edinburgh: Scottish Health Executive.

NHS (National Health Service) (2002/2003) *Good Practice in Consent.* London: NHS.

NHS (National Health Service) (2003b) *Consent to a Post Mortem Examination on a Baby or a Child.* London: NHS.

NHS (National Health Service) and Clinical Governance Support Team (2005) *A Practical Handbook for Clinical Audit.* London: DoH and Healthcare Financial Management Association.

NHS (National Health Service) Executive (2000) *The Vital Connection: An Equalities Framework for the NHS Department of Health.* London: NHS.

NMC (National Medical Council) (2002) *Code of Professional Conduct.* London: NMC.

Neill, S.J. (1996) 'Parent participation: Literature Review.' *British Journal of Nursing 5,* 1, 34–9.

Neuberger, J. (1994) *Caring for Dying People of Different Faiths,* 2nd edn. London: Mosby.

Nolan, J., Chalkladis, G., Low, J., Olesch, C.A. and Brown, T.C. (2000) 'Anaesthetic and pain management in cerebral palsy.' *Anaesthesia 55,* 32–41.

O'Brien, T. (1998) *Promoting Positive Behaviour.* London: David Fulton.

Office for National Statistics (2001) *Census 2001.* London: Office for National Statistics.

Oliviere, D., Hargreaves, R. and Monroe, B. (1998) *Good Practices in Palliative Care: A Psychosocial Perspective.* Aldershot: Ashgate.

Overholser, J. and Fritz, G. (1999) 'The impact of childhood cancer on the family.' *Journal of Psychosocial Oncology 8,* 71–85.

Olsen, R. and Maslin-Prothero, T. (2001) 'Dilemmas in the provision of own home respite support for parents of young children with complex healthcare needs: evidence from evaluation.' *Journal of Advanced Nursing 34,* 5, 603–10.

Oswin, M. (1991) *Bereavement and Mentally Handicapped People.* London: King's Fund Report KFC 81/234.

Owen, R. (2000) 'Relieving stress in palliative care staff.' *Palliative Care Today 9,* 1, 4–5.

Panke, J. and Ferrell, B. (2005) 'Emotional Problems in the Family.' In D. Doyle, G. Hanks, N. Cherny and K. Calman (eds) *The Oxford Textbook of Palliative Medicine.* Oxford: Oxford University Press.

Parahoo, K. (1997) *Nursing Research – Principles, Process and Issues.* Basingstoke: Palgrave/Macmillan.

Parkes, C., Relf, M. and Couldrick, A. (1996) *Counselling in Terminal Care and Bereavement.* Leicester: British Psychological Society.

Payne, S. (2000) 'Research involves small steps, not great leaps.' *International Journal of Palliative Nursing 6,* 2 (editorial).

Pearson-Vaughan, B. and Fitzgerald, M. (1994) *Nursing Models for Practice.* London: Butterworth Heinemann.

Perrens, C. (1996) 'A parent's dilemma.' *Paediatric Nursing 6,* 3, 93–9.

Peterson, S. and Greil, A. (1990) 'Death experience and religion.' *Omega 26,* 4, 239–53.

Pollution Prevention and Control Act. (1999) London: Stationery Office.

Porter, J. (2001) 'Interpreting the communication of people with profound and multiple learning disabilities.' *British Journal of Learning Disabilities 29,* 12–16.

Powncenby, J. (1996) *The Coming of Age Project – A Study of the Transition from Paediatric to Adult Care and Treatment Adherence among Young People with Cystic Fibrosis.* London: Cystic Fibrosis Trust.

Public Health (Infectious Diseases) Regulations. London: HMSO.

Quinton, D. (2004) *Supporting Parents: Messages from Research.* London: Jessica Kingsley Publishers.

Rainbows Children's Hospice (2006) *Basic Symptom Control in Paediatric Palliative Care,* 6th edn. Leicester: Rainbows Children's Hospice.

Ramirez, A., Graham, J. and Richards, M. (1998) 'The effect of stress and satisfaction at work.' *Lancet 347,* 9003, 724–8.

Ray, L.D. and Ritchie, J.A. (1993) 'Chronically ill children coping at home: factors that influence parents' coping.' *Journal of Paediatric Nursing 8,* 4, 217–25.

RCN (Royal College of Nursing) (2004) *Adolescent Transition Care – Guidance for Nursing Staff.* London: RCN.

RCPCH (Royal College of Paediatrics and Child Health) (1997) *The Essentials of Effective Community Health Services for Children and Young People – Report of a Working Party.* London: RCPCH.

RCPCH (Royal College of Paediatrics and Child Health) (2002) *The Future of Paediatric Pathology Services.* London: Royal College of Paediatrics and Child Health, Obstetricians and Gynaecologists, and Pathologists.

Read, J. (2000) *Disability, the Family and Society.* Milton Keynes: Open University Press.

Reed, M. (2000) *Grandparents Cry Twice: Help for Bereaved Grandparents.* New York: Baywood.

Richards, M.A., Corner, J. and Clark, D. (1998) 'Developing a research culture for palliative care.' *Palliative Medicine 12,* 309–403.

Riches, G. and Dawson, P. (2000) *An Intimate Loneliness: Supporting Bereaved Parents and Siblings.* Buckingham: Open University Press.

Riley, R. (1996) 'Children as customers too.' *British Journal of Community Nursing 1,* 158–9.

Roberts, K. and Lawton, D. (1999) 'Financial assistance for families with severely disabled children and transport costs.' *Children and Society 13,* 333–45.

Robinson, W.M., Berde, C., Ravilly, S. and Nohl, M. (1997) 'End of life care in cystic fibrosis.' *Paediatrics 11,* 2, 205–9.

Rogers, C. (1980) *A Way of Being.* Boston: Houghton Mifflin.

Roper, N. (1980) 'A model for nursing and nursology.' *Journal of Advanced Nursing 1,* 3, 219–27.

Rosenblatt, P. (1996) 'Grief does not End.' In P. Silverman and S. Nickman (eds) *Continuing Bonds: New Understandings of Grief.* London: Taylor and Francis.

Rosenblatt, P. (2000) *Parent Grief – Narratives of Loss and Relationship.* Hove: Bruner-Mazel.

Rowntree Foundation (2001) *Financial Implications of the Death of a Child.* York: SPRU and Joseph Rowntree Foundation.

Roy, C. and Andrews, H. (1999) *The Roy Adaptation Model,* 2nd edn. Stamford: Appleton Lange.

Royal College of Pathologists (2002) *Report of a Working Group of the Royal College of Pathologists.* London: Royal College of Pathologists.

Royal College of Surgeons and College of Anaesthetists (1990) *Pain After Surgery.* London: Royal College of Surgeons.

Rubin, S. (1993) 'The Death of a Child is Forever: The Life Course Impact of Child Loss.' In W. Stroebe, M. Stroebe and R. Hanson (eds) *Handbook of Bereavement: Theory, Research and Intervention.* Cambridge: Cambridge University Press.

Russell-Johnson, H. (2000) 'Adolescent survey.' *Paediatric Nursing 12,* 6, 15–19.

Sandler, A., Wareen, S. and Raver, S. (1995) 'Grandparents as a source of support for parents of children with disabilities: a brief report.' *Mental Retardation 3,* 248–9.

Saunders, J. and Valente, S. (1994) 'Nurses' grief.' *Cancer Nursing 17,* 4, 115–19.

SCIE (Social Care Institute for Excellence) (2004) *Resource Guide – The Blueprint Project.* London: SCIE.

Scottish Office (1997) *Protection of Children (Scotland Act).* Edinburgh: The Stationery Office.

Sheldon, F. and Speck, P. (2002) 'Children's hospices: organisational and staff issues.' *Palliative Medicine 16,* 5, 410–16.

Select Committee Inquiry into Palliative Care. (2004) London: Stationery Office.

Simons, J. (2002) 'Practical issues in the care of the dying child.' In A. Goldman (ed.) *Care of the Dying Child,* 2nd edn. Oxford: Oxford University Press.

Sloper, P. (1999) 'Models of service support for parents of disabled children. What do we know? What do we need to know?' *Child Care, Health and Development 25,* 2, 85–99.

Sloper, P. (2001) *Improving Communication between Health and Education for Children with Chronic Illness or Physical Disability.* York: University of York.

Smaje, C. (1995) *Health, Race and Ethnicity: Making Sense of the Evidence.* London: King's Fund.

Smith, R. (1992) 'Audit and research.' *British Medical Journal 305,* 905–6.

Smyth, M. and Robus, N. (1999) *Surveys of Disability in Great Britain. The Financial Circumstances of Families with Disabled Children Living in Private Households.* London: HMSO.

Speechley, K.N. and Noh, S. (1992) 'Surviving childhood cancer – social support and parents' psychological adjustment.' *Journal of Paediatric Psychology 17,* 15–31.

Speck, P. (1992) 'Care after death.' *Nursing Times 88,* 3, 20.

Spinetta, J., Jankovie, M. and Arush, M.W. (2001) 'Guidelines for the recognition, prevention and remediation of burnout in health care professionals participating in the care of children.' *Paediatric Oncology 35,* 2, 122–5.

Stein, A. and Woolley, H. (1999) 'An Evaluation of Hospice Care for Children.' In J.D. Baum, F. Dominica, and R.N. Woodward (eds) *Listen My Child has a lot of Living to do: Caring for Children with Life-limiting Conditions.* Oxford: Oxford University Press.

Stevens, M. (1998) 'Care of the dying child and adolescent: family adjustment and support.' In D. Doyle, G. Hanks and N. MacDonald (eds) *Oxford Textbook of Palliative Medicine,* 2nd edn. Oxford: Oxford University Press.

Stevens, M. and O'Riordon, E. (1996) 'Family responses when a child with cancer is palliative.' *Journal of Palliative Care 12,* 3, 51–5.

Stewart, A. and Dent, A. (1994) *At a Loss – Bereavement Care When a Baby Dies.* London: Balliere Tindall.

Stoter, D. (1995) *Spiritual Aspects of Health Care.* London: Mosby.

Stoter, D. (1997) *Staff Support in Healthcare.* Oxford: Blackwell Science.

Strachan, J. (1981) 'Reactions to bereavement: a study of a group of hospital residents.' *Apex 9,* 1, 20–1.

Strax, T.E. (1991) 'Psychological issues faced by adolescents and young adults with disabilities.' *Pediatrics 20,* 507–11.

Svavarsdottir, E.K. and McCubbin, M. (1996) 'Parenthood transition for parents of an infant diagnosed with a congenital heart condition.' *Journal of Pediatric Nursing 11,* 207–16.

Swartz, M. (1989) *Textbook of Physical Diagnosis.* Philadelphia: Saunders.

Sweeting, H.N. and Gilhooly, M.M. (1990) 'Anticipatory grief – a review.' *Journal of Social Science and Medicine 30,* 10, 1073–80.

Teague, B.R., Fleming, J.W., Castle, A., Kierman, B.S., Lobo, M.L., Riggs, S. and Wolfe, J.G. (1993) 'High tech home care for children with chronic health conditions: a pilot study.' *Journal of Paediatric Nursing 8,* 4, 226–32.

Tebbitt, P. (2000) *Raising the Standard of Care, Clinical Governance for Voluntary Hospices. Occasional Paper 18.* London: National Council for Hospice and Specialist Palliative Care Services.

Templar, D. (1993) 'Death anxiety scales.' *Omega 26,* 4, 239–53.

The Inquiry into the Management of Care of Children Receiving Complex Heart Surgery at the Royal Bristol Infirmary – 'Learning from Bristol.' Report presented to Parliament by the Secretary of State for Health, July 2000.

The Royal Liverpool Children's Inquiry (Alder-Hey). Report to Rt Hon Alan Milburn MP, Secretary of State for Health. www.rlcinquiry.org.uk

Thomas, K. (2003) *Care for the Dying at Home – Companions on the Journey.* Oxford: Radcliffe Medical Press.

Totterdell, A. (1990) *Five and a Half Times Three: The Short Life and Death of Joe Buffalo Stuart.* London: Hamish Hamilton.

Tuffrey-Wijne, I. (2003) 'The palliative care needs of people with intellectual disabilities: a literature review.' *Palliative Medicine 17,* 55–62.

Twycross, A. and Wilcock, A. (2001) *Symptom Management in Advanced Cancer,* 3rd edn. Abingdon: Radcliffe Medical Press.

Twycross, A., Moriarty, A. and Betts, T. (1998) *Paediatric Pain Management – A Multi-disciplinary Approach.* Abingdon: Radcliffe Medical Press.

UNESCO (United Nations Educational Scientific and Cultural Organisation.) (1991) *United Nations Convention on the Rights of the Child.* Geneva: UNESCO.

Unger, R. (1999) 'Some musings on paradigm shifts: feminist psychology and the psychology of women.' *Psychology of Women Review 1,* 2, 58.

United Kingdom Parliament (21 July 2004) *Select Committee on Health, 4th Report. Palliative Care.* London: Stationery Office.

Urquhart, J., Haslett, E., Mitchell, J. and Porteous, M. (1999) 'Millennium babies.' *British Journal of Obstetrics and Gynaecology 106,* 9, 100–1.

Vachon, M. (1993) 'Emotional Problems in Palliative Medicine – Patient, Family and Professional.' In D. Doyle, G. Hanks and N. MacDonald (eds) *Oxford Textbook of Palliative Medicine.* Oxford: Oxford University Press.

Vachon, M. (1997) 'Research into staff stress in palliative care.' *European Journal of Palliative Care 4,* 3, 99–103.

Vessey, J.A. and Swanson, M.N. (1996) 'Chronic conditions and child development.' In P. Jackson (ed.) *Primary Care of the Child with a Chronic Condition.* St Louis: Mosby.

Vickers, J. and Carlisle, C. (2000) 'Choices and control: parental experiences in paediatric terminal home care.' *Journal of Oncology Nursing 17,* 1, 12–21.

Viner, R. and Keane, M. (1999) *Youth Matters: Evidence-based Best Practice for the Care of Young People in Hospital. Caring for Children in Health Services.* London: Action for Sick Children.

Waechter, E. (1981) *Death Anxiety in Children with Fatal Illness.* Unpublished thesis, University of Washington, p.41.

Walter, T., Pickering, M. and Littlewood, J. (1995) 'Death in the news: the public invigilation of private emotion.' *Sociology 29,* 579–96.

Ware, J. (1996) *Creating a Responsive Environment.* London: David Fulton.

Webb, P. (2000) *Ethical Issues in Palliative Care – Reflections and Considerations.* Manchester: Hochland and Hochland.

Welsh Office (1998) *NHS Wales: Putting Patients First.* Cardiff: The Stationery Office.

Wendell, S. (1996) *The Rejected Body – Feminist Philosophical Reflections on Disability.* New York: Routledge.

While, A., Citrone, C. and Cornish, J. (1996) *Bereaved Parents' Views of Caring for a Child with a Life Limiting Incurable Disorder.* London: Kings College.

Whyte, D. (1997) 'A family nursing approach to the care of a child with chronic illness.' *Journal of Advanced Nursing 17,* 3, 317–27.

Wolfe, J., Grier, H. and Klar, N. (2000) 'Symptoms and suffering at the end of life in children with cancer.' *New England Journal of Medicine 342,* 326–33.

Woolley, H., Stein, A., Forrest, G. and Baum, J. (1989a) 'Staff stress and job satisfaction in a children's hospice.' *Archives of Childhood Disability 64,* 114–18.

Woolley, H., Stein, A., Forrest, G.C. and Baum, J.D. (1989b) 'Imparting the diagnosis of life threatening illness in children.' *British Medical Journal 298,* 1623–26.

Worswick, J. (2000) *A House Called Helen,* 2nd edn. Oxford: Oxford University Press.

Wortman, C. and Silver, R. (1999) 'The myths of coping with loss.' *Journal of Counselling and Clinical Psychology 57,* 349–57.

Useful Websites

Acorns Children's Hospice: www.acorns.org.uk
Acupuncture: www.myacupuncture.org
Association of Children's Hospices: www.childhospice.org.uk/sections/
media/achfactsheet.html
Department of Health Policy and Guidance: www.doh.gov.uk
Homeopathy: www.lmhi.net
Hunt's Pain Assessment Tool: www.ppprofile.org.uk
National Centre for Complementary and Alternative Medicine:
www.nccam.nih.gov
The Association for Children's Palliative Care: www.act.org.uk
UK Research Council on Complementary and Alternative Medicine:
www.rccm.org.uk

Subject Index

Author Index